MYSTERIOUS LINCOLNSHIRE

MYSTERIOUS LINCOLNSHIRE

DANIEL CODD

First published in Great Britain in 2007 by The Breedon Books Publishing Company
Limited, 3 The Parker Centre, Derby, DE21 4SZ.

This paperback edition published in Great Britain in 2013 by DB Publishing,
an imprint of JMD Media Ltd

DEDICATION

For Josie and Thomas, so they know the land that they were born in.

ACKNOWLEDGEMENTS

Pamela Kellagher, Mick Holmes, Charlotte Roke, Estelle Ashworth (and Paul Jackson), Brian Knotts and Claire Tyson (whose dog, Boca, is noted in Chapter 9), Shelly Hemming, Lincolnshire Archives, Lincoln Central Library, R.S., Rebecca Unwin, the staff at Lincoln Archives, the Folklore Society, Mr Hallam for his tour of RAF Scampton, Neville and Janet Codd, the staff at Lincoln Castle and at Lincoln Cathedral. Illustrations (3, 5, 7, 8, 9, 11, 13, 14, 16, 17, 18, 20, 21, 22, 24, 26, 27, 31, 36, 42, 47 and 49) are copyrighted Nicola Stone. Many thanks must go to Nicola, whose expertise with photographic equipment and suggestions for images compliment this work excellently.

ISBN 978-1-78091-304-9

CONTENTS

FOREWORD

One of the earliest memories of my childhood is of being told how at low tide, the roof of a submerged church could be glimpsed in the North Sea near the coast of Mablethorpe and that its bells could still be heard peeling. To this day I am uncertain where this legend originates, since the east coast has been no stranger to extensive flooding. Perhaps it stems from a tidal surge in 1287 when Mablethorpe's church was devastated on New Year's Day. If so, then this story has been retold for centuries; I remembered it while researching this work and found it to be representative of folklore in general across Lincolnshire.

For, in preparing this compilation, after endless trawling through so many periodicals, books and especially newspaper articles, spending countless hours at the archives and libraries, cross-checking hundreds of websites and travelling the length and breadth of Lincolnshire talking to so many who have encountered strange phenomena, one simple conclusion has reared itself again and again. People simply do not change in what they believe. We live in an age of DVD players, mobile phones, growing cities and towns, and technological advancement, and I trust that Lincolnshire is no more backward in coming forward than anywhere else in the UK. And yet the beliefs of centuries ago still persist. They have not gone, merely been replaced. In fact, after talking to hundreds of people all over Lincolnshire, there are very few who, after a moment's hesitation, will not cautiously admit 'Well, actually, one time this *really* strange thing happened.'

Today, in the 21st century, the very idea of the existence of a race of 'little people', such as the goblin-like Tiddy Folk, is something to be smiled at as a quaint fairy tale. Yet so many people will look you in the eye and claim that they have witnessed bright lights in the sky, or that so-and-so saw what they 'reckon was a UFO'. UFOs and their 'grey' pilots are undoubtedly the modern incarnation of the fairy folk, just as gigantic sea serpents allegedly seen off the east coast are the modern incarnation of dragons. Devils, imps and demons have been supplanted, first by witchcraft (until the late 19th century) and then by Satanists and cults in the late 20th century. The blazing-eyed phantom black hound known as Hairy Jack, who loped around Hemswell and Grayingham, has been replaced by the gigantic black cats regularly seen slinking away into hedgerows, their glowing eyes peering out at cyclists and ramblers in lonely country lanes.

But this is just an observation. This compilation is not a study of psychology. Think what you will of these reports and beliefs, and evaluate the evidence on its merits, or in some cases, if you wish, your *own* beliefs. Maybe – certainly – some of these tales are more than 'good stories'. Ultimately, it is up to the reader to decide whether they believe some of these accounts to be just possible, to be outright fabrication, or to be real events in time and space as the witnesses would have us believe. For, as to whether any of it is true – (i.e.) conclusively proving the existence of ghosts or giant black cats – well, the very nature of the subject matter of this book makes that impossible to verify. For example, a perceived sighting of a ghost is only 'real' to the person who sees it, not to the world at large.

Of course, some of the enigmas noted here *are* mooted in the real word. I for one can testify to the ease with which one could 'disappear', thanks to a near-suicidal manoeuvre on a rough track north of Guy's Head during an attempt to drive out to the Wash. The car became bogged down and insane attempts to get it moving again could have sent the car shooting over one of the 7ft dykes that bordered the track. The point is, that had the car gone over the edge and fatally crashed into the wet fields below, it could have been days before we were found – given that no one knew where we were and there really is an 'edge of the world' feeling about this part of Lincolnshire.

This act of stupidity aside, much of the content of this book is open for the reader to decipher. It truly is a question of belief, but when one's own friends and relatives look you in the eye and tell you quite sincerely of their own paranormal experiences, it becomes somewhat difficult to disbelieve them, especially since you have known them, and all their character foibles, for decades and know without doubt they would not in their wildest dreams see ghosts unless there were ghosts to see. I myself, while impressed by the witness accounts and not a total disbeliever, will continue to sit on the fence on the subject until I see a ghost, a UFO or large black cat with my own eyes. Yet many people are already past that point and claim to have seen the things that we all may or may not wish to believe were true. In short, the continuation of such sincere persistence in belief either means that these things actually *exist*, or our own desire to believe in them keeps us seeing things that we are 'not really seeing.'

Many people are quite content to tell you of the strange legends they know or what they have seen. Therefore, this compilation has been compiled, researched and sourced to the best of my ability in an effort to show how folk belief still manifests itself, only in different guises. However, for some of the legends out there it becomes nigh-on impossible to track down the truth since there are so many versions. This book is also not a history book, but it has been written in good faith and I apologise in advance for any unwitting historical inaccuracies. In truth, it is up to the reader to track down the 'reality' of these tales and to investigate them further if they are intrigued.

CHAPTER I

ENIGMATIC EVENTS FROM
COUNTY HISTORY

INTRODUCTION

The general perception, perhaps, of Lincolnshire is that of a quiet, rural and slightly removed part of Britain. While there may still be some substance to this opinion, it is naturally befitting for a region with 2,000 years of recorded history that it has, on numerous occasions, been the setting for periods of violent upheaval right up to and including the 20th century, which, when condensed, can paint a very different picture of the county. Of course, such a remark can be made of almost anywhere, but Lincolnshire's extremely diverse and tumultuous history provides the backdrop for some very intriguing incidents and historical mysteries not directly linked to the supernatural.

Currently there is a great deal of speculation concerning the Knights Templar mystery, thanks mainly to the film *The Da Vinci Code*, some scenes of which were filmed at Lincoln Cathedral. The Knights Templar were purged in England in 1312, but rumours have since clung to the order concerning lost secrets of immense religious significance and hidden treasures, including – just maybe – the Holy Grail itself. In Lincolnshire the order had established a Preceptory in 1185: Temple Bruer, which can be found still standing (although in some disrepair) off the A15 as one travels northwards

Temple Bruer, long abandoned by the knights themselves.

from Sleaford. After the Templars were abolished, Bruer fell into neglect and abandonment. Then, in 1833, the Reverend G. Oliver led an excavation of the site and his alleged findings put us in more familiar Templar territory. Stories circulated that Oliver's workmen had uncovered underground passages and vaults, in which were found centuries-old skeletons displaying signs of extreme violence. There was also evidence of excessive burning on some vault's walls – the supposition being that this chapter of the Templars were engaged in the secret torture and murder of their enemies. Such a claim was somewhat at odds with the image of the hard-working, wool-producing community of the knights of Bruer, and another excavation in 1907 dismissed the stories. No vaults or skeletons were found, but there were two flights of stairs that led down to a crypt…a rather more logical interpretation of skeletons and underground passages.

Since the release of *The Da Vinci Code*, the *Lincolnshire Echo* has regularly featured the latest theories – scholarly and not-so scholarly – as to where (if anywhere) in Lincolnshire the search for enigmatic ancient secrets and semi-mythological artefacts ought to be carried out. But behind this ongoing and popular mystery are other enigmas from way back in history that one might not perhaps associate with Lincolnshire. Writing in around AD835, the Welsh scribe Nennius states in his *Historia Britonum* that the great leader of the Britons, named Arthur, fought 12 battles against the Anglo-Saxon invaders, including the decisive clash at a place called Mount Badon *c.*AD500. The locations of all of the alleged battles ascribed to Arthur and his forces by Nennius are, to say the least, debatable, but there is at least the suggestion of a possibility that the semi-mythical King Arthur fought campaigns along the banks of the River Witham and the River Glen, which snakes through southern Lincolnshire.

Staying in southern Lincolnshire, while there is little doubt as to the actual existence of the famous Fenland rebel Hereward the Wake – a *thegn* supposedly from Bourne who led a revolt against William the Conqueror in 1070–71 – the problem for historians has not necessarily been his exploits. The questions of who he actually was, where he came from and what happened to him have had to be answered by sketchy half-clues in ancient documents, folklore and records written some 70 years after the rebellion. Writing about 1140, the scholarly Geoffrey Gaimar recorded that Hereward died violently. *L'Estoire des Engles* states that Hereward was remarried to the widow of Earl Dolfin and was subsequently murdered by his son-in-law Hugh de Evermue. The *Gesta Herewardi Saxonis*, written around the same period, claimed that a crowd of jealous Normans had attacked him in his house and in the eruption of violence that followed, Hereward killed at least 15 of his attackers before being struck down and hacked to death. It is reasonable to assume that if this is true, then it happened somewhere in Lincolnshire and maybe this was more than a spontaneous outbreak of violence. It seems that Hereward died no more than a few years after the siege of Ely and this could have been the premeditated assassination of someone whom King William still saw as very much of a threat. But for all intents and purposes, apart from his two years as a rebel warrior, the life – and death – of the *real* Hereward the Wake has been lost in the shadows of history.

And what to make of the mysterious abandonment of the mediaeval village of Gainsthorpe, off the A15 west of Hibaldstow, where these days a single, lonely farmstead is all that stands among the earth mounds of this long-deserted ghost village? A local curate commented in 1697 that the place had become the casualty of 'time, poverty and pasturage', but folklore claims that the population of Gainsthorpe were massacred by the inhabitants of surrounding villages sometime in the 1600s.

There were other mysteries through the centuries. A remarkable skeleton was discovered in 1747 at Amcotts Moor in the peatland of the Isle of Axholme. The skeleton of the woman, dated to the Middle Ages, was found in an upright position, as though 'standing' beneath the ground. Sometime in the latter part of the 1800s repairs were being carried out in the chancel of St Peter's Church in Bottesford when a mass of skulls were found in the interior, close to the eastern wall. There were no other bones and it was assumed they belonged to the victims of beheading. There was no fortress in the immediate vicinity from where they might have been relics, so how did they come to be there? In October 1931 the digging up of Haxey High Street unearthed the skeleton of a 'true' giant: that of a seven-foot tall man thought to have been a Roman warrior.

Nearer our own time, the last, fatal leap of 20-year-old skydiver Stephen Hilder over Hibaldstow Airfield on 4 July 2003 can now never be explained to everyone's satisfaction. An open verdict was recorded by the coroner in 2005, it being debatable whether Stephen had sabotaged his own parachute or someone else had tampered with it. To some, either explanation was as likely – or unlikely – an answer to the strange tragedy.

Throughout the centuries, in times of conflict there have been rumours of conspiracy and assassination, but in quieter times crime mysteries and enigmatic figures have surfaced to perplex us.

THE WORLD'S FIRST UNIVERSITY

Although not directly linked to the criminal, the well-known story of the world's first university being built at Stamford is none the less an intriguing chapter in Britain's mythological heritage.

In c.1136, the Welsh churchman and renowned scholar Geoffrey of Monmouth produced his expansive *History of the Kings of Britain*, drawing on as much local lore as actual fact. It covered a time period that began centuries before Christ up until the year AD800 and told the story of how refugees from Troy, under Brutus the Trojan, fled to the island of Albion, guided by the goddess Diana. This island was Britain and the Trojans defeated a race of giants that inhabited the place before setting up a capital called New Troy (modern-day London). This, Geoffrey tells us, was around 1070BC.

Born of this line of Trojan leaders was one Bladud (or Blaedud), who traced his lineage back to Aeneas – and was the father of Shakespeare's King Lear.

There are many tales relating to Bladud, including the story of how he was the founder of the world's first university – at Stamford in Lincolnshire. Bladud became the ninth king of the Britons in 863BC and he had returned to Albion from the famous schools in Athens. He brought with him four learned Greek sages, presenting them with the task of finding a suitable place in the kingdom for a great house of education. Thus, it came to pass that the university was built upon the banks of the River Welland at Stamford, a fine Athenian-style building with halls, colonnades and temples – the greatest seat of learning in the world in history.

Some years later c.850BC, this patron of knowledge was killed when he made a brave but doomed attempt to fly. Watched by a huge crowd in New Troy, Bladud had attached wings to his arms and leapt from a great height. He was caught by a huge gust of wind and though he flapped his arms frantically, he crashed into the Temple of Apollo and was fatally injured.

As the years – and the centuries – passed, the great Athenian university at Stamford is supposed to have passed into the hands of the Druids, the notorious priestly caste whose training lasted some 20 years before they were ready to mediate between the human and the divine. The heathen teachings flourished until the year AD192 when Lucius, King of the Britons, expelled the Druids and conformed Stamford University to a Christian school of learning. Then, in AD449, Stamford and its university was attacked by marauding Picts and Scots.

The invaders were repelled by the warlord Hengist, but by the early seventh century the university's days were numbered. In AD601 Augustine, the first archbishop of Canterbury, found Stamford's university peopled by a mix of both Saxons and Britons engaged in heretical practices. After hearing a report on this, an outraged Pope Gregory I ordered the university destroyed; there was considerable resistance, but by the year 605 the world's first university had been demolished and razed to the ground.

The 'truth' of any of this is highly questionable. Geoffrey of Monmouth's 12th-century account is the earliest surviving record of King Bladud himself, and was allegedly based on a lost source of Breton legends he had translated. The tale of Stamford's university is even more spurious, for the earliest known account is that in John Hardyng's rhyming *Chronicle*, written some time before his death in 1465. Hardyng, who lived at Kyme, was a man of antiquarian knowledge but seemingly not above bribery and forgery – his dealings with King James I of Scotland concerning important documents have indicated as such. Thus it is generally taken that the tale began with Hardyng in the 15th century and was elaborated upon by successive scholars and local historians.

Just a myth? Certainly, although one day maybe some scholar might uncover some feeble evidence for the university buried deep and lost within the papal archives. It would be marvellous if there were even an ounce of truth in the old, old tale.

SIMON THE ZEALOT

There is the fascinating prospect that one of Jesus Christ's 12 apostles came to Britain in the first century AD and was actually killed on Lincolnshire soil.

The apostle in question was Saint Simon the Zealot, or, alternatively, the Canaanite or Cananean. The Zealots were an extreme Jewish nationalist organisation that, in the year 66, fermented a violent uprising against the despised Roman occupiers of Judea. Jewish assassins known as the *sicarii* turned on the occupiers and the bloodshed continued for four years, culminating in a last stand by the Zealots at the temple in Jerusalem – the holiest of all Jewish places. A two-year-long siege ensued, but the revolt effectively ended when the Roman forces fought their way through a devastated city and massacred thousands, before burning and looting the temple on 8 September AD70. Hundreds more Jewish fighters killed themselves during a siege in their last stand against the Roman army at Masada the following year.

However, Simon had left the Zealots long before this carnage erupted – possibly after witnessing Jesus himself change water into wine at Cana, when he realised that spiritual power would settle the future of Israel rather than the bloodshed of the sword of fanaticism. He must have been seriously conflicted upon the event of Christ's crucifixion and Resurrection: when Christ rose again after his death on the cross he ordained that the Apostles were not to know the time when the Kingdom of Israel was to be restored.

Nevertheless, Simon travelled widely following Christ's ascension to heaven and preached evangelism on a truly – by first century standards – worldwide scale. He is reputed to have spread the word in Egypt, Mesopotamia (modern Iraq), Persia (modern Iran), Cyrene (modern Libya), Carthage (Tunisia) and Mauritania (west Africa); Armenian custom holds that he travelled there as well, and by the year AD44 Simon had passed through Europe and departed Spain for the chilly shores of the north-westerly European island of Britain. It is said that he visited the savages of the land and performed miracles – and he may also have accompanied the legendary Joseph of Arimathea on his visit to Glastonbury, Somerset.

It was after much travelling that some 16 years later Simon the Zealot returned to the inhospitable lands of England. In the year AD60, while preaching in eastern England, he fell foul of the hated Roman Procurator Fiscal Catus Decianus.

During the Roman era Caistor was indeed the site of a fortified Roman settlement, but in AD60 the Romans were newly arrived in the British Isles and the fort at Caistor is of uncertain date – it does not appear to date back to the first century. If there is any truth in the legend that Saint Simon returned to England, then the reason for his brutal fate in Caistor would have to be that in the year

The Roman-era wall boundaries the church at Caistor.

AD60, Roman forces were crushing various rebellions, including those by Boudica and her followers, and the warlike Druids on Anglesey. Having Simon the Zealot in England, whipping up religious enthusiasm would simply present another threat that had to be dealt with, so according to the legend Decianus had Simon arrested. The Apostle was dragged to Caistor, where he was crucified – a martyr's death.

Simon the Zealot was buried at Caistor on 10 May AD61.

However, another version of the saint's demise claims that he left England and travelled to Persia with Judas Thaddaeus, or Saint Jude. Both were reportedly assassinated in an unknown town known as Suanir, with Simon being killed with a saw and Jude being murdered with a battleaxe on a long pike handle. Both martyrs were, according to this version, buried in Persia.

Like the tales of Joseph of Arimathea, and even Christ himself, travelling to the British Isles, the story of the martyrdom of Saint Simon the Zealot in Caistor can now never be proved one way or the other.

DANISH INTRIGUE AT GAINSBOROUGH

Was the rule of the shortest-lived king England has ever known brought to an abrupt end by an assassination in Lincolnshire?

The ruler in question was Svein (Sweyen) Forkbeard, the 11th-century king of Denmark. The king of England at that time was Athelred II, and he ruled a land which for years had been subjected to Danish sea raids. In the year 1002 he announced that he knew of a Danish plot to invade the nation and overthrow him, and his army fanned out to brutally round up Danish 'suspects'. The anti-Danish sentiment snowballed and mobs began attacking Danish communities: on 13 November thousands were butchered in atrocities across central and western England in what became known as The St Brice's Day Massacre.

Athelred II undoubtedly instigated the massacres, with the irony being that it actually precipitated a Danish assault, irrespective of whether or not there had been an *actual* threat to his kingdom originally. For among those murdered in London was the Danish king's sister, Gunnhild, and the outraged Svein ordered devastating revenge attacks on England that carried on for years while Athelred managed to forestall a total invasion by paying Svein tribute money.

Such a chaotic situation couldn't go on forever, and in July 1013 Svein sailed into the Humber with a huge fleet of longships to claim the kingdom of England. His journey took him some 20 miles along the River Trent to the relatively friendly territory of Gainsborough – which, during this period, was part of a wide-ranging area of eastern England known as the Danelaw, where Danish communities had settled. As he disembarked, the people of Gainsborough – along with all who lived in the area of Danelaw – accepted Svein Forkbeard as king of England. Svein had conquered a third of the nation without a sword being drawn.

After gathering horses and supplies, and rallying many local men to his cause, Svein's highly-efficient army moved south-westerly towards the capital, causing much destruction and mayhem as they went. However, Svein's army met stiff resistance at London: many of his men drowned in the Thames during the battles, but as one by one surrounding towns capitulated to the Danish king, London found itself isolated and unable to resist the invaders. It was December 1013 and Svein Forkbeard, the king of Denmark, was also the king of England.

That winter Svein returned to Gainsborough, where he had left his son and heir Cnut in charge. Gainsborough Castle became the royal residence and held court to the king and his family as well as his officials, advisors and retinue. Among these, it seems, there was a treacherous assassin.

King Svein Forkbeard died at Gainsborough Castle on the night of 3 February 1014, and one story claims that his untimely death was due to a riding accident. One Florence of Worcester recorded that Svein had ordered the people of Gainsborough to pay 'a large tribute from the town where rests the uncorrupted corpse of the precious martyr, Edmund – a thing which no one has dared to do since the town was given to the church of that saint.' Florence claimed that while out riding, the ghost of Saint Edmund had appeared to Svein and run him through with a heavenly spear, forcing him to the ground. He subsequently died in writhing agony. However, Florence supposed that only Svein had seen his ghostly attacker on the day of the incident.

A more interesting account claims that he grew ill at a banquet, and although some kind of fever is a possibility, others claimed that a member of his inner circle had poisoned him to death. Perhaps he then went out riding and died of his sickness, falling from his horse in the process.

With the passing of so many years it is largely impossible to establish the truth. Reading between the lines it does seem, however, that there was something unnatural about his death. Superstitious villagers claimed that the king had indeed been slain by the ghostly hand of the martyred Saint Edmund himself, in divine justice for the havoc his tax collectors were wreaking on England, but a more likely candidate for any assassination attempt would be the ousted king, Athelred II. Athelred had fled to Normandy in the face of the Danish advance, and, although growing old and sick, he still had his eye on the kingdom of England for his son and heir Edmund Ironside. Like most other rulers of the age, Athelred was not above murder when it came to politics – and it would only require one traitor in Svein's household.

When Athelred retook his kingdom in 1014, the young King Cnut had all his hostages brutally mutilated before he fled Lincolnshire for Denmark. Horror followed upon horror as Athelred's army burnt to death every Dane they could find as they marched through the county; the people of the town of Gainsborough paid in blood for their support of Svein and Cnut.

Gainsborough Castle no longer stands, although its earthwork foundations can still be observed at the site east of Morton and off The Little Belt. Although they said locally that Svein Forkbeard was buried on Pingle Hill, this is not true – for the king lies buried in Roskilde, Denmark. But whatever the truth of King Svein's cloudy end, it is fascinating to speculate that Britain's shortest-ever lived ruler was the victim of an assassin during this turbulent period of Gainsborough's history.

LOST TREASURES

For generations there have been rumours of a hoard of treasure buried somewhere on the boundary line between Digby and Dorrington. The site of this treasure was marked by a large stone which had, in time, sunk into the ground, although folklorist Ethel Rudkin wrote in 1936 that the site where the stone sank was still known – one wonders if it still is. Not far away is Catley Abbey, disestablished during the reign of King Henry VIII. It is said that the monks hid a hoard of treasure nearby, which has yet to be discovered. However, these riches would pale in comparison to the fabulous treasures that legend says lie buried in the silt of the Wash.

In September 1216 King John had launched an offensive against rebel barons and the would-be usurper Louis Capet of France. The campaigning took him through Norfolk – and it was during this endeavour that some say John made a fateful decision to send his immense baggage train on ahead via a more direct, quicker route. Local guides were to lead the baggage train on its shortcut and rendezvous with the king and his soldiers on the other side of the Wash. Following these instructions, the baggage convoy (horses and wagons loaded up with stores, equipment, the king's wardrobe, his portable chapel and relics – and, of course, his royal treasure) is said to have got bogged down in the treacherous quicksand of the Wash somewhere between Walpole Cross Keys and Long Sutton; while crossing the tidal river known as the Wellstream the sea rushed in and swamped the stricken convoy. Not a single man, beast or item was ever seen again.

Could it be that King John's treasures are buried somewhere along the Nene?

The area where John's treasure was lost is now significantly inland and in some 800 years not a single piece of evidence of buried royal treasure has turned up in the area. There is strong suspicion that the whole story is a myth, but either way this event is said to have taken place on or about 12 October 1216 – six days before the king's death.

There is an added element of mysterious intrigue to this tale of mediaeval campaigning through the East Midlands. Legend says that, put simply, while he rested at the Cistercian abbey of Swineshead, east of Sleaford, John was poisoned by a monk called Brother Simon as he was about to molest a nun, who happened to be the sister of the abbot. Being a legend, there are varying unsubstantiated accounts of what happened. One story indicates that John was given three poisoned peaches as he ranted about a famine he would bring upon the country with a bread price hike, while another version claims his wine was poisoned by the monk on the orders of Pope Innocent III – with whom John had fallen out with some years previously over the choosing of the Archbishop of Canterbury. The suspicious king had ordered the monk to first sample the wine, and the monk had done so; the luckless assassin took a sip and is held to have died himself some time afterwards. It took a further two days for John to die at Newark, where the 'official' cause was logged as dysentery brought on by overindulgence.

In truth, this legend is unlikely but difficult to rule out completely. The biggest argument against John being poisoned is that he was apparently growing ill already after his exhausting campaigning in the saddle, and a bout of gluttony at King's Lynn was the aggravating factor. Therefore, any poisoning that occurred at Swineshead would have merely made an ill man worse.

A disastrous campaign and a nation in turmoil, lost treasure which, if it turned up today, would be priceless, and ultimately regicide? The legacy left by King John during his last, fateful journey through Lincolnshire is fascinating indeed.

THE ISLE OF AXHOLME'S LEGENDARY 'GIANT'

There are many stories told of a hermit and 'giant' named William (or Billy) of Lindholme, who, centuries ago, was supposed to have lived in the boggy and treacherous Isle of Axholme in North Lincolnshire. He was the son of a farmer brought up on a small hill just outside of Wroot and one tale alleges that his father harnessed his strength and used him to run the farm single-handedly. These liberties caused the young giant to lob a stone into Wroot in an attempt to crush his parents as they attended a party there. Indeed, many of the tales of William drift into the realm of the fantastic; William's parents called him to account for his actions in trying to kill them and leaving the fields free for the sparrows to attack. The giant youth sulkily replied that he had in fact captured all the invading sparrows and thrown them in the barn before he had tried to murder his parents!

Upon arriving home William's parents were aghast to find that he had actually been telling the truth: the barn was full of sparrows, most of which were dead or dying. However, there were several survivors – and these sparrows had turned completely snow white. These were set free and formed a colony of extremely rare white sparrows that inhabited the region.

Some accounts say that William possessed the powers of a wizard, and others went further. The giant's abilities, they said, were as the result of a pact with the Devil. When they came to build the causeway through the marshland across Hatfield Moors, to Wroot, William agreed to perform the task single-handedly at record speed – provided no one should attempt to see how he was carrying it out. However, one local horseman who rode before the giant to show him the route glimpsed an unnerving sight: William of Lindholme behind him, in the mist of a wall of stones, gravel and pebbles flying and landing, but the giant was being helped...by hundreds and hundreds of little demons in red coats, who scurried and flew around him. The villager whispered, 'God speed your work' and forced on his mount ever faster to escape the unholy causeway being built behind him. However, the desperately-needed causeway was never finished. For the villager had broken the deal by looking at William, and the demons had instantly vanished. The causeway had lost momentum and petered out at the same time, and the giant refused to undertake any more efforts to finish it.

William's own death was surrounded with rumours of Satan's involvement. His pact with the Devil meant that he knew when his time was up, and, as such, he prepared very carefully. He dug his own giant grave and then propped up an enormous flagstone next to it. When Satan came to take his soul he simply lay down in the grave and knocked away the pole; the flagstone crashed down on top of him and entombed him.

For centuries, generations grew up in the Isle of Axholme on these tales, but could it be that there is the barest of truths in the story of this mythological figure? The odd, out-of-place boulder allegedly thrown by William can apparently still be found in Wroot, although it stands on private land. Folklorist Ethel Rudkin heard that the boulder was so large it had sunk into the ground under its own weight and was difficult to locate. She was also told in 1931 by a native of Wroot that he had seen a pure white sparrow 'not over 30 years back'. The local knew the legends of William of Lindholme very well; William was also referred to as Tommy Lindum, or Lindrum. Of the legend of the Hatfield Moors-Wroot causeway, Rudkin was told '...the odd part of that is, that there is the beginnin's of a cobbled roo-ad there now – I've seed it – well! 'Ow did it get there if Tommy didn't maa-ke it?'

Ethel Rudkin wrote that the very wet, low-lying land to the north of Wroot housed a spring of pure water by a slight hill of gravel, where William had lived a hermit's existence. In 1727 the Revd Samuel Wesley and a Mr Stovin went to this region on the border land between North Lincolnshire and South Yorkshire and found a house in an advanced state of disrepair – built on the site of William's hermit's cell. Here, one of the floors was like that of an ancient chapel, with a stone altar at one end...and what they thought was the hermit's grave at the other. Standing before this was a large freestone slab with a weathered inscription which they could not read. The two intrepid investigators are alleged to have prised up the slab and dug into the grave beneath it; here they found one tooth, a skull and the thigh and shin bone of a human body – all of which were very large. Also found were a piece of beaten copper and a peck of hempseed.

Rudkin wrote, 'The freestone slab that was over the grave was gradually broken up by the inhabitants of the house that was built on the site of the cell and used for scouring purposes, so that there is no hope of ever reading that inscription and so throwing a little light, perhaps, on the identity of William of Lindholme.' But the native of Wroot, to whom Rudkin was told this story in 1931, also commented that there was an old box in the granary at Lindum (Lindholme Hall in Hatfield, South Yorkshire) where William's bones were now kept. He had personally seen them, he told her.

ACCIDENT OR SABOTAGE?

Following the Napoleonic Wars, there was a mood abroad in Britain for social change. Regular protests, riots, conspiracies and numerous abortive insurrections occurred, notably the Luddite uprising, the Peterloo Massacre and the Cato Street Conspiracy among others. Wealth and privilege were being questioned by the lower classes, and rights and reform were being demanded – the threat of revolution was in the air. On 19 July 1821 there were riots as the hugely unpopular King George IV was crowned. It was against this backdrop that Colonel Coningsby Sibthorp, one of two MPs for Lincoln, met his mysterious end.

Colonel Sibthorp came from a line of Sibthorps involved in Lincoln politics and he was an ardent supporter of the unpopular king. Indeed, he appears to have been ignorant of the true depth of his *own* unpopularity. On the evening of 23 February 1821 the colonel dined at the house of a Dr Cookson at 24 Eastgate, Lincoln, before being collected by horses and a carriage to take him back to his own home in Canwick. Also travelling with him were his brother, his sister-in-law and their daughter, who had also dined at Dr Cookson's house.

The carriage set off and turned right into Priorygate, and somewhere near Priorygate Arch one of the wheels suddenly flew off. As the carriage tipped crazily the coachman was thrown from the box and the startled horses bolted, finally tipping the carriage over in a horrendous crash outside 13 Minster Yard. The colonel was seriously injured and gently carried into number 13 (which happened to be the home of an aunt), where it was clear he had been paralysed with spine and leg injuries. He never really recovered and died on 9 March 1822 at his home in Canwick, aged 40.

To the end Colonel Coningsby Charles Waldo Sibthorp considered the whole incident an accident, despite it being very clear from the start that the linchpin in the wheel had been deliberately removed. Reporting the circumstances of the crash, the *Lincoln, Rutland & Stamford Mercury* noted that three men had been overheard in Lincoln discussing a plot to sabotage the colonel's carriage the very night before. It was also noted that the coachman had picked up the politician from the White Hart and then his relatives a short time later, so the saboteurs may have thought that their enemy was travelling alone. Not that it mattered, the newspaper noted for the benefit of its readership. Anyone attempting to injure or kill the colonel would clearly accept that other people might get hurt, such were the times.

The true circumstances by which the linchpin became removed from the coach have never been established. But it is tempting to speculate that the mood of revolution touched Lincolnshire, and that the colonel was its unlucky victim. Not by bullet, sword or knife, but by sabotaging his carriage – in itself somehow indicative of the nature of protest in a rural town far away from London itself.

Minster Yard, Lincoln: site of the accident.

The Mary Celeste of Railway Folklore

On the night of 19 September 1906 the *Scotch Express* thundered into Grantham station when it should have been slowing down, and it derailed at points in the track before winging a bridge and crashing over on its side. Fourteen people were killed in the disaster, but the mass of contradictory witness statements meant that *why* the express crashed would forever be a mystery.

Lieutenant Colonel P.G. von Donop, the Government Railway Inspector, was charged with uncovering what had happened. Fellow engine drivers claimed that the driver of the *Scotch Express* may have shot through Grantham because of a time constraint. Some witnesses spoke of the express driver, Fred Fleetwood, having been heard yelling to people as the train passed between Peterborough and Grantham. Some claimed that, mysteriously, the locomotive footplate had been deserted as the train hurtled towards its doom; others even claimed that some supernatural force had guided the train towards disaster.

There was a persistent rumour that Fleetwood, the driver, may have had a drink problem. Von Donop traced the source of this allegation to the girlfriend of the train's fireman...the fireman, one Ralph Talbot, had apparently thought Fleetwood was an alcoholic, and he had claimed he would stun Fleetwood and take over the train if he suspected the man was drunk. And von Donop had indeed come across reports among the mass of confusing evidence that two people had been spotted 'fighting and gesticulating' at the footplate...

A signalboxman who had witnessed the train hurtle towards Grantham station claimed that, as it flashed past, the light from the firebox briefly illuminated the locomotive footplate. Two figures were glimpsed, struck rigid with terror and staring fixedly in front of them.

Von Donop eventually had to admit defeat. The handbrake at the footplate had only been partially applied before the crash, and there was no evidence of mechanical faults. His report ruefully noted 'The primary cause of this accident must forever remain a mystery'. To those who swore they had seen the driver and the fireman engaged in their own suicidal, pitched struggle at the footplate, the crash of the *Scotch Express* wasn't perhaps so much of a mystery.

World War Two Urban Legend

The infamous rumour that the bodies of thousands of German soldiers had been washed up on the shores of the British coastline during World War Two also circulated in Lincolnshire, as writer Naomi Royde Smith's diary entry in September 1940 indicates: 'It began with a reported tocsin in Cornwall, spreading to Hampshire, heard by many...The Germans had landed somewhere in Dorset; in Kent; in Lincolnshire. This was officially denied. Then a whisper started that the corpses of German soldiers, in full battle dress, had been washed up all around the coast. Presently the horrid detail that each corpse had its hands tied behind its back was added...Then the tale grew into patent absurdity. The whole of the Channel from Weymouth to Devonport was covered with the corpses of stricken armies...The entire population of the Reich must have perished.'

By the time this rumour touched Lincolnshire, it may have sounded frighteningly plausible: after all, was not the air war being fought from RAF bases scattered all over the county? The Germans had attempted an invasion in the late summer, and all had perished disastrously! One story claimed that the bodies were charred because the sea was set on fire. Another theory held that the Germans had held an ill-fated rehearsal for their invasion of Britain and that violent weather conditions had sunk their barges. In Lincolnshire – as in other parts of the UK – people saw no such bodies, but this was explained away by the authorities somehow containing the whole situation.

In fact, the rumours got so bad that on 16 October 1940 there was an official denial of the story. In classic *X-Files* mode, this failed to stop the stories – for, of course, the government wished to avoid exciting the population until the situation had been assessed.

The interesting thing about this is that it appears to be the classic early example of an urban legend sweeping the nation, county by county, like wildfire, with very little evidence to support it (except, perhaps, the bodies of bailouts being washed ashore). There is also perhaps a heavy element of wishful thinking: if thousands of German soldiers had died attempting to invade Britain, then the war was surely not long to end…

It is easy to see how an anxious populace speculated when confronted with odd incidents during the war. Typical of this was the story of one Stan Jeshey, who, in 1940, saw what looked like a battle taking place out in the North Sea. Stan and a friend ran into sand dunes at Theddlethorpe-St-Helen and through binoculars watched what appeared to be enemy aircraft bombing a convoy of 40 vessels in the distance. Above them, three Spitfires droned and circled, but did not intervene to help the besieged vessels.

From this the lads decided that it must have been a mock exercise. But then the six o'clock news noted that a convoy of vessels *had* been attacked in the North Sea, but no damage was inflicted. However, the next day Stan found dozens of tea chests washed up on the beach and floating in the sea – clearly, there *had* been casualties during this mysterious incident. It was dusk, so he was unable to investigate any further. The following day they were gone.

It was put out that all the chests had been salvaged by fishermen and found to contain raw rubber. Quite where they came from, and what became of the unlucky ship that had carried the cargo, was unexplained. But the tacit acknowledgement of an 'incident' followed by a denial of any damage done – when clearly there was evidence of such damage – would certainly make people wonder to what extent misinformation was being put out as the 'official line'.

VANISHING ACTS

T.F. Thistelton-Dyer's *Strange Pages From Family Papers* (1900) mentions a perplexing disappearance that took place in Lincolnshire *c.*1750. It was on the day of a wedding, and following the service the bride, groom, family and the assembled guests repaired to the bridegroom's residence to await the dinner hour. Some chose to ramble in the garden, others to rest in the house. Then something happened to spoil the happy occasion.

A servant appeared and summoned the bridegroom away to a quiet corner. He told his master that there was a stranger at the door who wished to see him, and at this the bridegroom left his guests to see what the man wanted. He was, quite literally, never seen again. Gradually the party broke up as people fanned out to search for him, and despite extensive enquiries being made, the new bride was left mystified and heartbroken at the fate of her lost husband.

On 8 September 1815 the *Lincoln, Stamford & Rutland Mercury* reported on the death of Mrs Iremonger, who was 'advanced in years'. But accompanying this short report is an intriguing enigma. Mrs Iremonger had been married to Mr William Iremonger, a grazier who had left his residence in Alford on horseback and simply vanished without trace. Mr Iremonger had disappeared after leaving his house some 20 years previously, in 1795, and the newspaper remarked 'he is supposed to have been murdered'.

John Codd, groundskeeper to Mr Ald Gibbotson of Lincoln, vanished without trace somewhere between Newark and Lincoln on 1 November 1809. It was a Wednesday, and Mr Codd had been at Newark Fair. At about three o'clock in the afternoon he was observed to climb on to his horse at the White Swan Inn in Newark and set off in the direction of Lincolnshire. Some time later, the *Lincoln, Stamford & Rutland Mercury* reported that his horse had been found wandering about a mile from Newark in the borderland between Lincolnshire and Nottinghamshire. One stirrup was missing and the bridle was broken – signs that Mr Codd had fallen violently, or been pulled from his mount. Nine days later the newspaper reported that no sign had been found of the missing man; the only witness to the mystery – the horse – could, of course, not help the investigators.

What is likely to have happened in both these mysteries is that the missing men had been attacked by the footpads that were still a danger to travellers in Lincolnshire in the early 19th century. On the other hand, a shoemaker from Aubourn called Pearson seems to have been deliberately targeted. In the early 1830s he was shot and wounded by a man named King, who was transported. In 1832 Pearson, by now recovered, simply vanished after leaving a public house in Bassingham. In 1858 a skeleton which was found in the River Brant was *assumed* to be his, but clearly the circumstances of the mystery were never going to be explained and there is no indication that the case was ever resolved.

Gutch and Peacock's *County Folklore Vol 5: Lincolnshire* (1908) notes a strange story told by the rector of Wispington, north-west of Horncastle. A local miser died (names and dates are deliberately withheld so perhaps this had happened in the near past) and he was laid out in a coffin. The following day he had vanished, only to have been replaced by stones. The rector hinted darkly that Satan had come and taken the body, but what is more likely is that criminals stole the body. After all, if the man were a miser perhaps they expected to find evidence of his reputed hoard about his person, and the stones were laid in his place to compensate for the weight.

Of course, for ships to go down at sea, or crash, is hardly unknown off England's eastern coast. And when ships vanish without trace the details of the mystery can be generally attributed to bad weather conditions or poor-quality vessels. Nonetheless, there is still something of an eerie, supernatural element concerning ships and crews that are simply never seen again. Perhaps it is the fact that the final resting place of those lost will never be known, nor will the last moments and heroism of their lives; perhaps it is the association with a kind of mysterious Mary Celeste-style misfortune. Perhaps it is the tiny chance that those lost may have survived somehow.

The *Grimsby News* reported just such an enigmatic tragedy on 23 November 1894. The previous week, the steam tug *Sarah Joliie*, of Liverpool, had entered Grimsby and the master had reported that they had sadly lost a large, full-rigged barque that they had been towing. The lost ship was the 1,720 tonne *Culmore* and when it was being towed, it was being crewed by a personnel of 22 including Captain J. Reid.

The tragedy had occurred on or about the 14 November as the tug towed its charge through the choppy waters of the North Sea. For a week there had been severe weather conditions: fog had blanketed the mouth of the River Humber and parts of the North Sea, and heavy rain lashed at the tug and the barque it towed to port. The two vessels were caught in an immense gale, and the rope attaching the *Culmore* snapped. This was somewhere in the vicinity of Spurn Head.

The *Culmore* was quickly lost to sight, due to the fog and the fact that it was night time, and the cries of the crew on board the barque as it drifted away were quickly lost to the ears of those on board the steam tug. It was enough for the battered steam tug to limp to Grimsby, but a week later it put to sea once again in an attempt to locate the lost vessel. Unfortunately, neither the lost barque or any of its doomed crew were ever seen again and the steam tug returned to Grimsby empty-handed.

In the early morning of 13 March 1928, a 32ft long Stinson aircraft named *Endeavour* took off from RAF Cranwell and flew westwards into atrociously-bad wintry conditions. The craft was piloted by captain W.G.R. Hinchcliffe, a highly-experienced fighter pilot of the Royal Flying Corps, who had claimed several kills during World War One – and he should have known better than to attempt to cross the Atlantic in the sub-zero temperatures. Especially since he had a co-pilot, the Honourable Elsie Mackay, a 34-year-old English socialite who yearned to be the first woman to fly the Atlantic – in an age when aviation records were beginning to be claimed and time was running out. At about 11:30am their aircraft was reported over County Waterford, Eire, 280 miles west of RAF Cranwell. What was thought to be the *Endeavour* was next spotted two hours later by the lighthouse keeper at Mizzen Head, County Cork – 400 miles west of RAF Cranwell. After that the *Endeavour* vanished off the face of the earth, never to be seen or heard from again.

Similarly tragic is the case of Captain William Schaffner, a 28-year-old American flying with the RAF. The captain's Lightning jet, *Foxtrot 94*, took off from RAF Binbrook on the night of 9 September 1970 on an exercise trying to intercept another aircraft. The Lightning flew too low and crashed into the sea off Flamborough Head; it did not sink immediately, though, and around 11pm a Shackleton reconnaissance aircraft thought they saw Captain Schaffner climb out on to the wing of the floating jet and then lower himself into the sea. Eventually, as the Shackleton's searchlights probed the darkness for their comrade, the Lightning jet fighter sank beneath the waves and settled on the seabed, its nose pointing upright. As the days dragged on into weeks a team of divers were sent down to inspect the Lightning on the seabed. They found the plane intact, with the canopy still in place. But the cockpit was eerily empty...an official veil of Cold War vagueness surrounding the incident and the good condition of the submerged jet for years fuelled speculation that the captain's jet had encountered a UFO off the east coast, a suggestion that was offensive to the captain's family. This legend has now largely been laid to rest: accidents such as Schaffner's do happen, and the real mystery is how he managed to become free of his cockpit, close it again, and then vanish off the face of the earth with his emergency dinghy in (relatively) smooth seas, while a Shackleton with a searchlight above him was trying to pick him out.

In May 2006 it was announced that detectives from the major investigation team were again reopening the case of nine-year-old Christine Markham. The little girl had disappeared without trace on 21 May 1973 after leaving her home in Robinson Road, Scunthorpe, to go to school; she had walked part of the way with two older siblings who had to catch a bus to their own school. As the bus moved off they had seen through the window their little sister turn around and wander away, apparently in the direction they had just walked. Unfortunately the little girl had earned for herself the reputation of a truant, who often took herself off and returned home later than normal, and it was not until 19:30 that evening that she was reported missing. Christine was never heard from again, although investigators logged some 33 possible sightings of her in the general area on the day she went missing, drawing the conclusion she vanished that evening – as opposed to vanishing on her way to school. But the police were playing catch up and by the time the trail ran abruptly cold they had formed the dreadful conclusion she had been abducted.

In 2002 modern forensic techniques provided a link between a bouncer called Kappen from Port Talbot and the so-called 'Saturday Night Strangler', suspected of murdering three teenage girls in Wales in 1973. On 11 June 2002 Humberside police announced they were re-investigating Christine Markham's disappearance – as Kappen had been in the area at the time. In the autumn of 1973, Kappen had lodged in the Gainsborough area and he was thought to have worked as a contracted lorry driver in Scunthorpe. This was some weeks after Christine's disappearance. However, any links to Kappen could now never be established – for he died in 1990 at the age of 49.

The Christine Markham story is made all the more poignant because of the agonising lack of closure for her family and those who knew her. She is North Lincolnshire's Gennette Tate, the little girl who one day simply didn't come home.

What is worrying is that in this era of modern forensic detection (not to mention air, sea and land searching capabilities), people can still vanish forever. On 21 November 1996 Ruskington man Michael Hewerdine was last heard of going to meet a man in Sleaford. He rarely travelled beyond the local area, and yet never returned from his enigmatic assignation. It is likely that the missing man has been murdered. Britain is a relatively small, crowded island, but in such instances as this, the quiet countryside of Lincolnshire suddenly becomes very ominous: miles and miles of lonely woodland and barely-inhabited hills and fenland, with ample places for people to vanish off the face of the earth.

CHAPTER 2

SAINTS AND MIRACLES

INTRODUCTION

One of Lincolnshire's oldest and most famous stories concerns King Oswald of Northumbria, an exceptionally-pious Christian ruler whose fortunes changed when he was killed in battle by his rival, King Penda of Mercia, in the Welsh Marches in AD642. Oswald was beheaded and his arms chopped off as the spoils of war, and the rest of his corpse was buried on the battlefield. In c.675 the slain king's remains were unearthed by his niece, Queen Osthryth, and transported to Tupholme Abbey near Bardney. When the cart carrying its grisly burden arrived at the gates of the abbey it is said that the monks treated the remains of the dead king – an enemy of Mercia in their eyes – with no respect, and they dumped them in a nearby field and merely covered them with a tent. To their horror, a bright light illuminated the spot and blazed up from the site towards the heavens.

The effect on the monks was immediate: they recovered the corpse and brought it into the abbey, fearing the wrath of God after their shameful treatment of their dead enemy. They vowed never to close the doors of Tupholme Abbey again, spawning the local phrase, 'You must have been born in Bardney' of someone who habitually leaves their door open.

Of course, many such stories are associated with the grand houses of religious significance in Lincolnshire. For example, St Mary's Church at Stow is held to stand on the site of a miracle. Around c.AD670 a Northumbrian queen called Etheldreda – whose duties to her husband were second to her duties to the cloth – fled south when her husband, King Egfrith, began to demand his conjugal rites. Etheldreda's journey took her southwards, heading for an estate that she owned in Ely, Cambridgeshire. She entered North Lincolnshire, it is thought, at Winteringham.

Perhaps the most familiar miracle associated with Etheldreda is the story of her staff. The weather was ferociously hot and she was exposed. She was suffering from fatigue and, at a point which some say was Stow in Lincolnshire, she stuck her staff into the ground and then fell asleep. When she awoke the staff had put forth leaves and branches which shielded the holy woman from the sun's rays. It afterwards grew into an immense ash tree, which towered above all the others for miles around. According to Thomas of Ely, it was the largest ash tree in Lindsey, a gift from heaven to protect Etheldreda from the heat of the sun. The exact spot became known to pilgrims as Etheldredastowe and the original wooden church was built there. Nowadays, the village of Stow is dominated by its huge church on that very site, sometimes referred to as Stow Minster, which is, indeed, of Saxon origins, with significant Norman additions.

The 'Miracle of Stow' may in fact have occurred at West Halton, where a church is dedicated to Saint Etheldreda. But Stow is the favoured site, and St Mary's Church – far too big for the village it stands in – is sometimes called the 'Mother of Lincoln Cathedral'.

In fact, there was something similar in Lincoln itself. One Giraldus Cambrensis tells us that the exact site of Lincoln Cathedral '...on the brow of a hill beyond the River Witham had been pre-signified by certain visions, miracles, signs and wonders' and there is a recurring theme of miracles occurring at the tombs of Lincoln's earliest bishops within Lincoln Cathedral. The Episcopal ring of Bishop Remigius de Fecamp, the cathedral's founder, was removed from his tomb in 1124 and held to have the ability to produce cures after being dipped in water. And upon Bishop Robert Grosseteste's

The remains of Tupholme Abbey, Bardney.

death on 9 October 1253 he is said to have appeared in spirit form before his enemy Pope Innocent IV – the pontiff had been planning to have Grosseteste's body disinterred and his bones and ashes scattered. Grosseteste's ghost looked at the Pope and said to him, 'Is it thou, Sinibald, thou miserable Pope, who wilt cast my bones out of their cemetery, to thy disgrace and that of the church of Lincoln? Woe to thee who hast despised, thou shalt be despised in thy turn!' Grosseteste's tomb in the cathedral was said to distil an oil as proof of his sanctity.

It is clear that some of these tales are pure folklore. During the reign of Henry IV, a vision of St Margaret herself is held to have appeared within the church at Quadring and killed one Simon Greenleaf, Lord of Nut Hall, who had been dabbling in the occult. But it is equally clear that some of the stories – notably that of Bishop Hugh d'Avalon – contain a strange ring of truth. It is certainly true to say that Lincolnshire has produced some of England's most notable holy men, from Saint Botolph, Guthlac of Crowland and Gilbert of Sempringham, to Bishop Hugh himself. And some might consider that the founders of Methodism, John and Charles Wesley, rank alongside these great men in terms of devotion. On 9 February 1709 John, then aged five, had to be rescued from a terrible blaze at the rectory in Epworth. It was an escape so narrow that his father Samuel described the saving of his son as 'almost a miracle', and a neighbouring clergyman called it 'an account of a very remarkable Providence'. One can imagine that in later years the followers of Methodism saw God's hand in the escape.

Nearer the present time, religious symbolism is sometimes seen in the most mundane of settings, and signs from God – such as speaking in tongues and the stigmata – are not unknown. An apparition of 16 hovering virgins has purportedly been seen 'many times' over fields in Manby, and there is a contemporary account of a vision of Jesus Christ himself, bathed in a red glow, stepping from an image of divine mercy before a praying schoolgirl in Lincolnshire. Even angel sightings have been reported...

The Crowland hermit

Guthlac was the son of a seventh-century Mercian nobleman. The first recorded indication of the strength of his faith was his announcement at the age of 24 that he was quitting his life as a successful soldier and mercenary to lead the life of a monk at the monastery in Repton, Derbyshire. After two years it appears that the drunken irreligious lifestyle of the monks clashed head-on with Guthlac's devotion and self-deprivation, and he obtained permission from the abbot to become a hermit. The genuineness of his piety, it seems, during this time at the monastery won over the attitude of his dissolute fellow monks.

Guthlac hired a boatman named Tatwain and told him to take him deep into the Lincolnshire Fens in Croyland (modern-day Crowland), to the most inaccessible island he knew of. Tatwain did as he was bid, taking the hermit and his servant – one Beccelm – by boat through the dank and gloomy reeds of the wetlands to a tiny island in the middle of the most inhospitable reaches of Lincolnshire, a haunted place where the only things that moved in the shadows of the trees were a few savage, local tribespeople. The date is recorded as St Bartholomew's Day, 24 August, in the year 699.

In this fog-shrouded atmosphere, the three built a small cell each and a tiny chapel. Guthlac lived in this godforsaken marshland for some 15 years until his death, and he took to wearing animal skins and living off a piece of barley bread and a cup of stagnant water, which he took after sunset. Apart from bouts of illness, he may have succumbed to a kind of marsh fever.

His island was repeatedly plagued by demons, monstrous creatures that came out of the gloom: they appeared as 'many horrible shapes with great heads, fiery mouths, scaly bodies, pointed chins, crooked legs and unwinking eyes as big as saucers'.

It seems that the dank island became something of a spiritual battleground, with repeated visits from angels – the only thing, at times, keeping Guthlac sane while the monsters tried to tempt him. The nightmarish entities ridiculed the hermit beyond his endurance and one day – real or imaginary – when it seemed the world had ended, Guthlac found the creatures had dragged him before the gates of hell. The poem *Guthlac A* tells us that hell's gates, where damned spirits were awaiting entrance, was under some cliffs. It is said that the only thing that saved Guthlac from losing the conflict and being taken to an unknown fate was the spiritual appearance of his patron, the first-century apostle St Bartholomew, who handed him a scourge with which to whip the creatures back and beat them off.

These tales of the hermit's spiritual and mental conflict gradually spread beyond the fenlands, throughout the kingdom of Mercia, and pilgrims began to make the hazardous journey to the little island in ever-increasing numbers in order to receive spiritual advice and cures. One day, Ethelbald (or Athelbald) – an exile with a link to the throne of Mercia – arrived at Guthlac's cell.

Ceolred ruled the kingdom of Mercia at that time, and Ethelbald – a cousin of Ceolred's and therefore a rival – had been forced to flee in fear of his life. Ethelbald made several visits to the hermit, and on one occasion he was given some startling information. Guthlac prophesied that Ethelbald would eventually become king of Mercia, and Ethelbald promised him in return that if the prediction came true, then he would build an abbey on the site of the hermit's little chapel.

On 11 April 714 Guthlac died. He is believed to have been buried in a lead coffin from Wirksworth in Derbyshire. A year later, his corpse – apparently undecayed in the manner that would befit an incorruptible saint – was moved to a shrine. Ethelbald came there to pray and one night saw a vision of Guthlac, who again repeated to the astonished Ethelbald that he would be king of Mercia within one year.

In the year 716 the prophecy came true, just as Guthlac had promised. King Ceolred died after becoming insane during a fit at a banquet, and the path was opened up for Ethelbald to take the

Stow Minster.

throne. On St Bartholomew's Day later that year, Ethelbald — now king — laid the foundation stone of the abbey he had promised the hermit on his pilgrimage.

Today much of the abbey is in ruins, but Guthlac's tiny cell is marked for tourists and pilgrims.

GILBERT OF SEMPRINGHAM

The 12th-century Lincolnshire saint Gilbert was born at Sempringham, the son of a wealthy Norman knight, Sir Jocelin, c.AD1083.

While Gilbert's mother was pregnant with him she dreamt that the moon came down from the skies and settled in her lap, which she took as a sign of her child's coming greatness. However, Gilbert was born a cripple, much to his parents' dismay, and they considered a career in the church the best way for him to distinguish himself. Thus they sent him to France to be educated as a clerk in the holy orders. When he returned to England he served as clerk to the Bishop of Lincoln for two years before returning to serve the church in Sempringham — where he set up the Order of Sempringham.

A miracle, of sorts, is attributed to him in *The Book Of Saint Gilbert*. Father Gilbert was travelling when necessity forced him to seek overnight lodgings at the dwelling of a couple in Stamford. The lady of the house prepared a couch for Gilbert to rest on and then discreetly confided to his holiness

The site of Guthlac's cell is marked for pilgrims.

that, though she and her husband had been married years, the good lord had failed to bless their union with a child. She hoped that her guest's presence under her roof might convince the almighty that she was worthy of bearing a son.

It appears this hopeful plea was answered, for that very night, when her husband returned home, a son was conceived which, nine months later, they named after Father Gilbert. When Gilbert learned of the news, he had the family sent a cow so the infant would not go without, thus choosing to treat the lad as if he had been one of his own.

Those of a cynical nature may suspect that the holy man's interest in the boy was less than spiritual, but this suggestion is at odds with what is known of Gilbert: he had a deep concern for the welfare of children, and he was responsible for opening a school for the offspring of the peasants in Sempringham.

He lived to be over 100 years old (possibly 106) and was entirely devoted to his faith, dying at Sempringham. Upon his death on 4 February 1189 many people reported that they witnessed marvellous lights in the sky, which indicated that a great servant of God was leaving this earthly plane. In France, where King Henry II of England was campaigning, the monarch is reported to have said, 'Truly I knew he had left this earth, for all these ends (referring to his misfortunes in war) had come upon me because he is dead.'

In subsequent years miracles of healing were reported to have occurred at his tomb in Sempringham, which many see as the fulfilment of his mother's prophetic dream during pregnancy.

He was canonised in 1202 by Pope Innocent III. Today the site of his burial is unclear, but there are those who think he may lie before the decorated archway in ancient St Andrew's Church, Sempringham, where there is to be seen a coffin-sized depression in the ground. Outside the wall of the church can be found a memorial to Saint Gilbert and the Gilbertine nuns.

BISHOP HUGH

Of exceptionally-worthy memory was Bishop Hugh d'Avalon of Lincoln, formerly Prior of Witham, Somerset, and a learned man who earned the respect of the clergy, royalty, three popes and the common people for his generosity, sense of justice and his spreading of the faith in the 12th century.

By all accounts Bishop Hugh was an extremely attractive and witty man, whose personality embraced all. Men, women and children all experienced his human charm. Chroniclers recorded anecdotes about him playing with babies, where the infants would gurgle happily, much to the evident joy of the bishop. He was thoroughly chaste and took his vows of celibacy extremely seriously, but, unlike some of the clergy, he entertained widows and mothers at his table, blessing them and listening to their fears and problems. His charm even extended to members of the animal kingdom, notably his famous swan, whose behaviour wildlife experts still have some trouble in explaining. Such stories of an entirely human bishop no doubt fuelled the fondness which almost all felt for Hugh, who had come to England of noble Burgundian stock and ultimately went on to champion a diocese for 14 years, which, at that time, extended from the Humber to the Thames.

Hugh was also exceedingly gifted as a diplomat and a politician. On occasion he acted as both an ambassador and as judge at the royal and papal courts. His charity extended to ethnic minorities and the underclass: Jews, the poor and sufferers of leprosy were all groups he championed. His personal courage was not in doubt either, for he risked his own life, while the Bishop of Lincoln, defending a group of Jews from a bloodthirsty mob during a riot in Stamford. His greatest achievement, however, was his overseeing of the rebuilding of Lincoln Cathedral after an earthquake in 1185 destroyed much of it. Much of the western and eastern transepts are credited to Bishop Hugh, which greatly enlarged the original cathedral built by the first bishop, Remigius. Although the immense Angel Choir was built after Hugh's death and canonisation, it was nonetheless built to provide a fitting place for a shrine to the new saint.

There were numerous miracles that were purported to have occurred in Bishop Hugh's lifetime (and beyond), which are described fully in Father Herbert Thurston's *The Life Of Saint Hugh Of Lincoln* (1898). A cripple was cured after using the hod that Hugh had used himself, when he had pitched in and helped the masons in the rebuilding of Lincoln Cathedral. It is also recorded that Hugh cured a madman in Lincoln by blessing him with his sacramental relic ring and reading the first few verses of Saint John's gospel over him.

Perhaps the most famous story concerning Bishop Hugh is that of his swan. Hugh had already displayed an almost mystical affinity with certain members of the animal kingdom, with birds and squirrels attracted to his company while he was at Witham in Somerset. When Hugh took up residence at the Episcopal manor house at Stow, north of Saxilby, a beautiful swan very quickly 'adopted' the holy man as its master.

The utterly bizarre behaviour of the swan was originally chronicled by both Adam of Eynsham in his *Magna Vita Sancti Hugonis* and Geraldus Cambrensis in his *Life*. Both claimed to have witnessed first-hand the bird's strange devotion to Hugh and it is generally accepted that the story of the swan is genuine and not fable spinning.

Geraldus Cambrensis wrote of the swan that it was much larger than a normal swan, by the same proportions by which a swan is larger than a goose. Its appearance was unusual – apart from its size it did not have the usual swelling and black mark on its beak. Part of the swan's beak was bright yellow, and so was its head and upper neck, while the rest of its body was brilliant white.

When it first arrived at the manor, no one could recall seeing the giant bird before. Within a few days it had killed all the other swans, with the exception of one female. However, when Bishop Hugh arrived at the manor house '…this royal bird' allowed itself to be captured without any difficulty. The swan was presented before the bishop, where it astounded all present by allowing the holy man to feed it. Soon it took to snaking its long neck up the bishop's ample sleeve so it could lay its head upon his breast. It would hiss quietly as though 'talking' to the bishop.

The great bird acted as both pet and guard dog to Bishop Hugh, guarding him while he slept and allowing no man, animal or anyone to get near him while they walked together. On frequent occasions it attacked the bishop's chaplain and Adam of Eynsham, the biographer. Geraldus Cambrensis noted, 'Curiously enough, it was friendly and tame to nobody except the bishop; as I have seen myself, it kept everyone else away from its master when it was with him by hissing at them and threatening them with wings and beak, emitting loud croaks as is the habit of swans. It seemed determined to make it quite clear that it belonged only to him and was a symbol sent to the bishop alone.'

When Hugh was absent from the manor house, those who remained would know when he was returning by the strange performances of the swan. Three or four days before the bishop arrived back the swan would start to act up, displaying much excitement and making loud croaks and cries. It would fly over the surface of the river and beat the water with its wings. Sometimes the swan would leave the pond and waddle majestically into the hall as if it hoped its visit would coincide with the bishop's return.

However, when Hugh visited Stow at Easter 1200 the swan would not come anywhere near him. When it was finally captured, it was reported as hanging its head in grief and looked utterly wretched. Hugh was, at this point, in poor health, and with hindsight the swan's behaviour has been interpreted as taking leave of its master for the final time. However, it is written that the swan of Stow did not pine away and outlived its master by many years.

Bishop Hugh died on 16 November 1200 at a house owned by the bishops of Lincoln during a

A depiction of Hugh and his swan, by the good bishop's tomb at Lincoln.

visit to London. As he breathed his last in his bed, his last words were that God provide a good pastor for the church at Lincoln.

Hugh's body was washed in preparation for the long journey back to Lincoln. The journey made its sombre way through much of eastern England, and it is written that the people and clergy of London accompanied it for miles beyond the city boundary. As the procession made its way northwards, whether in town or country, huge crowds turned out and swarmed the cortège, with many trying to touch the bishop's coffin. The remarkably-bad weather proved no obstacle to the grief of the people, who – in scenes which must have been exceptional – crowded the streets and roadsides no matter what their sex, health, status or race. The rain and wind had failed to put out the candles that surrounded the coffin, and many saw this as a miracle.

As the bishop's funeral cortège made its sombre way through Lincolnshire to Lincoln, the people of Stamford turned out to see the procession. The bells tolled in the churches and monasteries, yet, despite extremely bad stormy weather, the torches and candles attached to the hearse continued burning and cast an eerie light on the assembled throng, as well as the train of monks singing requiems that followed the hearse.

A local shoemaker, known in Stamford for his extreme devotion, made for the hearse when the procession had stopped. Bowing his head under the bier, the shoemaker prayed that he too should be allowed to meet his maker as the bishop had done. He returned home and, having confessed his sins, taken the sacrament and made a will, he quietly passed away that very night. The tale is first related in the 13th and 14th-century text *Flores Historiarum*, written by the monks of St Albans and Westminster.

After five days and nights the cortège halted at Ancaster, west of Sleaford, and upon resumption it was met about a mile outside of Lincoln by a truly-incredible gathering that included three archbishops, the kings of England and Scotland, bishops, abbots, magnates, landowners, the clergy, and immense throngs of common people such as had never been seen in Lincolnshire before. The site of this remarkable episode is described as '…at the foot of the hill almost a mile away from the city' and is likely to have been somewhere in the location of Canwick Hill.

The funeral continued into Lincoln despite the heavy rain and muddy approach. In Lincoln the Jewish community came out to pay their respects, ever thankful to the bishop for having stood up for the Jewish community in Stamford a decade earlier during ferocious race riots.

Apart from the strange fact that the weather could not dim the lights around the coffin, the journey was accompanied by numerous supernatural events of the type that took place at Stamford. A knight is said to have had a cancer of the arm cured after touching the coffin, and as the ceremony got underway within Lincoln Cathedral itself there were excited claims of miracles in the crowds that had swarmed outside the building. Several people claimed that a blind woman had had her sight restored and demanded that the bells of the cathedral be tolled and a *Te Deum* be chanted. The excitable crowd were calmed when it was promised that the 'miracle' would be investigated after the funeral. No sooner had this taken place than rumours swept the crowd of another incident. A man in the crowd was wandering around in a daze, sobbing and holding up a purse; he had stolen it, he shouted, and because he had committed a crime on this of all days, he had lost his sight. The purse was wrestled out of his hand and returned to the woman, and at this the man claimed that his vision had been restored.

Bishop Hugh was buried by the north wall of the chapel of Saint John the Baptist in Lincoln Cathedral the following day. It had been noted, particularly by the dean of Lincoln, how Hugh's face had appeared lifelike when it had been arrayed prior to burial. Many saw the pure whiteness of his features, tinged with pink, which gave him the appearance of being merely asleep.

Bishop Hugh was canonised in 1220. During the investigation into the bishop's worthiness as a candidate for canonisation, the committee found substantial evidence of some 29 miracles that were alleged to have been performed at his tomb in the cathedral. All were well attested, with statements from those who had allegedly been cured as well as witnesses to the miracles. Among those healed at the tomb was a member of the Knight's Templar, but the number of women and children healed outnumbered the men. Maladies which were cured included blindness, deafness, cancer, crippling immovability, paralysis and insanity. All would have taken place between 1200 and 1220, and they must have occurred in Lincoln.

Typical of the astonishing miracles was the case of a woman who had been struck down for years with crippling paralysis, which left her bent and with no feeling anywhere in her legs. It was written that '...her ankles were permanently bent up to her buttocks...' and she had spent three years in the care of laymen, who confirmed her awful condition. Two women who took her to church also testified to the seriousness of her state. The woman was taken to Hugh's tomb in a basket and spent the night there. Upon waking she found herself in considerable pain as her muscles stretched and her bones cracked; after this torment she found that she could stand and walk. Another layman went on record to say that he had seen this happen for himself.

All in all, Bishop Hugh is rightly considered one of the most important men to ever be associated with Lincoln. In the 14th century there was one last strange reminder of the wonder that Hugh had inspired two centuries earlier. During the tenure of John Bokyngham (Buckingham) as bishop of Lincoln (1369–98), thieves stole a golden reliquary containing Bishop Hugh's skull during a robbery at Lincoln Cathedral. They stripped the reliquary of gold and jewels but apparently did not open it up, quickly throwing it away into a field. Here, it is said, it was watched over by a crow who only left the scene when the robbers had been arrested and the clergy came to recover the sacred relic.

LITTLE SAINT HUGH

Contrastingly, the murder in the 13th century of a little boy in Lincoln called Hugh was an outrage in more ways than one. The boy's death heralded an ugly fuelling of anti-Semitism in England that lead to the expulsion of the 3,000-strong Jewish community by a royal edict, ordered by King Edward I on 18 July 1290, some 35 years after the events in Lincoln. In the 14th century, Chaucer used the basis of the boy's death in one of his *Canterbury Tales*, ensuring the legend did not die. More sinisterly, in 1930's Germany, Hitler and his Nazi propagandists seized the ancient story as evidence that other countries in Europe had dealt with their own Jewish 'problem' in the past as the German regime were now justified in doing themselves in their own country.

The outrageous anti-Semitism – and the mini pogrom – that followed Hugh's death is not in doubt. The spiritual miracles and supernatural occurrences that were reported concerning the boy's death may have been merely more propaganda designed to highlight the boy's innocence and fuel the blame culture.

Hugh was born around 1246, son of a Lincoln woman named Beatrice. It is said that he sung in the choir at Lincoln Cathedral, and his journey to and from the services took him through Lincoln's Jewish quarter, where he sang his favourite song, the *Magnificat*. In 1255 Lincoln had a small but thriving Jewish population of about 70 homesteads around the Steep Hill area of the city, and their wealthier-than-average status had, it seems, already made them a focal point for low-level discontent brought on by ignorance of their Jewish ceremonies, xenophobia, and plain jealousy of their wealth.

In the summer of 1255 little Hugh disappeared, apparently while out playing with a ball in the vicinity of the Jewish neighbourhood, near a house at the foot of Steep Hill owned by a Jew called

Copin. What his true fate was after he vanished can now never be known, as the official version – more than likely tortured out of suspects as the investigation progressed – certainly cannot be trusted. It seems reasonably certain that Hugh was missing for a number of days while his mother Beatrice and a search party looked in vain for her lost son. What comes after is shrouded in uncertainty.

Little Hugh's body was found at the foot of a well in the garden of Copin's house. The search party may have uncovered the corpse, but another story alleges spiritual intervention – although whether this legend was circulating at the time of the murder or grew in the years that followed is, of course, impossible to tell.

Beatrice was told by some of Hugh's friends that they had seen her son near Copin's dwelling. As she neared the property she was apparently led to the well in the garden by the ghostly sound of Hugh singing the *Magnificat*. As she peered over the edge, Beatrice saw her murdered son lying at the bottom of the well, yet the strange singing continued to implore her with the words, 'The lead is wondrous heavy, mother; The well is wondrous deep; A keen penknife sticks in my heart; A word I do not speak.'

As the search party grimly recovered the boy's corpse, people whispered that all the bells rang at once and books in the city began to read themselves aloud. A ballad recalled the events thus:

> And all the bells of merry Lincoln
> Without men's hands were rung
> And all the books of merry Lincoln
> Were read without men's tongue
> And never was such a burial
> Since Adam's days begun.

Other phenomena continued during the slain boy's funeral, where the ghostly voice continued to sing the *Magnificat* so continuously, that the priest in charge of the service implored the voice to stop. The spirit of the dead child apparently then told the priest that the Virgin Mary had appeared beside him at the bottom of the well and placed a grain of rice underneath his tongue, and he would continue to sing her song as long as it was there. The priest gently removed the rice from underneath the dead boy's tongue and the haunting singing stopped...

When a blind woman claimed that she had recovered her sight after touching the boy's body, he was finally buried as a martyr in Lincoln Cathedral.

At the time, King Henry III's Justiciar, John de Lexington, was in Lincoln and he took control of the investigation. He ordered Copin's arrest, and, perhaps with other alleged murders in mind (there had been similar cases in Bury St Edmunds in 1181 and Norwich in 1144), the case took shape. Copin was charged with murder in what, it can be imagined, was a heavily-charged atmosphere. He was encouraged to implicate everyone involved, first by torture and then by promises from Lexington of being spared execution. Eventually, Copin told a dreadful, garbled 'confession', of which there is more than one version.

Hugh had been playing with a ball with some friends near Copin's house on that fateful day, when the ball got knocked into Copin's garden (or through his window into his house). The children were wary of recovering the ball until Copin's daughter appeared and lured Hugh on to the property with an apple. Another account states that he was seized when he sneaked on to the property to recover his ball. Yet another version claims that the Jews simply kidnapped the boy and dragged him into Copin's house, in spontaneous anger at his singing the *Magnificat*.

Behind the walls of Copin's household, Hugh was held captive for 10 days and kept alive on milk. He was tortured regularly and – as the desperate search for the lad continued outside – he was finally whipped and then subjected to a mock crucifixion as part of a diabolical Jewish custom, during which he was killed.

This story was elaborated as Copin's controversial confessions kept coming. The story changed to allege that Hugh was kept prisoner with no food while Jews from all over the kingdom gathered in Lincoln to watch a mock 'trial', at which the little prisoner would be tried to avenge the execution of Christ, a practice that occurred every year with religious fanaticism. Following much feasting, the assembled Jewish crowd selected one of their number to represent Pilate and Hugh was sentenced to torture and execution. The boy was subsequently crucified and killed, with some accounts saying that his throat was cut. This whole version of the tale rings false, as it is highly unlikely the boy could be hidden in such a small section of the city for so long while a search party hunted for him.

Following the ceremony, the murderers carried the body to a river where they tied lead weights to it and dumped it in the water. It refused to sink. This element of the story may have been the first to spread by word-of-mouth the mythology of the boy's divinity, which subsequently developed in the other supernatural tales.

Thus thwarted, the band carried the body back to Copin's house and threw it down the well in his garden while they decided what to do. It was at this point that the search party – or Hugh's mother – found the corpse.

With a shaky confession in his possession, Lexington went back on his word and sentenced Copin to death, along with 18 other Jews that Copin had implicated. It is recorded that Beatrice petitioned King Henry III when she heard that Copin may be given his life for the confession, and the king ordered Lexington to pass the death sentence in the case. Copin was dragged behind a horse past the crowds to Canwick Hill, where he was strung up and hanged, while his 18 co-accused met their fates in London. Ninety-one other Jews linked to the incident were imprisoned, and the following year some of them were sentenced to death. Many more may have been killed were it not for the intervention of the Benedictines, who secured their release on the understanding that heavy fines were paid as punishment to the Earl of Cornwall.

The shrine in Lincoln Cathedral to the dead little boy became the focus of pilgrimage. Whether or not Hugh was murdered by the Jews, by Copin on his own, by someone else, or even if he fell down the well trying to get his ball, the rot had set in and the days of England's Jewish community were running out…a disgraceful episode in Lincoln's history fuelling a shameful chapter in England's history. Hugh's shrine was mostly destroyed in the chaos of the English Civil War, but visitors to the cathedral can still see the base halfway down the south aisle. In the late 18th century, so the story goes, investigators forced open the stone coffin and found the skeleton of a little boy aged about eight, encased in lead.

In 1934, when the Nazi's were peddling Hugh's story as historical justification for their own outrages, the City Mayor George Deer told 80 assembled members of the Jewish Historical Society that the city accepted the Jews were treated scandalously during the episode of almost 700 years ago. Canon J.H. Srawley, Chancellor of the Cathedral, added to those gathered in the Jew's Court that the saga of Hugh was buried, and 'it is the end of the matter for all sane men'.

THE OTBY SKINNING

It is told that centuries ago, two outlaws lived in a cave in the Lincolnshire Wolds at Otby (north of Market Rasen and east of Osgodby). A young farmhand, named William Hooker, perchanced to be driving cattle this way when he overheard the two villains plotting to rob a farm at Osgodby. Billy warned the farmer and the two bandits were forced even deeper into hiding in the Wolds.

Before they fled, however, they swore revenge on the youth who had betrayed them. At length they snuck back to Otby and ambushed William as he toiled the fields one day on his own.

Poor William Hooker was mercilessly beaten and then the flesh cut from his body in a brutal skinning by the two robbers. They then threw the bloody remains of his skin over a hedge to dry, but the hedge began to wither, and, very quickly, it dried up and died. No vegetation would grow at this spot afterwards.

Despite his vicious treatment, the young farmhand did not die. The two robbers left him, writhing in agony in the dirt. However, the boy's two torturers had carved away the skin from every part of his body – except the palms of his hands. William, in his torment, managed to put his palms together in the fashion of one who is praying…and the angels saw him and took mercy on him.

The story goes that the skin on his palms began to spread, until it covered his hands, then his arms, and eventually his entire body.

HEALED BY AN ANGEL?

It was Whit Sunday 1658 when a shoemaker named Samuel Wallis answered a knock at the door of his Stamford home. Wallis had been sick with consumption for some 13 years.

It was six in the evening and Samuel was reading *Abraham's Suit For Sodom*. His nurse was absent, so he crawled with difficulty to the door; upon opening it he saw on his doorstep a white-haired, white-bearded old man with a fresh complexion. The old man wore a 'little narrow band, coat and hose of a purple colour, and new shoes tied with black ribbands'. His stockings were very white. The man was dry and his feet untouched by the mud, despite the fact that it had been raining heavily outside. His hands were ungloved and as white as snow, and he had a white stick in his hand.

Upon being invited in for a beverage, the old man drank for some time and then asked Wallis what ailed him: consumption, came the reply. At this the strange guest suggested a possible remedy for Wallis's complaint…a herbal concoction of two leaves of red sage and one of bloodworte soaked in beer. Wallis, he stated, should replace the leaves every four days and take the potion for 12 days. The old man then bade the shoemaker farewell with the words, 'No, friend, I will not eat; the Lord Jesus is sufficient for me. Very seldom doe I drinke any beer neither, but that which comes from the rocke. So, friend, the Lord God be with thee.'

The old man was never more heard of after leaving Wallis's home, and his remarkable recovery (after taking the old man's advice) attracted much excitement in Stamford. The incident reached the ears of one Dr Worthington, who, in 1661, wrote of it to a friend, making the supposition that the old man may, in fact, have been an angel.

Curiously, the same pattern of events was repeated in Moorland, Staffordshire, at around the same time, and the popular opinion was that the old white-haired healer was indeed an angel. It was even put forward that the mysterious stranger was the Wandering Jew, Cartaphilus, who was a porter to Pontius Pilate. Cartaphilus is held to have struck Jesus Christ as he was being dragged out of the Judgement Hall after being sentenced to crucifixion, jeering at Jesus for loitering. In reply, Jesus told Cartaphilus, 'I am going and you will wait until I return'. Thus, the spiteful Cartaphilus was destined to wander the world until the Second Coming.

MODERN RELIGIOUS PHENOMENA

It is somehow strange to contemplate that signs from God occur in modern Lincolnshire, but nonetheless they are reported. On 5 June 2000 *The Times* reported that a fence had been put around a tree in the grounds of North Sea Camp prison in Freiston, after a 25-year-old prisoner, named

Mohammed Tair, of Derby, claimed he could observe the name Allah in Arabic within the branches. A chaplain visiting the prison confirmed the man's observations and prison officials erected the fence as protection. Similarly, on Christmas Day 2005, an image resembling Jesus Christ was found to have mysteriously appeared on a wardrobe in a converted loft room in the Wyberton home of the Luckham family.

On 30 August 2004 a stand at a religious festival on a showground at North Carlton, two miles north of Lincoln, collapsed during a concert, injuring 12 people. Eyewitness Sean Cuthbert, aged 35, said that he trusted in the Lord and thankfully there were no fatalities, with most of the injuries being minor. He added, 'The Devil is at work in lots of places, so it is important that we do not stop the festival.' The cause of the accident was not immediately apparent.

The following year, 28-year-old Ed Hollamby, wheelchair-bound and suffering from a mysterious, crippling arthritic muscle ailment, was taken to the Grapevine Christian festival at North Carlton. Ed's friends presented him before a stage where Solihull pastor David Carr was holding a praying session. Mr Carr merely looked at him and stated, 'In the name of Jesus you are cured my son.' Immediately Ed experienced a joyous sensation akin to 'one of those tin diving suits being taken off me – the relief was amazing'. The pain that wracked his body began to subside and, with the help of some of the church support workers, he was helped to his feet and managed to walk. The more steps he took the better he felt. 'I spent the rest of the festival dancing around with my daughter,' Ed told the *Lincolnshire Echo* on 1 September 2005. 'God cured me.'

In May 1992 a 42-year-old widow living in Lincoln showed her bishop the palms of her upturned hands, and the astonished man noticed that there were round tender areas of scarred skin which, he was told, occasionally seeped blood.

Heather Woods, the sufferer in question, was a deacon in a small Episcopal church. The first sign that she was suffering the stigmata – the wounds of Jesus Christ's suffering on the cross – was an incessant itch on her left hand, which was, in turn, followed by a blister-like mark that had a halo-shaped mark around it. The shock of this was compounded when similar marks appeared on her right hand and then both of her feet. All the wounds were alike, about the size of an old tenpence piece at their height, and they began to seep blood and a clear fluid. Other wounds followed: a crescent-shaped red slash on her right side, and on two occasions her forehead was scarred by a vivid cross.

The advent of the first stigmata on her left hand was accompanied by other religious phenomena. Heather had a vision of Jesus Christ being baptised, and four days later she had an agonising vision of him on the cross. She was told that in 63 days her old life would transfigure and her life would take on a new beginning.

Heather was falling ill, and over the next two months her health deteriorated so badly that her friends wondered if she might die. However, upon the night of her worst torment, Heather experienced another miraculous vision, which apparently heralded the turnaround of her health and the beginning of her 'new life'. The very next day, she appeared to grow stronger and gradually began to recover.

In what must have been a tumultuous few weeks in her life, Heather also began to experience the phenomenon known as automatic writing. She received spiritual messages, and when one of these messages 'came through' she would grab paper and a pencil and write, trance-like, whatever was imparted. Often she knew not what she had written until after the event, and she wrote with her left hand – even though she was right-handed. Witnesses noted that this 'automatic writing' was clear, but the style varied from paragraph to paragraph.

On Good Friday the following year, Heather attended a service and an astonishing event occurred that led to her case being widely publicised and televised. Heather's sympathy with the suffering of

Jesus Christ was so profound that the mark on her side had begun bleeding again recently, and others present, who examined the injury, testified to the reality of this event after she complained of severe pains in her side during the service. Two days later, on Easter Day, a mark had appeared on her forehead — sympathetic of the scratches on Christ's forehead caused by the crown of thorns. This mark remained visible to witnesses for several days afterwards.

Genuine religious phenomena, or, more scientifically, was Heather Woods suffering some kind of self-produced skin disorder brought on by her devotion and torment of Christ's time on the cross, a kind of autosuggestion producing the marks? Either way, the incident was highly mysterious and remarkable.

As if to top all this off, a highly-reputable religious website notes the claims of a teenage girl in Lincoln who stated that, one night in February 1999, she and her family watched what they described as an appearance of angels. The mesmerising display continued for some three hours — at one time there were possibly hundreds of the entities. The teenager wrote that they gradually appeared nearer the ground, so it was easier to make out specific details as to their appearance. They seemed to be made of blue light, but their shape resembled that of a person. They appeared to wear robes and she could make out gigantic wings which spread all the way down their backs. The figures made circles and spun this way and that; they formed a heart shape and then made themselves into what resembled a fountain with flowing water. For three hours the angels put on this miraculous display, at one time forming a crown with a cross on it, then a dove; sometimes they danced around what seemed to be a giant hole in the sky that reminded the teenager of a great, sparkling blue jewel. This would fade and then reappear, and after an hour of amazement the family began to pray before the angels. There is also some suggestion that several of the neighbours, alerted to the family's prayers, came outside and saw the fantastic event for themselves. One of the children wrote of the family's experiences in a letter to Pope John Paul II. She drew many illustrations of the event and received a warm reply from his Holiness.

Clearly, over the years and centuries, faith in the county has not been dimmed.

The eye of the Lord: this stone 'angel' was positioned in Eastgate, Lincoln, to glare at clergy who frequented a nearby pub in the 1600s.

CHAPTER 3

HE LOOKS UPON HIM AS THE DEVIL
LOOKS UPON LINCOLN

In the past, it was believed that Satan and his demons presented a very real threat to the good people of Lincolnshire. Indeed, Lincoln's most famous story of the supernatural concerns the Lincoln Imp: a tiny, malicious-looking stone gargoyle who sits cross-legged and leering at visitors high up in the Angel Choir, in the grandiose East End of Lincoln Cathedral. A popular version of the myth tells how Remigius, the first Bishop of Lincoln, prayed for divine intervention from the Virgin Mary (to whom the cathedral is dedicated) when a horde of demons assaulted the site on the eve of its consecration in 1092. Immense gusts of wind blew up and buffeted the Satanic hordes back, but one imp managed to get inside the cathedral; here, he became petrified to stone as the guardian angels of the cathedral protected the place from the evil little creature. Maybe this story has something to do with the fact that Remigius died in the days preceding the consecration of Lincoln Cathedral in 1092. Such a tragically-timed coincidence perhaps provided the bedrock for myths of Remigius exhausting himself and expiring while defending the cathedral from Satanic mischief, in the days running up to the dedication. The fact is that he was already very ill and simply did not live long enough to see his cathedral dedicated. Furthermore, the Angel Choir was not completed until the late 1200s, so however one looks at this version of the Lincoln Imp story it is largely impossible.

But the most popular version of the legend tells how the Devil sent two imps to Lincoln in the 14th century to cause chaos within the great cathedral. They tripped over the bishop, upset furniture and caused general mayhem, until an angel appeared and ordered them to stop their behaviour. At this, one imp flitted away but the other taunted, 'Catch me if you can!' and threw rocks at the angel – who instantly petrified the creature. And to this day, the evil little monster grins maliciously down at the tourists and sightseers, as he had been when mocking the angel immediately before its wrath transformed him to stone all those centuries ago. However, irrespective of whether he was merely a stonemason's gargoyle or genuinely a petrified imp, the legends surrounding the Lincoln Imp have now become part of Lincolnshire folklore.

The buffeting gusts that chill those who walk past the south-westerly part of the cathedral have been mentioned earlier, as the remnants of a miraculous wind that threw back the Devil. Other tales speak of it as an evil wind, responsible for blowing the imp into the cathedral through the great west doors.

Another tale of devilry stems from an era when the clergy at the cathedral had fallen into wicked ways. The Dean was a foolish, evil man, and his monks were a bunch of sinners. By this time, with these folk in charge, the Devil had decided to grant the cathedral a stay of execution, and one day he passed through Lincoln with his friend the wind. As they chatted, the Devil told the wind to wait outside for a moment while he popped in to see his friend the Dean.

The wind did as he was bid, but the Devil never reappeared. The wind, they say, still waits outside for him and this is the explanation for the south-westerly gusts!

But could it be that Satan himself has kept a sinister presence at Lincolnshire's most holy site? A small well stands outside the cathedral near the Chapter House, and children were told that if they ran backwards round the well seven times and then looked through the little holes that once allowed people to spy inside the gloom of the well, they would see the Devil leering back at them.

The Lincoln Imp.

Is he trapped inside? Perhaps it is just as well that this trick only worked on All Hallows Eve and the holes are no longer there!

Many places in Lincolnshire harbour link to the Devil. Coinciding with the fear of such supernatural evil went the fear of witchcraft, and studies on the topic by eminent folklorists have shown that such superstitious beliefs persisted well into the 19th and early 20th centuries in Lincolnshire. Nowadays, the witchcraft, spells and accusations of bygone eras have been replaced by cults and Satanists. As the old saying goes, 'He looks upon him as the Devil looks upon Lincoln…'

THE BLACK HUNT OF BURGHLEY WOODS

In 1127 King Henry I of England gave the abbacy of Peterborough to an abbot called Henry of Poitou. The 12th-century Peterborough chronicler Hugh Candidus recorded how there was much protest, as the abbot's acquisition of Peterborough Abbey was a strategic move aimed at reaping profits; thus, 'miserably was the abbacy given between Christmas and Candlemas at London'.

As soon as the abbot arrived 'on the Sunday which one sings, *Exurge, quare obdormis, Domine?*', a hellish spectacle was visited upon the area, which was chronicled as fact and talked about across England. In the deer park in the town of Peterborough, and in all the woodland between Peterborough and Stamford, a ghastly, demonic hunt was seen crashing through the trees, through Lent and up until Easter.

Many reliable witnesses saw the huntsmen, and the monks heard the winding of the horns at night from deep inside the forest. It was reckoned that there were some 30 demonic huntsmen in all: 'These huntsmen were big, black and ugly, and all their dogs were black and ugly with wide eyes, and they rode on black horses and black goats'.

The entire incident is clearly a criticism on the excesses of the abbot, but it is possible the huntsmen were real: many people of 'unquestioned veracity' saw and heard them, and Hugh Candidus certainly believed the rumours: 'This was on his (Abbot Henry's) arrival. Of his departure we cannot yet speak. May God provide!'

THE EVIL UNDER THE BRIDGE

It was once said that where Pilford Bridge crossed the River Ancholme in a small valley between Normanby-by-Spital and Toft-next-Newton, an evil, malevolent entity lurked. Locally, it was whispered that the force that resided under the bridge was a witch, but not a live witch; it was more a kind of nasty, malicious energy, which haunted the bridge so badly that, in the end, three parsons were called out to try and end the matter.

The spirit had taken to pushing people off the bridge and into the water, and now the three parsons stood by the grassy banks of the river and asked the spirit what it wanted. 'Life, I want, and life I'll have!' came the sinister reply from under the bridge.

At this, those assembled chucked a live cockerel into the water. When the entity fell on it and ripped it to pieces and began eating it, the parsons managed to trap the spirit in an iron pot and bury it at the site. The exorcism had worked.

Folklorist Ethel Rudkin heard this legend from a native of Willoughton in the 1930s, who told her that if they were to raise the pot, even today, the spirit would come out again and be as bad as ever.

Could the witch still be trapped under Pilford Bridge?

WHEN THE DEVIL VISITED LINCOLNSHIRE

What would the Devil want with the inoffensive county of Lincolnshire? Who knows, but over the centuries Satan himself seems to have taken a frighteningly-frequent interest in the goings-on here. Folklore associates many places in Lincolnshire with Satan. One of the earliest legends of Satan appearing in the county is set at the Benedictine abbey in Croyland (Crowland).

Towards the end of the year 869, the Abbot Theodore sat in desperation in his quarters at the abbey, while the uncontrollable monks had ignored his pleas and embarked on a drunken, debauched party. But the blasphemy had being going on for months: one monk was even reckoned to have sold his soul so he could discover the elixir of life. Suddenly, the very walls of the building shook with an immense rumbling of thunder, and the revellers stood in terror as a monstrous form emerged from a cloud of foul-smelling smoke. It was Satan himself, '...so fearful in countenance, so diabolical in its malignity' that all fell cowering before the vision.

Satan had a dire message for them all. They were doomed, he laughed: God had turned his back on them and their sinful ways and cursed the abbey, and within 12 months the place would lie in ruins and they would be damned. The story goes that nothing happened for months, and the wary monks began to breathe a sigh of relief. But in mid-870 a monk in the tower on lookout duty spotted ominous, faraway black shapes on the distant horizon of the North Sea. The following day the shapes revealed themselves to be a fleet of Viking longboats.

The Norse raiders had no difficulty in navigating the marshland of the Lincolnshire Fens, and soon they were swarming on to the little island of Croyland and charging towards the abbey, swinging their battleaxes. Inside the abbey, alarm bells were rung to summon the monks to prayer and ask for deliverance. It was a hopeless endeavour, for had not Satan himself warned them what was coming? Abbot Theodore was brutally murdered as he took mass, and some 80 others were caught and butchered along with him.

The raiders tipped over and smashed tombs and entirely ransacked the monastery in an attempt to find treasure. The corpses of the massacred clergy were heaped on a pyre and burned, as was Croyland Abbey, before the raiders sailed on to Peterborough Abbey to continue their campaign of pillage and murder.

In North Lincolnshire can be found the tiny hamlet of Dragonby – although you would never find it unless you were looking for it. Nevertheless, this little place off the A1077, between Scunthorpe and Roxby, is a haven of supernatural phenomena: ley lines traverse the region, phantom hounds lurk in the surrounding countryside, and a petrified 'dragon' lies in the hills behind Dragonby. At one time Dragonby was called Conesby Cliff and local lore claims that the hillsides echo to the ghostly pealing of a submerged church. The church had sunk into the hillside during harvest-time hymns as the Devil sat on the roof laughing his head off; when the congregation emerged they found the church door now opened into a long underground tunnel which led all the way to hell. Satan had taken their souls because the community had fallen into avaricious ways and their hypocrisy in church had attracted him.

It would appear that stories of an appearance by Satan in the county began circulating some time in the 15th or 16th century, when the famous 272ft-tall tower named The Boston Stump was added to St Botolph's Church in Boston and completed c.1520. The tower, as would be expected, is very exposed to the elements, and an incessant blustery wind whips round the pinnacle. As with Lincoln Cathedral, folklore claims that this wind is the Devil puffing and snorting in anger or exasperation – a reminder of an encounter on the site in the seventh century between Satan and the Saxon monk Botolph, which the Devil lost. The church is alleged to have been built on the site of a monastery founded by Botolph c.AD654.

The Devil could take many forms. The story goes that in the 1790s a group of young boys were playing near a sinister wooden framework in Melton Ross, North Lincolnshire, when their attention was captivated by a hare. The boys were larking around at the site of one of Lincolnshire's most notorious landmarks: Melton gallows, which stands in a field near the edge of the A18 road midway between the villages of Melton Ross and Wrawby. Some claim the gallows were erected by King James I to curb outbreaks of bloody feuding between the wealthy de Ros and Tyrwhit families, and the tales of long-ago lawlessness no doubt intrigued the young boys. At the site of the gallows, they were playing a deadly game: 'hanging' themselves from the branch of a nearby tree in a dangerous imitation of an execution, with each boy seeing how long he could hang for before his pals hoisted him up and he could breathe again.

As the next little boy placed the noose around his neck for his 'turn', the hare pathetically bounded past – for, as the children noticed, it only had three legs. Leaving their friend in the tree they chased the animal for a laugh into the woods. There, the three-legged hare found new speed and he led the boys on an exhausting chase between the trees ever further away from their friend, until it escaped completely.

This animal, locals speculated afterwards, had been Satan himself. For when the boys returned to their friend, they found him hanged with the noose around his neck, swinging from the bough.

It was also thought that a tremendous gale that battered north-west Lincolnshire in the late 19th century was the work of Satan. No one could recall such ferocious weather, and soon they were saying that the prolonged gusts were the Devil showing his fury – for two exceptionally-pious women had died in one parish of late, and he had missed his chance to take them for his own. Perhaps Ann

Powell, a 69-year-old widow found dead in her home in West Street, Alford, in July 1906, wasn't so fortunate. In an article on the devout Ms Powell's bizarre demise, veteran *Lincolnshire Echo* journalist Peter Reynolds noted how a fire from a paraffin lamp had burned Ann's nightdress off her, but she had actually been killed by at least four tremendous blows to the back of her head from a billhook, and the miserable room was splashed with blood. The curious verdict of suicide was passed on the death, but locally they thought differently. To some it was clear the old woman had been murdered, but why? Or by whom? Or what? Rumours swept sleepy turn-of-the-century Alford that the deeply-religious Ms Powell had expressed a wish to die like a Christian martyr and, indeed, a book on the subject was found before her corpse. But how could such a barbaric incident have taken place without anyone seeing or hearing anything strange? Ann Powell had greatly feared that something dark and sinister was coming for her in the days preceding her strange death, and locally there was much speculation that she had, indeed, been killed and taken by Satan himself.

Ethel Rudkin's *Lincolnshire Folklore* (1936) noted how, in Lincolnshire, the Devil was referred to as Old Nick, Old Harry, Old Sam, Sammiwell or The Old 'Un…never 'the Devil'. Some believed that the Devil returned yearly to Lincolnshire and perhaps you may just glimpse him these days should you find yourself in a stable in Willoughton at midnight on 24 April, St Mark's Eve. For it was then that the horses would go down on to their knees and begin talking to each other, as would the cattle in the fields, and it was thought that if one could prevent this bizarre behaviour (by stopping a horse from kneeling) one would conjure up the arrival of Satan, who charged in astride a monstrous black pig. It was said that he had been crossing the lonely countryside overseeing the annual harvesting of fern. Rudkin wrote in 1936 that in living memory, two men had shared a nervous night in a stable in Willoughton trying to pluck up the courage to attempt this. But at 10 minutes to midnight an immense wind blew up, blowing the stable doors open with a mighty crash, and as the stable echoed with bangs and din in the wind the two fellows bottled it and ran back to their homes.

Another way to snatch a glimpse of Satan, folklore claims, was to run round the church seven times and then stick pins into the door; this trick apparently worked at the church at Glentham, where it was said that if you ran round the church seven times, sticking a pin in the belfry door each time, on the seventh occasion you could look through the keyhole and espy Old Nick himself. On the edge of the River Rase at Tealby, just east of Market Rasen and on the edge of the picturesque Lincolnshire Wolds, lies a stone which locals refer to as the Devil's Pulpit. When the moon is full, goblins and demons danced on the stone. Sometimes the Devil himself would appear when the Bayons Manor clock chimed midnight, and he would drink from the water of the brook. Its location was described to Ethel Rudkin as being beyond the park, which lies opposite the fantastically prominent All Saint's Church. One needed to then follow the stream for some time before coming to the 'large hump of stone' on the right. This was the Devil's Pulpit, and Rudkin was told by a local in Caistor that there were still those who avoided the spot for fear he might be there.

However, the church at Dorrington is apparently the best place in the county to spy Satan. If you dare to peer through the keyhole of the sturdy church door on a bright moonlit night, Lucifer himself can be seen rolling glass marbles on the floor…and Rudkin noted that a certain G.H., still living in 1934, claimed that he had watched a white rabbit cavorting on Church Hill, Dorrington, which had transformed itself into the Devil before his very eyes.

Perhaps these days the Devil has transferred his attentions elsewhere. If not, we are in good hands; as 6 June 2006 approached, Lincoln Cathedral's sub-dean Canon Alan Nugent commented, '…I can assure people that if the Devil has anything special planned I will be doing everything in my power to try to stop it.' For some believed the date – 06/06/06 – heralded the arrival of the Antichrist, who would establish a counterfeit kingdom on earth, thus beginning Armageddon.

LEGENDS OF WITCHES

The history and study of witchcraft in Lincolnshire would probably be enough to fill a book of its own. Stories of encounters with witches have been retold down the centuries, with perhaps the most familiar being the story of Blind Byard. Byard was a blind old nag chosen by a knight during the time of the Crusades as his mount to fight a witch called Old Meg, who lived on heath land at Ancaster and who pursued a vendetta against the surrounding hamlets. Because Byard was blind, the knight figured he would not see the witch nor be afraid of her. But during the confrontation Old Meg is said to have leapt on the horse's rump and dug her talons into his flesh – causing the poor horse to produce three almighty leaps covering 60 feet in an effort to shake her off. The soldier eventually killed Old Meg with his sword, and accidentally also slew his faithful horse. The site of this encounter is now known as Byard's Leap (at the A17-B6403 junction), and two complete sets of horseshoes in the ground mark part of the gigantic leap for visitors to see.

A story from Swineshead tells of an old witch named Mad Kate who lived near the ancient remains of a motte-and-bailey castle called the Manwar Ings. Kate was suspected of bringing about a plague on homes and crops, and so eventually a lynch mob gathered. They set off for the Manwar Ings to see if she had kept an appointment with Satan; sure enough, as darkness fell, they spotted the old woman through the gloom atop the bank at the Manwar Ings.

As the crowd bore down on Kate, torches and noose in hands, something forced them back in utter confusion. An immense thundering of hooves announced the arrival of a sinister black-cloaked entity that rode a powerful jet-black steed. The horse snorted and dripped sweat, and the mysterious stranger reined in the beast just long enough to grab Kate and swing her behind him on to the saddle, before galloping off into the blackness of the night. Kate was never seen again, and the frustrated mob had to be content with torching her cottage and killing her 'familiars' – the black cats she lived with.

This set of horseshoes marks the landing place of Byard's almighty leap.

Christopher Marlowe's *Legends Of The Fenland People* tells how an ancient British burial mound just east of Revesby was supposed to host Sabbaths between the Devil and his followers. His appearance is described thus, '...he would invariably assume some frightful shape, such as that of a lion, or bear or hydra-headed monster, and by his very appearance terrify the assembled witches into compliance with his desires.' In the early 17th century a Captain of the Guard passing through Lincolnshire is said to have stumbled upon such a black mass during a moonlit ramble, when he encountered 100 half-naked women consuming the victim of a sacrifice. They attacked him, and dumped him outside the inn at Revesby, where he eventually recovered from terrible injuries. Marlowe, writing in 1926, pondered that, for all he knew, such rituals still persisted in remoter parts of Lincolnshire in some form.

Marlowe also noted the story of a beautiful and alluring young witch who had once lived near Louth. She was called Fanny, but legend has named her Fan o' the Fens. Fanny was alleged to have kept the spirits of those she pursued vendettas with in little bottles, and she was blamed when another local girl, during a bout of illness, vomited live newts and a frog. When a carter from Stixwould announced that he had vomited a live snake after passing Fanny's house and shouting curses at her, the young witch was subjected to a ducking, during which she nearly drowned. She was then flogged, beaten and chased from the parish.

SATANIC GUARDIAN OF THE WINCEBY BOULDER

On 11 October 1643 Roundhead and Cavalier forces clashed in battle at the town of Winceby. It was a small battle, but a chaotic and bloody one: Cromwell's horse was killed under him, and names like Slash Hollow and Slash Lane adorn the places where Cavaliers were cornered and slain. It was said that Slash Hollow – a dry valley at the site – ran ankle-deep with blood that day. The battle was decisive, and on 20 October Lincoln itself surrendered to Parliamentary forces. Legend has it that after the battle victorious Roundhead soldiers threw the bodies of the hundreds who died into a pit in the ground. Some said that treasure and riches were also thrown into the hole with the corpses. Finally a gigantic stone was hauled over the mass grave.

Gradually the corpses of the Royalist soldiers decayed, and as they did so the gigantic boulder sank into the ground, deeper and deeper, year by year.

Over the years the legend of the hidden treasure grew and there were a number of fruitless attempts to move the boulder: some spoke of how anyone who wanted to be successful would need a team of horses stretching into the next parish. However, one day a farmer, using a team of horses, eventually began to feel the stone give a little, but it proved that the treasure had an unwelcome guardian. In his excitement at his impending success, one of the farmer's assistants uttered an oath, 'Let God or the Devil come now for we have it!' At this the Devil appeared in front of the terrified farmer. The chains were snapped, the horses were thrown over and the boulder rolled back into place.

In the early 20th century a certain gentleman from Lincoln was allowed to see the buried boulder for analysis. It was a dark-blue-grey colour and extremely resilient: he tried in vain to chip away a piece of the boulder with his iron, without success. The stone was simply too tough. Superstition still clung to the object, for the surveyor's boss warned him against disturbing the 'Old Lad'. To this, the surveyor replied that if Satan appeared, then he would send him after his boss.

The Winceby Stone was eventually shifted with heavy machinery, and it is unclear where it now lies. But mysterious grooves noted on its surface by the surveyor provided several theories. The stone was deposited in Lincolnshire during the natural upheaval of the Ice Age, and the marks were probably scored by ice. Others said that when the stone began to surface again after being buried, ploughing machinery hitting it caused the grooves, or maybe Cavaliers sharpening their swords before the battle were responsible.

But others claimed that the curious marks were the footprints of Lucifer himself…and that even to this day, at the site where the massacred Royalists were buried with the treasure, groans can be heard mingling with the whistling wind.

A PERSISTENCE OF SUPERSTITION

Studies by folklorists at the turn of the 20th century produced fascinating evidence that accusations of witchcraft persisted much longer than one might think.

Recurring patterns of belief were repeated right across Lincolnshire, although there were precious few clues as to how one actually *became* a witch. Ethel Rudkin was told that to become a witch, in Crosby at least, meant making a pact with the Devil. A notorious witch in Crosby, near Scunthorpe, told a young girl who wished to become a witch to come to her house at midnight. Dutifully the young girl turned up, and was told by the witch to stand up, bend over and put her finger tips to her toes. She must then say, 'All that I 'ave a-tween me finger tips an' me toes I give to *thee*', meaning the Devil. The young girl did as she was bid, but halfway through the ritual a strange little old man walked in and sat down in the chair opposite, watching her. This spooked the girl badly, so she changed the chant to, 'All that I 'ave a-tween me finger tips an' me toes I give to…God Almighty!' At this, the strange old man stood up and disappeared out of the room, and as the witch screamed blue murder the young girl fled from the house.

A typical encounter with a witch went something like this. Rudkin was told of a nasty witch who had lived at nearby Burton-upon-Stather, who, if displeased, would attack her enemies' livestock. On one occasion when a local man was unable to supply her with milk and butter, she cursed the cow, snapping, 'May your cow turn into a bull!' Rudkin learned that hereafter the cow took on the form of a bull, which became wild and uncontrollable. The animal's milk went to curd and it took to charging everyone and everything until, one day, it slipped and broke a bone. It had to be put down after that. On another occasion the witch cursed a farmer's entire herd, giving it a blight referred to as scour. Normally the farmer would be able to control such a blight, but this one looked like it was going to wipe out his entire herd. Suspecting his herd had been witched, he cut seven locks off one cow and burnt them at midnight on his own, without telling anyone what he was up to. This strange ritual apparently worked, for afterwards the cow began to get well again, and so he performed the odd ritual on the rest of the herd.

SHAPE-SHIFTING

North of Sleaford, Dorrington had a tradition of witchcraft. There is a fascinating piece of folklore that claims that the witches infested a hillside near the village, and one evening local shepherds took a pot-shot at a flying witch and hit her with an arrow. The shot witch is said to have dropped the coffin-shaped stones that peppered the Ewerby Waithe Common nearby. She had apparently stolen them in the first place from 'a temple which stood on high ground not very far off'. In the 19th century, witches were held to gather at the church on St Thomas' night, 21 December, and anyone who has visited St John and St James' Church at Dorrington can vouch for its lonely, eerie setting. It is situated isolated on a hill, about a mile and a half outside the parish, by (what is now) the B1188 and surrounded by windswept panoramic views of the Lincolnshire countryside.

Perhaps the witches chose the church due to the legend that a Saxon chieftain had been forced to build a chapel there on the site of a pagan temple, because demons frustrated his attempts to build it elsewhere by continually moving the stonework back up the hill. In the 19th century Dorrington's most notorious witch was a certain Mrs H, who was held to be able to transform herself into an animal. When in human form the old woman went about dressed in a black skirt, and a black alpaca shawl with a red fringe. As she walked through Dorrington, those that she passed by would halt and not move until she had gone on her way. It was said that she could pass through the keyhole of her own door, but it seems that villagers thought she could also invade their houses. One man who had offended her found the old hag stood at the foot of his bed as he was about to retire; the malicious witch lifted the bed up three times, with the man in it, crashing it to the floor again as an apparent show of her power before she vanished. At some point Mrs H was found in her home, laid on the floor and bloodily battered – apparently by an intruder, but locals claimed she had incurred the injures while in the form of a giant rat, which a local had kicked. It is not clear if she recovered from the violent assault.

Lincolnshire witches were also believed to be able to shape-shift into magpies, dogs and toads; more commonly, though, it was black cats and hares, of which there are several accounts. Perhaps the earliest reference to this belief dates back to the 17th-century *Harleian MS*, which notes how auditors were overthrown by a mysterious hare that darted around Bolingbroke Castle, Old Bolingbroke, vanishing in cellars and terrifying pursuing hounds in the 1650s. The hare was thought to be either a ghost, or a witch who had been imprisoned inside the castle. Folklorists of the 19th and early 20th century obtained many first-hand accounts of black cats and hares being kicked, savaged or shot – only for the local 'witch' to be seen displaying similar injuries the next day. One lady recalled having to go to Rowston to see two old men on business. The two bachelors were eccentric, but they put their eccentricity down to their mother being a witch. They recalled her darting about as a hare and coming into the house through the keyhole. One day their mother had been blasted by a farmer with a shotgun

The church at Dorrington, playground of witches and Satan himself?

while in the guise of a hare, but she managed to struggle back to the house. There, she had died in human form from a gunshot wound to the side.

Of this type was an incident noted in Gutch and Peacock's *County Folklore Vol 5: Lincolnshire* (1908), which had apparently occurred within living memory near a village somewhere north of Northorpe (presumably the Northorpe between Gainsborough and Scunthorpe – there are three in Lincolnshire). An old man in the village was rumoured to possess the ability to turn himself into a dog, in which form he would roam the fields attacking cattle. One farmer claimed that he had caught a black dog pestering his cattle and when he raced into the field he watched the dog shape-shift into the man from the village who everyone reckoned was a wizard. Miss Mabel Peacock wrote that in Lincolnshire '…the belief in shape-shifting still exists, that is certain'.

Indeed it does. Sometime around the first half of the 1990s a witness claimed that he had been motoring steadily back home through Lincolnshire from Norfolk very late one night. In a dark, rural location crowded with trees, the motorist's eyes were drawn towards an animal in a field to his right, about the size of a horse or deer. As his direction took him closer to the animal it approached the road, and as he drove past it the witness stated that, although it had the body and legs of a horse, it had a man's face. He formed the impression it was a flesh-and-blood creature, and it frightened him. This bizarre episode was called in to the *This Morning* TV show in 1996 and there has since been speculation that perhaps the creature encountered was either a witch 'shape-shifting' or a half-transformed victim of a witch's spell.

THE WITCHES OF WILLOUGTON

Ethel Rudkin found several Lincolnshire locals who knew of the antics of the witches on the other side of Lincoln, to the north. A native of Willoughton did not know of the exact spot where they held their 'conventions', but 'I know as they did used to meet somewheres, ter discuss their business, an' suchlike.'

In the 1800s the women of the village would work the land, and truly-strange stories began to circulate about one of their number named Becky L. The women were, for want of a better word, attacked on at least one occasion by bizarre creatures that appeared on the land '…striped, like mackerel, they were, only yellow and blue; headless *things* and without legs…' The women would lash out at these weird creatures but never actually hit them. They would hop and bound out of the way much like rabbits. But all Becky had to do was shout at them, 'Now, begone, you devils!', and the strange pests would disappear.

Another man claimed the spot where old hags would gather was nearby Bliber (Blyborough) Top. In the mid to late 1800s it was reckoned that witches congregated at somewhere called 'The Cot' at Bliber Top, using their powers to stop horses in their tracks. If a wagoner whipped his horses with a gad (whip) made out of wicken, it meant the spell was broken and the horses could move on again, and there are plenty of accounts of how the wicken tree was possessed of strange powers that could thwart witches' plans. Typical of this is the story of a vindictive witch at Ludford called Owld Nancy, who was recorded as pursuing vendettas against her neighbours in the mid to late 19th century. She was reputed to go about in the form of a white hare, but she could also manifest as a cat. The cat would annoy a farm worker called Bob (against whom Nancy appeared to have a particular hatred, perhaps on account of her belief he had 'wronged' her daughter). Whenever he fed his horses, a cat would appear hissing and spitting, which so frightened the animals that they refused to eat. Bob became worried that he would get the sack, but it seems his boss, the farmer, was somewhat sympathetic to his plight; eventually a friend suggested to Bob that he bury a piece of wicken over the stable door, and this apparently stopped the harassment of the black cat.

Fantastic tales were also told of one Betty W, who held the position of Parish Clerk in Willoughton for some years. Betty was blamed for filling the church with an explosion of soot from the chimney during a wedding feast she had not been invited to. But by far the strangest story concerned Betty's husband John, who allegedly came home one day and found a number of little tailors sitting cross-legged on the table, sewing frantically. Upon his entrance, however, they vanished before the startled man.

A Willoughton villager called Mrs Smith had been afraid of being witched, so she had invited Betty W around and asked her to take a seat on the best chair in the house. Betty did so and sat on pins hidden beneath a cushion, which drew blood. This kind of trickery was believed to deprive a witch of the ability to harm her attacker, and there are numerous accounts of slashings, prickings and stabbings of old women who were suspected of casting spells on their neighbours. The level of accusations – everything from nervous breakdowns to outbreaks of livestock ague – blamed on local old women paints an almost disturbing picture of parts of Lincolnshire in an age when rationalisation was supposed to have taken hold. In 1885 a Lincolnshire clergyman, R.M. Heanley, received a complaint from a 'respectable wheelwright' that his pig had been overlooked at sale. The offended pig seller confided to the clergyman '...thou and me knaws the party that hes dun it...' and went on that if only he could draw the blood of the witch, all would be well again. But, he complained, then the ignorant magistrates at Spilsby would make him pay for attacking her.

Betty W died in 1841, and '...the woman as laid 'er out found she'd gotten a "witch-pap" like a little pap, it were, a-tween 'er two natural ones – but that weren't at all surprisin'. A *real* witch, she were.'

THE END OF SUPERSTITION IN LINCOLNSHIRE?

It was reported in January 2004 that during renovations at a rural farmhouse in Navenby, builders had come across a green bottle-like object buried in the foundations. Partially smashed by the workers, it was found to contain some bent pins and other relics. After sitting idle in a cupboard for some time, the object was taken to an open evening held by Lincolnshire County Council's archaeology department, by the owner of the house, Jo Butler.

Here, Finds Liaison Officer Adam Daubney identified the bottle for what it was – a witch bottle designed to protect the house and throw back the spell at the one who had cast it. Further interesting finds followed. The bottle contained human hair as well as pins, and a substance which may have been urine, one theory being that whoever made the bottle wanted to make the witch feel as though they were passing pins when urinating, and thus be exposed.

The most remarkable discovery of all was the artefact's age. For although such protections were commonplace in the 1500s and 1600s, the Navenby bottle was dated to around 1830 – which confirmed, beyond doubt, that in this part of Lincolnshire, fear of dark, supernatural spells still lingered a lot longer than was previously thought. And whoever had made the witch bottle had suspected someone of casting malevolent spells upon them...

It can only be wondered if the witch bottle brought to light the suspected evildoer and what the results were. The bottle was preserved and put on display in the Museum of Lincolnshire Life in Lincoln later that year.

Prior to World War Two, Ethel Rudkin travelled the region collecting first-hand accounts of remedies, superstitions and many tales that had been passed down by word of mouth. She clearly appears to have recognised that perhaps times were changing and old superstitious beliefs ought to be chronicled before they died out, as Europe was marching in the direction of political instability and, three years later, war. But much of what she gathered together had still been practised in living memory and perhaps even today such fearful beliefs in witchcraft – or the witches' activities themselves – haven't died away completely in some parts of the county. As late as 1979, *The Witch's Gospel* by Charles Bowness described a pair of covens in Lincolnshire that were dedicated to the pagan witch tradition. The covens had existed for a very long time, and those who participated worked robed under the direction of a male Magister, supported by a male lieutenant who carried a blackthorn rod and a lady who acted as his medium. Author Ronald Hutton, on a visit to Lincolnshire, found that these covens appeared to have been in existence since at least the 1940s.

THE DEMON CHURCH

The 13th-century St Botolph's Church in Skidbrooke has stood abandoned for many a year now. It has not been used for Christian worship for some 30 years, but its remoteness in marshland and copse-shrouded eerie setting seem to have made it the focal point for gatherings of a sinister kind. Even before this there was reputed to have been the ghostly figures of hooded monks still haunting the place. A correspondent to the *Lincolnshire Echo* of 11 February 2006 noted how, late one night, in the hollow, empty shell of the church, he and some friends had clearly heard phantom footsteps crunch on the stone floor. Local lore tells ancient, vague stories of spells and witchcraft, and it is said that St Botolph's has been put under a curse.

Stories first appeared in the 1970s and 1980s that the empty mediaeval church had become the haunt of Satanists, so much so that it earned the reputation as the so-called Demon Church. There were persistent reports of fires burning in its grounds and strange activities taking place; by January 2004 locals were so disturbed by the goings-on that they forced a meeting between local church leaders and the Churches Conservation Trust to try and decide what action to take – one sad but extreme option being to demolish the church.

The Rector of Louth, Canon Stephen Holdaway, reported that the church was being desecrated with animal sacrifices, and that the stone pillars were being daubed in black with Satanic symbols. He added, 'This sort of activity shows no respect for the people who are buried there.'

The 65-year-old churchwarden, a Mr Benton, claimed that he had been called out at three in the morning after reports of activity, but had been unable to act after the cultists became aggressive and he feared being attacked. He believed that many of the cultists were coming in from Grimsby, and a Skidbrooke resident confirmed that the headless carcasses of sheep and chickens were being found at the church.

The Bassetlaw Ghost Research Group, six months earlier on 7 June 2003, had set up a base camp in one corner of the old church during an all-night investigation. They reported that the gloomy, oppressive atmosphere of the place appeared to be almost trying to force them to leave. Strange noises were heard, and there were ominous flashes in the sky when the weather was calm. Parapsychologist David Wharmby also stated enigmatically to the *Louth Leader*, 'We saw small babies among the gravestones and grass.'

In the hamlet of Skidbrooke itself, the dark rumours surrounding the church had forced one woman to have her house blessed by a priest. The woman said, 'I felt such bad vibes. The whole place (St Botolph's) really freaked me out. People think it's a load of nonsense but there is such a thing as black magic, and it's dangerous.' The reputation of St Botolph's had become so notorious by the end

The approach to St Botolph's, Skidbrooke.

of 2004 that on Halloween, a small bunch of locals, including churchwarden Benton, were forced to form a vigilante patrol at the lengthy entrance of the church. That night they turned away scores of paranormal investigators and devotees to the art of black magic, telling them, 'Go away! You are not wanted here.'

They certainly are not, either by the locals or the Churches Conservation Trust, and the situation as to what to do with St Botolph's at present remains unresolved.

MODERN URBAN LEGENDS

Twenty years or so on, there are those who will tell you a 'true' story that they remember doing the rounds when they were at secondary school. It concerns a girl pupil at the school concerned taking part in an Ouija board experiment. The story goes that the board 'told' the girl she would be dead within 24 hours. This frightened her and she left the table and dashed outside, whereupon she was hit squarely by a car in the road and killed.

Those who recall this story from their teenage years are in their 30s now, and versions of the tale vary depending on who tells you it. According to some, the incident took place during a lunch break and the girl was killed right outside the school; others say the girl died following an Ouija board experiment at someone's house after school hours. One consistent feature of the tale is that in recounting the story, the teller always notes that it happened to a girl in a different school year to their own, usually a couple of years earlier.

This story has been around at least 20 years, and it is usually cited as a 'true' story whenever groups of 30-somethings gather and end up relating spooky tales. It is almost certainly an urban legend and is probably retold in various guises about schools up and down the United Kingdom. In Lincoln, this eerie tale has somehow attached itself to the City School on Skellingthorpe Road.

In 2007 I was told of a woman in Waddington who awoke in the night and found her bedroom populated with ghosts, and the poor lady had to manoeuvre between these wraiths in order to get to the bathroom. Coming back to her bedroom they were still there, so in extreme terror she bravely tried to ignore them and got back into bed. The spirits were of all ages, backgrounds and eras – and their glassy eyes appeared to stare right through her. The appearances of the ghosts became a nightly ritual, and the woman concerned eventually realised it was all to do with a mirror she had been given as a present. She was deeply religious and the mirror (as I understood the tale) had been presented to her by someone who wished her harm – as it allowed the souls of the dead to travel between dimensions in order to torment whoever owned the mirror. Those who appeared were the wraiths of those from the local community, who had been evil or immoral in life. Upon understanding this, the woman smashed the mirror and the ghosts came no more.

It is possible that this tale is another example of an urban legend, but the person who told me the story assures me that it happened recently, and she also knew to whom. She was also convinced of the story's authenticity.

THE DEVIL IN DISGUISE

In February 1999 a teenage girl and her family in Lincoln claimed an extraordinary encounter with angelic beings. Five months later there was an equally-remarkable encounter with a frightening, malicious entity that appeared within the family's own house.

The teenager was babysitting five of her siblings while the rest of the family were at church, and her description of the creature was frighteningly specific.

She was wearily led upstairs by her eight-year-old sister's insistence that something was in one of the children's bedrooms. There, a figure stood with its back to them – not a ghost, or made of light, but a real solid flesh-and-blood creature. The entity had curly blonde hair which fell to its shoulders. It wore a brilliant white robe, and wore no shoes. Gigantic, feathery white wings were spread across its back, which reached from ear level to its ankles in length, and the creature was surrounded by a kind of yellow glow. The teenager watched this creature from her vantage point for some minutes, fascinated by its beauty, but she already appeared to have formed the impression that the entity was somehow different to the angelic creatures she had seen earlier that year in February.

It was. Eventually the thing turned round to look at them, and from the front it looked very different. Its skin was grey, wrinkled and layered, like old leather. Its blazing red eyes had no pupils, and it leered at the children as it watched their awe turn to shock and horror.

Pandemonium ensued within the troubled house as the entity chased the screaming children to the downstairs living room, where they barricaded it out. Their screaming brought a small crowd of concerned neighbours out into the streets, and when the children's father arrived and ventured upstairs he found beds tipped over and images of Jesus Christ thrown from the wall. Eventually he managed to get the story from his shaking children and ultimately believed this tale beyond doubt.

If we are to accept that this Lincoln family saw angels earlier in the year, then one must also accept the possibility that the children also saw a demon. Perhaps the creature appeared to test their faith, or strengthen it, or to make them mindful of complacency. The website upon which these claims appear is certainly a genuinely non-sensational religious concern. And it is notable that this encounter coincides with a letter which the family received from his Holiness Pope John Paul II, dated 28 July 1999, in which he says that he will pray for them upon learning of their original angel sighting.

Chapter 4

Portents and Curses

Introduction

Portents of death and omens of doom have taken many forms in Lincolnshire over the centuries. Certain places have gained the unfortunate reputation in centuries gone by of being 'unlucky'. A Bronze Age round barrow, high on the Lincolnshire Wolds north-east of Tealby, can be found right next to the B1225, and is reputedly a place of ill-luck – with a visit to it invariably followed by misfortune, illness and...rain.

The county is littered with long barrows, round barrows, and ancient relics from other eras, and it is notable how many of the boulders deposited during glacial shift have stories of superstition and misfortune attached to them. It is perhaps human nature that out-of-place geographical curiosities should become the objects of fascinated awe and sinister belief. But such belief is more universal: for example, a battered old pot kept hidden away at East Halton is rumoured to be cursed, and even stranger is the notion that the stranding of huge fish heralded some coming misfortune, or that a cormorant which settled on St Botolph's Church in Boston forewarned of impending disaster.

Some may remember the short-lived rumours claiming that the Red Arrows were jinxed.

Some may remember the thankfully short-lived rumours in the late 1980s that the world-famous Red Arrows air display team were jinxed. The talk began with a concentration of accidents in a short space of time...which was possibly all that it took, given the Red Arrows' otherwise outstanding safety record. Towards the end of 1987, two of the display team's Hawk Jets touched wings during manoeuvres and both crashed into land at Welton. Three months later, in January 1988, a pilot, Flight Lieutenant MacLachlan, was killed when his Hawk crashed after a roll went wrong. After this tragedy, the Red Arrows were briefly banned from air displays, but reinstated in May.

Barely a month passed before the jinx struck again. One of the Red Arrows developed engine trouble on the runway...the pilot was forced to eject as the plane caught fire. Since then, unrelated fatal accidents involving *former* Red Arrows pilots have occurred during flights, and on 12 January 2007 two of the planes grazed each other above Scampton, but the story of the 'curse' has hopefully been laid to rest for good.

Cursed stately homes and doomed family lines are perhaps more familiar territory to those with a fascination with the supernatural. In the late 17th century Sir William Massingberd is held to have killed a servant in the grounds of the now-demolished Bratoft (Braytoft) Hall. His subsequent home, Gunby Hall, at Gunby near Burgh-le-Marsh, attracted the rumour that no male of Massingberd's descend would inherit Gunby, as it was cursed; the Massingberd family were long established in Lincolnshire's social elite, having risen from the ranks of yeomanry in the Middle Ages to the title of baronetcy. But when Sir William died on 1 December 1723, the hall – and the Massingberd name – passed to his sister Elizabeth.

There are other such houses, but perhaps the title for the 'classic' cursed mansion goes to Cadeby Hall. The owners of Cadeby would tell uneasily of a phantom coach and four horses, which would pull into the grounds and up the driveway – for the ominous vision was a sign that someone in the family was going to pass away the following day. The omen always appeared in the evening and would slowly fade from view in front of the witness, leaving them to run terrified through the halls knowing that a death was inevitable...

Cadeby Hall is a great big depressing block of a building, three stories high, and can be found at Wyham-cum-Cadeby, near Ludborough. Perhaps the story of the Curse of Cadeby Hall can be linked to another piece of folklore attached to the place. The grim discovery of a child's skeleton found in a hollow tree in the grounds of Cadeby Hall spoke of evidence to the old rumour that, years earlier, a seven-year-old boy had vanished while playing – and the child's vengeful mother had cursed the hall. At any rate, the estate of Cadeby came into the possession of the Vicar of Roxby, Hugh Hammersley (1663–1714), who promptly lost it in a marathon gambling session with the Pelham family.

One wonders if the phantom coach and horses was seen in 1885, when George Nelson, aged 16, was thrown from his horse and killed on Barton Street. A headstone by the side of the road at Cadeby Hill sadly commemorates this, '*This stone marks the spot where George Nelson, of Cadeby Hall, was killed, January 16th 1885*'. Cadeby Hall (at the time of writing) stands derelict and boarded up, although there are suggestions of restoring it to its former glory.

Even today, there are beliefs rooted in portentous events. Throughout the 20th century a strange prediction arose to the effect that the changing of the local vicar in Horncastle pre-empted widespread flooding in the region, a circumstance that had been evidenced in 1919–20 when 23 people died in the Great Louth Flood. A new vicar was installed at St Mary's in 1959. On 7 October 1960, 7.24 inches of rain fell on the town in a mere six hours; scores of shops and homes were deluged and destroyed, and one man was drowned. The vicar changed yet again in 1980 and this time the area was flooded not once but three times, between 1981 and 1984.

Maybe, just maybe, the proof of forthcoming disaster is all about us, and we ought to be very careful indeed.

THE VOICE OF LINCOLN CATHEDRAL

In 1185 a great earthquake took place, and it was chronicled by one Hoveden as '...such as there had not been seen in England since the beginning of the world.' Lincoln Cathedral was destroyed, shattered in two and split from top to bottom. At this period in the cathedral's life, the see of Lincoln was vacant, and the destruction of the cathedral must have terrified the populace for more reasons than just the shock of the earthquake. The see of Lincoln had been technically vacant once before for nearly 17 years upon Bishop Robert de Chesney's death in 1166, and a prophet of the time – the monk of Thame – had predicted that the see of Lincoln would never be filled again. However, when tensions between the church and the royal house eased, the position was filled and the prophecy was proved wrong. One can imagine, then, that the people in 1185 thought the earthquake might be God's ultimate anger being displayed at the holy see of Lincoln being once again vacant.

After all, in June 1123, after Bishop Robert Bloet's death, had not a great fire almost consumed the town of Lincoln itself prior to the consecration of his successor, Alexander? Another fire tore through Lincoln Cathedral during Alexander's reign sometime in the 1140s: clearly God had an opinion on who championed the diocese. In 1186 Hugh of Avalon was made Bishop of Lincoln and the vacancy was filled.

To those who witnessed the following strange incident *c*.1237, it must, indeed, have seemed like the cathedral was possessed of some kind of supernatural 'voice' when it was displeased. That year, the crusading Bishop Grosseteste rallied against the corruption and sinfulness he had seen at the cathedral in the two years since he had ascended his seat at Lincoln.

The bishop's rage echoed round the stony interior of the massive cathedral, 'Were I to be silent on these matters, surely the very stones themselves would fall?'

As if to emphasise the bishop's point, the central tower of the cathedral promptly collapsed inwards, killing several of the people assembled. Perhaps the old building had itself had enough of the ungodly ways of the clergy.

SIGN O' THE TIMES – ELIZABETHAN PORTENTS

In 1564 a 'monstrous fish' was cast ashore in Lincolnshire, which measured 'six yards between the eyes and had a tail 15-feet broad'. Twelve men were able to stand upright in its gigantic mouth. Such an oddity was regarded as a portent – although its exact nature is unspecified. But the date noted for the capture was 17 November, so it is likely that the find was in some way being linked by the chronicler to a perception of Elizabethan misrule, given that the date was the anniversary of Elizabeth I's accession to the throne of England.

By contrast, the publication *Strange and Wonderful News from Holbitch In Lincoln-Shire* (1693) concerns a strange incident which was seen as being God's support for the Protestant rule of William and Mary. Whig politicians declared that the beaching of two monstrous fish, a male and a female, near Holbeach, was a sign from God that the entire ocean was the sovereignty of the British monarchs.

Cautionary tales were also popular in Elizabethan and Jacobean England, particularly when they concerned God's wrath on blasphemers and sinners. In 1581, it is said, a Lincolnshire youth who constantly swore by God's wounds and God's blood incurred the wrath of the almighty: the lad died with his own blood gushing forth from his ears, nose and mouth.

John Foxe's *Book Of Martyrs* (1563) mentions a curious incident which occurred in an un-named town in Lincolnshire, during the reign of Queen Mary I (1553–58). A certain bailiff had been a locally-renowned professor during the reign of the previous monarch, King Edward VI. However, in the early

Lincoln Cathedral.

years of Mary's reign, the bailiff 'turned to be a terrible troubler of many good men and women, went and bought copes and vestiments, in the first beginning of her reigne, to have the masse up again, and to shew himselfe a diligente workeman that waye as though the gospel had never been in his mouth.' One takes this to mean that upon the accession of a Catholic queen, the bailiff became something of a religious tyrant, his inner demons allowed to run riot.

However, one day, as he rode with a companion from a wedding, a raven flew over the pair of them and 'shit on his bearde'. At this, the bailiff fell from his horse, vomiting and crying that he was damned. Three days later he had died, leaving 'his diligence in papistry to the rest of that brode' with a dire warning that should sinners stray from the path of the true gospel, then they would meet a similar ignominious ending. Clearly he had learned his lesson and blamed Catholicism for his downfall.

John Foxe apparently liked this simple cautionary tale of which religion to choose, for the story is elaborated on in the 1583 edition of the *Book Of Martyrs*. The bailiff is called Burton, and he hid his inner Papist sympathies from King Edward VI. When Mary came to the throne, however, he gave vent to his religious beliefs: he forced mass upon poor curates at the point of a dagger, and his wicked ways led him into adultery. The updated version tells how the bailiff is defecated upon by a crow (not a raven) as he rides along 'the Fennebanke' in Crowland.

THE DEAD CART

In days gone by it was widely believed that in the dead of night, something called the Dead Cart squeaked and trundled through the lanes and dirty streets of the hamlets and villages of Lincolnshire. Alongside the River Trent, it was thought the hollow rumbling noise made by its wheels foretold a tragedy. No horses pulled it, and legend has it that it moved of its own accord – piled high with the lifeless bodies of those who were to die in the coming year. Those who spied it as it made its grim nightly journey would see, it was whispered, their own cadaver heaped with all the others on the Dead Cart.

A similar story, of sorts, is told of Burton, north of Lincoln. St Mark's Eve falls on 24 April, and it was the belief in some quarters that if one wished to foretell who was going to pass away in the coming year, then you should hide in the church porch. On this mystical date at midnight, the spirits of the unlucky villagers would march past the witnesses into the church.

Gervase Hollis, a colonel in the service of Charles I, noted a curious tale he had been told by a household chaplain in Burton. In 1631 two fellows had ensconced themselves in the porch of St Vincent's Church in the village. They became petrified with fear as an apparition of the local curate (with a book in his hand) appeared, followed by the wraith of a man – one of their neighbours – in a winding sheet. The church doors closed behind these two phantasms, and the two terrified spectators heard from within 'muttering, as if it were the burial service, with a rattling of bones and noise of earth, as in the filling up of a grave.' Four more times this happened: the other wraiths were two more men, an infant and an old man, each in a winding sheet and led by the spectral curate.

In the following weeks, three of the men of Burton passed on, as did a newborn; in January, an elderly messenger from Derbyshire arrived in Burton at death's door and expired – and the two spies who witnessed the whole episode at St Vincents on 24 April, confirmed that all the dead were those whose ghosts they had seen enter the church on the dreadful night.

An almost identical legend has attached itself to St Nicholas' Church in Haxey – only here, it is said, one of the two intrepid spies fell asleep before midnight and his fellow (who stayed awake) saw the ghost of his friend among the doomed procession entering the church. His friend, in order to cheat his fate, fled Haxey shortly afterwards, intending to live rough until the next 24 April had passed and he might consider himself safe. But, not suited to living off the land, he attempted to hide away in marshland, where he eventually became ill and died of starvation: a bizarre attempt to cheat his own death, which ultimately ended up killing him.

A WEATHER WARNING TO COUNTY FOLK!

Could it be that unknown forces kept an eye on the sinful folk of Grimsby in days gone by? The antiquarian Revd Abraham de la Pryme certainly thought so. Writing c.1700, he pondered that a firestorm that terrified the townsfolk on 3 July 1610 had been divine retribution for the vice and corruption that plagued Grimsby. The Abbey House was hit by a 'great sheet of fire from out of Holderness, over the Humber', which set it afire, killing all those inside and burning the place to the ground.

Weather was often taken to be the word of the Lord – or his anger – in days gone by. In a newsletter dated 12 February 1627, in correspondence to one Joseph Mede, it was written that violent thunder and lightning that had terrified the folk of Boston was a 'visible sermon'. Mede himself was apparently open-minded to this suggestion. Commenting upon the reports that fire had rained down on Boston from Heaven, he wrote, 'Things of this nature are lyable to fabulositie, but all is not false which so may talke of and from divers places.'

And on Christmas Eve 1724, the townsfolk of Grimsby again incurred the wrath of the almighty. A drunken crowd enjoying a pageant on the eve of Christmas Day were frightened when an immense storm gathered overhead and put a chaotic stop to the revelry: a warning that such merriment before the sacred day would not be tolerated!

CURSED AND UNLUCKY STONES

Wyche is a tract of land between Orby and Hogsthorpe, not far south-west of Chapel St Leonards on the east coast. Chronicler of folklore Ethel Rudkin wrote in the 1930s that the biggest farm in Wyche was Wych Farm, and that 'Some two miles from this farm, down a green lane and across a 40-acre field' there was a large pear-shaped boulder that locals claimed 'turned over' when the clock struck 12. Quite what this signified isn't mentioned.

Perhaps the strange ritual was linked to rumours that odd, out-of-place glacial remnants (such as the boulder at Wyche is assumed to have been) were haunted, or cursed. There are numerous such tales; for example, the Drake Stones are still to be found outside the gateway of St Edith's Church in Anwick, north-east of Sleaford, and consist of one large and one small 'glaciated boulder of Spilsby Sandstone'.

Local lore has it that c.1651, a local farmer was ploughing a field called 'Drake's Stone Close' when his horses and plough were sucked into the earth and lost forever in a kind of quicksand or bog, and the incident let loose a drake which 'flew away with a discordant quacking' from the depression in the field. The following day, villagers found that the ground in the field was once again firm – but a large boulder now indicated the site of the accident.

A legend arose that the stone stood on the site of treasure, guarded by the drake. In the early 19th century, around 1832, an enterprising treasure hunter attempted to move the Drake Stone with a team of oxen. Chains and ropes were all secured, and the mighty beasts pulled for all their worth. The stone began to budge slightly...and then the ropes began to snap, and the oxen collapsed in exhaustion. This violation of the Drake Stone is said to have released the drake a second time, and the guardian spirit of the treasure flapped its wings in anger over the terrified treasure seekers.

The Ven Edward Trollope wrote, as early as 1872, that the stone had, at one time, 'stood upon another', indicating that perhaps there were numerous glacial deposits in the area. In the early 20th century the local vicar, Revd Dodsworth, intrigued by the piece of folklore, set about locating and digging the boulder up. The transportation of the stone to the church is supposed to have resulted in its splitting into the two pieces we see now.

Rudkin wrote that workmen had often noticed two drakes sheltering beneath the stones, which were usually spoke of in the singular, and this had earned them the name the Drake Stone. During the 20th century, 'drake' has become misidentified as 'dragon', with claims that a monstrous dragon guarded the boulder in days past.

Before it had been moved, the Drake Stone had apparently earned the reputation for being unlucky, and it is not the only such boulder. A great stone in a field in Wroot – just shy of North Lincolnshire's border with East Yorkshire – didn't seem to want to budge either, despite a team of six horses straining at it. It stayed put and, one by one, all of the farmer's six horses fell ill and died, generating the rumour that it was bad luck to try and shift the stone. Through the generations, the legend grew that the stone was cursed and should not be moved. Neither should it be allowed to be grassed over...or the land above and around it would soon be wet with red blood. Folklorist Ethel Rudkin heard that the boulder was so large it had sunk into the ground under its own weight and was difficult to locate. But in the mid-1970s it is alleged that the stone *was* moved – and that the person who shifted it suffered a tragic bereavement inside of two years.

Then there was the Crosby Stone – or Stock Stone – of Crosby, hidden away in a stackyard in the 19th century by a farmer, angry at the local layabouts congregating round it. During this period Crosby's fortunes began to wane as the prosperity of the nearby, growing town of Scunthorpe began to put it in the shade. In 1901 the stone was remembered as townsfolk dug a pit to plant a tree commemorating King Edward VII's coronation. A Mr Hornsby suggested setting it at the base of the tree, and since he was the only person old enough to remember where it was buried it was thought wise to recover the Stock Stone before it was lost to the ages. It was placed at the foot of the tree, protected by railings, to symbolically improve the prosperity of Old Crosby, and perhaps this is why they say locally that to move it will bring ill luck upon the town.

THE SACK STONE OF FONABY TOP

Perhaps the most well known of all the 'cursed stones' is the Sack Stone of Fonaby Top, north of Caistor. As a holy man, Saint Paulinus of York, made his way through Fonaby on an ass *c.*AD627, he spotted a farmer in a field sowing corn and asked if any corn could be spared for his hungry beast: the grumpy farmer denied having any. Paulinus pointed to a large sackful of corn that stood in the field, and he asked if that was corn. The farmer grunted that it was full of stones he had cleared from the field. Paulinus saw through the lie straight away, and in temper declared, 'Then a stone it shall be!' The sack of corn turned divinely into a huge stone – in the shape of an open-mouthed sack, which became known as the Sack Stone.

And so the story goes, although others said that centuries ago, a farmer at Fonaby Top had cursed the Almighty after blustery winds blew his seeds about even as he tried to plant them. He – and his sack of corn – had been instantly petrified into stone for his blasphemy, although with the passing of time only the stone sack of corn remained. Gloomy misfortune had began to attach itself to this unique landmark. To move it brought trouble, they said, and successive generations of ploughboys and farmers exerted themselves in rolling the stone to one side to plough under it before carefully moving it back. But sometime in the 19th century there *was* an attempt to move it which has gone down in local lore, and it must have been quite an event at the time.

The farmer at Fonaby House Farm got sick of ploughing round the obstacle, and so resolved to drag the Sack Stone to Fonaby Bottom. Right from the start it seemed the stone did not want to budge, and it eventually took a team of 22 straining horses to get it downhill to a water trough, where cattle took to standing on it to drink.

Very soon it became apparent that the cattle that stood on the Sack Stone to reach the water were falling ill. And so were the team of horses that had dragged it out of the field and down the hill. The farmer's crops failed, and when his eldest boy fell sick he began to take notice of what people were saying: the stone did not like to be moved! Preparing himself for back-breaking exertion, the farmer set to his task with merely the help of a young lad and a single solitary horse – all the help he could muster. But the stone almost carried itself up the hill, and the little team of three returned it easily to its old spot in the north-west corner of the field.

A Mr B inherited the land from the luckless farmer and he apparently took the 'curse' very seriously. Three of his workers were dismissed from his service for either moving the stone or plotting to remove it. Fascinatingly, Ethel Rudkin talked in the 1930s to an old Caistor woman who remembered working in the service of Mr B. The then manservant at the farm premises had claimed that his uncle had been one of those who had watched the legendary, disastrous attempt to budge the Sack Stone in the 19th century.

More misfortune had followed. When the land came under the ownership of a Mr A, the stone was moved to the north hedge side of the field – and a high mortality rate began to occur during calving. So once again the stone was dragged back and all the trouble ceased. In 1840 building work started on nearby Pelham Pillar – a monument to Charles Anderson Pelham, the future Lord Yarborough. In 1849, as work on the 128ft tower neared completion, a mason chipped a piece off the Sack Stone as a memento – and later fell from the pillar to his death.

The Drake Stone(s) stand before the church in Anwick.

There are held to be many other non-specific tales of people who experienced bad luck or died violently because they tampered with the stone. The earliest known photograph of the Sack Stone was taken in 1890, and it certainly does appear to resemble three great boulders piled on top of each other, with the top one resembling the 'open mouth' of the sack.

Sometime prior to the outbreak of World War One, the Sack Stone was finally budged. The circumstances are slightly unclear as to how. One account claims that the owner of the farmland successfully had the stone dragged from its centuries-old resting place in 1911. As if in protest, in 1914 it spontaneously split into three pieces; within days World War One had started, although locals denied this was some bizarre sort of prediction by the stone. But Ethel Rudkin wrote that the splitting of the stone into three pieces had prompted the farm foreman to move the pieces out of

Pelham Pillar, at Fonaby Top.

the way, the farmer perhaps being reassured by the possibility that the Sack Stone had now 'died' and could not harm his livestock. Today only two pieces of the moss-covered stone remain on the field's edge, one of them being the 'sack mouth'. The farmland is private, and the two leftover pieces of the stone can only be viewed with the permission of the owner of Fonaby Top.

Death Foreseen...

In 1859 a shopkeeper called Thorpe, who lived in the vicinity of Lincoln's South Common, awoke from a disturbing dream...he had dreamed that an acquaintance of his – a labourer named John Graham – had been found drowned, and Thorpe had helped to recover the body.

John Graham lived near to Thorpe, and was a man of notorious character. In June of that year he had been released from prison for attacking police, and he had a reputation locally as a poacher. The following day, Thorpe ran into Graham and told him of his bizarre dream the night before. Perhaps, he insisted, it would be better if Graham were to avoid water that day...?

The poacher laughed off the omen, and he told his friend that he would do no such thing: in fact, he was going fishing that very day in a stretch of water known unappealingly as the Sincil Drain, with another man called David Palmer.

That night, Graham's mother waited anxiously for her son to return. When he did not, she set out to look for him and approached Palmer for information. Palmer told her that they had indeed gone fishing that day, but the frustrated Graham had moved along the water's edge to a spot on the bank where he had thought he may have better luck with his fishing. Palmer had eventually lost sight of him.

In the darkness, Graham's mother found the body of her son lying dead in two feet of water. It was feared that he had suffered a fit and rolled down the bank into the Sincil Drain, where he had drowned. Thorpe's prediction of his death had been strangely accurate...had it been more than coincidence? Had it been a true premonition?

If so, then such 'premonitions' could take various forms. Folklorist Mabel Peacock noted an instance in the early 20th century of a man at Aslacoe Wap (a now-defunct ancient administrative district covering several parishes north of Lincoln) who first 'saw' several men carrying a coffin while he was gardening. Shortly after this he saw his wife at the same spot in the orchard in spectral form. Afterwards, the man's wife died during childbirth. Perhaps more bizarre is the claim of one Ivor S. Jones (submitted on the Ghost Club website) that he was introduced to a Mrs Squires while visiting Lincolnshire during the inter-war years. Mrs Squires, it seems, claimed she could 'smell' death in her nostrils, and whenever she smelt it, someone about her (formerly fit and healthy) was about to die.

The Boston Cormorant and other Death Birds

Boston's St Botolph's Church is arguably the parish's most famous landmark, with its impressive 272ft-tall tower known as The Boston Stump – although its claim to be the biggest parish church in all of England is the subject of some debate.

Botolph is held to have confronted the Devil on the site, and the church itself has a remarkable history. John Cotton, the 17th-century vicar of Boston, was one of the Pilgrim Fathers who famously founded Boston, Massachusetts, in the US. In 1612 militant puritans attacked the church, and in 1643 Parliamentary soldiers, who are said to have used the church as a base, further damaged it. It is unclear how the tower gained its odd nickname, but it has been suggested that pilots in World War Two used it as a landmark and referred to it as the 'stump on the horizon'.

Apart from all this, there is also the story of a gloomy portent that settled on the Boston Stump in September 1860 – a big, black cormorant. This agitated the people of Boston, who knew of the unlucky bird's association with maritime misfortune. Sailors had long held that to spot one while at sea meant certain disaster; it was also considered an 'unclean' bird, associated with departed glory. The story was recorded by a Mr Charles Ingamells in the *Stamford Mercury*, and his account states the date concerned was 8 September – a Saturday.

The bird remained atop the tower all day and was still to be found there the next morning. With the superstitious townsfolk in a quandary, the church caretaker, Mr Hackford, took matters into his own hands and shot it on the following Monday morning. The bird was found to measure four feet six inches from tip to tip of its wings.

The people of Boston wondered what all this heralded. Sure enough, news eventually reached them that the passenger steamer *Lady Elgin* had sunk on Lake Michigan after colliding with a schooner on 8 September. Some 400 people died in the disaster…among them Boston's local MP and his son. A statue to the MP, Herbert Ingram, was erected two years after the disaster, and it can still be seen in the market place near the Boston Stump.

The carcass of the notorious cormorant was stuffed by a taxidermist. The whereabouts of this odd relic is now lost to the ages, although it is to be hoped that, just maybe, it resides, dusty and forgotten, in someone's attic. However, the curious association between birds, death and disaster goes beyond the Boston cormorant and John Foxe's fatally-defecating raven. In 1893 two birds of an unrecognised species were witnessed larking around in the vicinity of a house in Caistor, where the owner was dying. The superstitious locals noted that the two strange birds had already visited the house on two previous occasions as a precursor of death. At the grange at Linwood, south of Market Rasen, rooks are said to have deserted their nests *en masse* after a suicide at the property. By the start of the 20th century, there was still a belief in Willoughton that the appearance of a pigeon – the 'death dove' – foretold calamity, and that rooks in Grayingham would desert the rookery for a year on the death of the head of a house. The Revd R.M. Heanley chronicled around this time that in the Lincolnshire Fens, swifts represented '…to the popular mind the souls of the lost, vainly bewailing the opportunities of grace which during their lifetime they neglected.' Strange as it is, this curious belief dies hard. In January 2007 I was told that a woman who resided in the village of Waddington became worried by the repeated appearance of two blackbirds, which, every day, merely alighted on the fence and looked about. They would then take off again, and this always happened at the same time of day. The lady became concerned that it foretold bad news, and shortly thereafter the family were torn apart by a catastrophic argument that is still, apparently, unresolved. After the fight, the two strange birds came no more.

CURSED TO DEATH

While compiling anecdotes for her *County Folklore* in 1936, Ethel Rudkin was told by a native of Willoughton of this allegedly-fatal curse: in order to cause an enemy to wither away and die, one had to catch a frog and stick it full of pins while still alive, then bury it. As the frog dies and withers away, so will one's enemy fade away and die. Furthermore, Rudkin was also told of an incident – apparently within living memory – of when this curse had been successful.

This native of Willoughton had, at one time, known a girl. She had had a suitor, but at length had chosen to marry another. The original beau would not stop from pestering his former sweetheart and soon friends began to notice how ill she was looking. She was encouraged to go and consult a wise man in Lincoln, who was a specialist in such incidents.

The Boston Stump.

The girl did so. During the interview, the 'wise man' drew a face on the surface of a mirror and asked the girl if she knew whom it represented. She said yes, it was her former lover. She was then told that this was the fellow who was causing her to become ill, most likely because the jealous man had placed a curse on her with a frog stuck full pins. But now that she knew who wished her ill, the curse would be prevented from working. But the wise man warned the girl that if she ever revealed to another whom her antagonist was, then the curse would instantly be reactivated again and she would begin to waste away once more.

The girl came home and in time began to grow well again, getting fatter and healthier. But her husband, perhaps vengeful, pestered her continuously to tell him who the cruel person had been who wished her such harm. Eventually she caved in, and she told her husband that it had been her former boyfriend. And with that, she once again became ill, wasting and pining away until she lost her life.

An interesting incident noted in *County Folklore Vol 5: Lincolnshire* (1908) indicates that such 'curses' may, in fact, be self-fulfilling prophecies brought on by the 'victim's' own state of fear. At Martin, between Metheringham and Woodhall Spa, there was an old clerk who church watched. When a farmer grumbled about the rates for the church, the clerk replied, 'You need not trouble for you'll not have time to pay them.' This so spooked the farmer that when he died three months later, the locals directly attributed his fear of what he had heard to his death.

OMENS OF LOVE

Folklorists have collected so much lore surrounding love and marriage that it suggests that affairs of the heart ranked only second to fear of witchcraft in terms of superstition, well into the 20th century and possibly up until the present day. Much superstition involved bizarre rituals to divine one's future husband, and they had to be performed on St Mark's Eve, 24 April. For example, there was a belief among the young women of North Kelsey that if they were to walk backwards to the Maiden's Well – and thence around it three times – they would see the face of their future husband in the waters if they looked in. Failing this, there were other alternatives for a young lady to find out who her intended was. If she could procure a piece of wedding cake at a friend's wedding, she should pass it through a ring and then place the crumb underneath her pillow. As she slept that evening, she would dream of the man who would be her future husband. If the young lady wished the man to turn up at her house, the ritual was a little more disgusting. Some were taught that if they gutted a pigeon and hung its guts above the door, for some reason this would prompt the man the girl would marry to come to the premises.

In Willoughton, if a woman wished to regain her errant lover, or get her own back, after he had behaved stupidly, then she must catch a frog (or toad) and put it in a jar. Paper was tied over the jar and pins stuck in the paper. Then, for nine nights in succession, the wronged woman had to tip the jar upside down so the frog was impaled on the pins, and leave it while she recanted, 'It's not this frog (or toad) I wish to prick; But my true lover's heart I wish to stick.'

As if to evidence the seriousness that young women took in such matters, *Drakard's Stamford News* of 24 February 1832 noted the death of one Elizabeth Bruff, spinster, in her apartment in the Workhouse at Bilsby near Alford. The paper reported that, 'Though she had long been quartered on the Parish funds of Bilsby, £35 was found in her cupboard, tied up in a piece of old stocking and it is thought she had property elsewhere. With the aid of two tame crows and a favourite hen, she practised in the occult sciences for which she was in high fame among the frail damsels who search after destinies; two of these were the last persons that saw her alive, which was about 36 hours before she was found lying cold and stiff across the hearth of her apartment.'

The Revd George S. Tyack noted in his *Lore & Legend Of The English Church* (1899) the belief in southern Lincolnshire that should a death bell toll for a married woman on the same day that the banns were announced for a young bride-to-be, then that prospective bride would die before 12 months were up. Such an incident had occurred in 1888, and thus proved that the portent was 'true'.

Variations on this theme continued well into the 20th century. It was a common belief in Scawby that if a married woman should discover two curls in her hair on her temples, where before the hair had been straight, then she would shortly become a widow. Ms Rudkin heard in the 1930s how a woman in Scawby had felt 'somehow different' as she cleansed a bedroom in the family home. The lady's straight hair had curled over each temple, and she screamed as she looked at herself in the mirror – for she knew the old legend. Within a fortnight her husband was brought home ill, he never recovered and died soon afterwards. World War Two produced a new generation of such beliefs: the so-called 'jinxed girls' – who were pointed out and avoided like the plague by the flyers and men of Lincolnshire RAF bases during the conflict. My own grandfather remembers hearing that at RAF Elsham Wolds, high in blustery North Lincolnshire, they were beautiful young women whose boyfriends were killed or missing in action...and of how potential suitors would give them a wide berth for fear of the same fate happening to them. My parents, who reside in Bracebridge Heath, have heard that the inoffensive village became attached with the same 'curse', and one can perhaps envisage the stigma levelled at these unfortunate, shunned women – whom, it can be imagined, were viewed almost as enticing Sirens by the men.

EAST HALTON'S CURSED POT

Deep in the cellar of Manor Farm in East Halton, North Lincolnshire, there lies a battered, centuries-old cooking pot. This object is contained in a cask, and it is kept trapped in a specially-made steel cage built into the dank wall of the cellar – out of the way and preventing it from being tampered with. Why? Because this object is reputed to be cursed, with a number of deaths linked to it.

The origins of the curse are shrouded in uncertainty, but there is a story of how the cellar was – at one time – linked by a two-mile long underground tunnel to nearby Thornton Abbey. It is said that a hunchbacked dwarf was murdered there in mediaeval times by the monks for an unknown reason; the corpse was reduced to ashes and spirited away by the monks down the underground tunnel to the cellar, where the remains were left in the cooking pot.

Others say that within the pot is a ghost, or sprite, trapped inside during an exorcism. Folklorist Ethel Rudkin was told that the ghost was linked to Thornton Abbey, and it caused so much disruption that the terrified occupants of Manor Farm had it 'laid' in a pot and covered with pins and earth, before being hidden away in the cellar.

Around the early 20th century the Atkin family purchased Manor Farm. The father of the family apparently had already heard of the sinister reputation associated with the ancient cooking pot kept hidden away in the darkness of the cellar.

There was a story of how a boy had dismissed the curse of the pot and tossed it into the village pond. Later that day the boy was killed when a wagon ran him down in the lane. A superstitious local who recovered the pot from the water and returned it to the cellar also died tragically within a day.

And it seemed that the previous occupants of Manor Farm had decided to leave after a baby had died there.

Atkin warned his children to stay away from the pot, but, one evening, six-year-old Charles accidentally knocked into it while playing with his brother John in the forbidden cellar. The very next day the two boys were playing by the Humber when Charles was killed — crushed under the wheels of a haycart as he larked around.

John Atkin recalled some 70 years later how the association of the pot and his brother's death had left a lasting impression; this was perhaps due, in some part, to his father ordering the cellar bricked up, sealing the pot into the gloom.

In February 1932 folklorist Ethel Rudkin visited Manor Farm to see the pot for herself. She was led down a stone stairway into the cold cellar, a room about eight feet square. The old iron pot was visible, sat right in the centre of the cellar. Ms Rudkin was told by the farmer's wife that she had tried to move it once — but the handle had snapped off in her hand and after that she dared not touch it. The farmer's wife had been informed of the pot's sinister legacy by the wife of the previous owner: it seems the evil legend of the old pot had been passed down to subsequent owners for decades. Rudkin peered into the pot and noted twigs on top of the earth, which resembled fir, but whether they were there ritualistically or by accident, she could not say.

In 1974 a businessman called John Morton and his family purchased Manor Farm, and Mr Morton was well aware of the evil pot that lurked in the bricked-up cellar. Nevertheless, he ordered the cellar broken into…but to be on the safe side he had the object entombed in the cage in the cellar wall, where it still resides today. The local minister, the Revd Bob Kenyon, was called in to perform a service of exorcism upon the pot.

Can such things really be? Perhaps one day, when the legend has been forgotten again, an unsuspecting owner will release the pot from its curious hiding place…unaware of what he might have unleashed upon himself.

ECCLESIASTICAL PREMONITIONS OF DEATH

Writer David Bridgeman-Sutton bore witness to a remarkable incident. He was with his friend David Rutter, the Canon and Precentor of Lincoln Cathedral. The two men had a fine night ahead: they were having tea at their London club, before going on to a concert and then supper. Between bites of a muffin, Canon Rutter became paler and progressively more agitated, before standing up. 'There's something wrong at Lincoln,' he announced. 'I must phone the cathedral.'

Shortly afterwards, Canon Rutter returned to the table, even paler, and he announced, 'The Dean collapsed and died earlier today.'

This was in the late 1960s, but there is a strange parallel to this story from way back in history. According to the chronicles of Florence of Worcester, which was penned in the early 12th century, a strange prophecy preceded the consecration of Lincoln Cathedral. The great date was set for 9 May 1092, the whole process being facilitated by the cathedral's founder Bishop Remigius, who bribed King William II to allow the dedication to go ahead at relatively short notice. The reason is that Remigius was by this time very sick and was afraid that he would not live to see the great building consecrated.

The entire English episcopate assembled in Lincoln, with the exception of Bishop Robert de Lozing, or Lozinga, of Hereford. He refused to do so after studying the movement of the stars, and this astrology had 'told' him that the consecration would not take place because Remigius would die in the days before the due date.

Astonishingly, the dire prophecy proved accurate. According to various sources, Remigius died sometime in the 72 hours before the cathedral's consecration date. One source, Hugh the Chanter, tells us that Remigius died the very night before. As a result, the consecration was delayed and the cathedral was eventually dedicated in the reign of Bishop Remigius' successor, Bishop Robert Bloet.

KIRTON-IN-LINDSEY'S CURSED VICARAGE

In September 1996 the *Daily Mail* ran a story speculating on local rumours and claims from an ex-resident that the old St Andrew's vicarage at Kirton-in-Lindsey was jinxed. There seemed to be an aura of foul deeds and ill luck in the village which centred on the place.

The R family first pulled up outside the stately vicarage, with its four red-bricked chimneys and plum and apple orchard, in July 1986. The Scottish couple fell in love with the place and the sale went through. But by the time the couple, and their four children, moved into the vicarage and renamed it St Andrew's Place, Mrs R was already familiar with some of the grim rumours attached to the building.

The family were the first non-clerical occupants since the vicarage built in 1865. Before them, the reverend had lived there – but he had fallen into disgrace after being convicted of assaulting a 15-year-old boy parishioner. Before that, the previous vicar had been killed in a freak accident when his tractor-type lawn mower had run him over in the garden. Mrs R also learned that the vicarage was said to be on the exact site where three 'ley lines' converged (arrow-straight alignments of 'earth energy', which are held to pass through such sites as churches, monoliths, long barrows, pagan burial sites, etc).

The family moved in around Christmas 1986, and just days after the housewarming Kirton-in-Lindsey was shaken by the brutal murder of a spinster in her 40s, one Ann Whittaker. Ms Whittaker was a neighbour of the newly-established R family, and she died at the hands of a teenage burglar; her mother was also badly injured in the robbery and died later in hospital.

Within a year, the vicarage had itself been robbed while the family were on holiday, and their car was stolen on a separate occasion and burnt out. Worse was to come. Mr R was a dental surgeon in Scunthorpe and on occasion his nurse would stay at the spacious vicarage to facilitate car pooling to work the next day. Mrs R quickly realised that her husband was having an affair, and when the truth came out it transpired that the clandestine affair had been going on for three years; to add insult to injury, it had started around the time Mrs R's mother had died. Although the affair ended, the family of six gradually fragmented and disintegrated under the usual traumatic circumstances. By the time Mrs R finally closed the door of the vicarage behind her forever in 1993, she was glad to have left the place, claiming it was jinxed.

Next door to the now vacant St Andrew's Place, another drama was playing out. The doctor who lived next door scandalised Kirton-in-Lindsey by embarking on an affair with a teenage patient, which resulted in his getting struck off the medical register. His supporters started a hate campaign against his mistress, while his own son, also a qualified GP, took over his father's position as the village doctor. However, the extent of the scandal ultimately led the doctor's shamed son to kill himself with an overdose. This tragedy led to the doctor being reinstated in 1996.

The *Daily Mail* noted that a young boy who lived in a house by the bottom of the orchard had recently killed himself, and Mrs R told the newspaper that 10 years after first moving in, she was now convinced that the old vicarage was cursed. Reporter Ceri Jackson speculated, 'By bizarre coincidence, the vicarage is built on the site where three ley lines converge. With some dating back to 4000BC these lines criss-cross the country, forming an invisible grid believed to be forces of enormous energy linking ancient monuments and sites of pagan rituals on which many of our oldest churches are built.'

CHAPTER 5

FAIRY AND GOBLIN LORE

INTRODUCTION

Figures from fairy lore pepper the folktales of Lincolnshire, and it is apparent that many of the stories appear to contain messages. For instance, the well-known tale of the Tiddy Folk of the Ancholme Valley would seem to be almost metaphorical: a powerful, ecological fable concerning the end of a way of life. Although no doubt widely believed by the superstitious locals of Lincolnshire, the creatures of fairy and goblin lore – in particular the ones that allegedly inhabited wet and inhospitable places – would seem to be manifestations of the fear of those primitive folk, of flooding and crop failure. The appeasement of such creatures was, in fact, the appeasement of nature herself.

It is clear that some of the stories told of folk from the other realm are fairy tales. Centuries ago, it was said that the River Trent had a will of its own, and every so often it would flood in an attempt to drown the good Christian folk of Lincolnshire who lived nearby. So a wizard who lived in the Lincolnshire Wolds used his slave to sort out the problem. This was not so difficult, because his servant was an enormous giant, slow, stupid and obedient, whose head touched the clouds. The giant tore up some hills from the next county and plonked them down along the banks of the Trent, thereby frustrating the river's attempts to rid itself of the human settlements. However, once a year, the river would attempt to wash the hills away with an almighty wave – and this is the explanation for the immense, unpredictable tidal surge (known as the Trent Aegir) that hits the Trent on a regular basis.

However, some of the stories recorded by eminent folklorists were told to them as though they were *factual* events, and the wealth of names accredited to the fairy folk across Lincolnshire is testament to a depth of belief that now little survives: some called them the Hyster (or Hyter) Sprites, and they believed them to be tiny and sandy coloured, and to have green eyes. They were held to return children who had become lost in the Lincolnshire Fens. In the Carrs (or wetlands) further north they were known as the Greencoaties, and the area was also the land of the Tiddy Mun Without A Name, Tiddy Men, Tiddy Ones, Tiddy People, the Strangers and the Yarthkins – which were, in description, more like a gnome or goblin. Sometimes the fairies were referred to as Hookies.

Yet, the possibility of the existence of the little people, either terrestrial or from another realm, still fascinates. J. Mitchell and R.J.M. Rickard's *Phenomena* (1977) describes the possible scenario thus, '...part of the general pattern of events would be that from the earliest time there was intimate contact between our race and another, more diminutive and less material; that the link between the two peoples gradually weakened: and that the smaller race retreated from areas of human habitation into the wilder regions...' This 'smaller race' played an important part in daily life up until the Middle Ages, and traditional ceremonies aimed at appeasing them persisted for centuries afterwards. Some even speculate that the little people retreated into the upper atmosphere and make a connection between them and the modern UFO phenomenon – the UFO phenomenon being today's equivalent of the fairy folk.

Fear of bogles, goblins and all manner of boggarts persisted well into the Victorian era. And it is worth noting that belief in fairies and pixies lasted beyond the infamous Cottingley fairy sensation of 1917, with reports of such sprite-like entities not unheard of in our own age. It is also a truism that across the nation, Lincolnshire included, fairies rarely took on the familiar image of the gentle, winged sprite. More often than not, they were wizened, ugly and frightening...

BOGGARTS

In days gone by there lived in Lincolnshire a race of things called boggarts – hideous, hairy, short troll-like creatures with muscular arms. They were thought to inhabit the northern Lincolnshire marshland known as the Carrs, but they could pop up anywhere and had the reputation of being extremely nasty and unpleasant.

Boggarts were said to pounce on travellers and pursue them, terrified, along the lanes; they lurked by the River Trent near Gainsborough, at Woofer Lane in Wildsworth, and they hung around a lonely crossroads called Lidgett's Gap at Scawby. The tales suggest that they could appear and disappear almost at will, accounting for the surprise they are said to spring upon unwary travellers. There is an intriguingly-named place at Kirton-in-Lindsey named the Boggart Field, which, to this day, has the reputation of being haunted. Further north at Barton-upon-Humber the ringing of the Barley Bell was reckoned to scare off the boggarts and other nasties that lived in the wilds around the town. This practice, however, was discontinued in 1860.

But one story tells how a Lincolnshire farmer managed to trick one of these nasty monsters. In mediaeval times, a farmer purchased a piece of land adjoining his own at Mumby, east of Alford. Before long he was confronted by the intimidating sight of a vicious-looking boggart, who claimed the land as his own and ordered the farmer to give it up. Unlike some, the farmer was not easily cowed by these creatures, and he argued the toss with it and threatened to get the magistrate involved.

This panicked the boggart, so he suggested that both he and the farmer share crops. The monster could quite easily have killed the man there and then, but a plan was forming in its slow-witted brain whereby if they shared the crops, each would get half but the farmer would do all the harvesting...but the sneaky farmer had a plan to get rid of this greedy creature. He asked the boggart what he wanted, that which grew above ground, or that which grew below ground. The creature deliberated for a while then chose that which grew above ground.

Upon hearing this the farmer sowed the field with potatoes, so naturally when harvest time came about and the boggart came to collect his produce, he merely found a huge pile of old stalks awaiting him.

For the following harvest, the hairy monster chose to have that which grew beneath the ground. So upon this, the wily farmer planted wheat, and the furious boggart found himself faced with a great load of stubble – while the farmer raked in all the grain.

At this point the boggart was getting wise to what was happening. So he angrily suggested that wheat be sown again at the next season – and that at harvesting time, they both mow at the same time and each took what he had harvested. In other words, a race.

When that time came around, the farmer was starting to get somewhat worried. The creature might be stupid, but it was powerfully built and would no doubt collect the lion's share of the wheat in the field. He decided to take himself off to visit the village wise man, and the old soothsayer suggested that on the boggart's side of the field he laid iron rods in the ground that would continually blunten the creature's scythe.

The farmer did just that, and he buried iron rods (procured from the blacksmith) in between the first few rows of the ripening wheat. At harvesting time, he ploughed through the wheat at a good rate, while his competitor kept having to break off to re-sharpen his scythe on the whetstone. In the end, the boggart gave up in disgust and told the farmer he could keep the lot. Perhaps now fearing the farmer was stronger than he, he shouted a few insults at the mortal and then vanished for good, throwing himself into a large hole.

The creature never returned to claim the land. But he remained in the area, and he amused himself with a form of highway robbery. He would attack and scare travellers in the darkness at night and retrieve whatever they dropped when they fled in terror. If the travellers had had the farmer's courage, they would have told the monster that their treasures were worthless and he would probably have accepted it!

BOGLES

Bogles haunted all the nasty, gloomy and swampy places that boggarts did, but their antics are more confined to the realm of the fantastic, as opposed to the earthbound. In the wetlands (or the Carrs) they dwelt under fields of crops, and farmers would perform complicated, drawn-out rituals to protect their houses and appease the bogles, and which would hasten spring along – for when there were no crops, bogles were particularly mischievous. One story tells how bogles could control the Green Mist (that heralded the start of spring) and thus the harvest. A young local girl, ill with fever, stated aloud that if only she could see the cowslips bloom, then she could die as content as possible by summer. The following day, the Green Mist descended in the area; spring had sprung, and with it the young maiden began to make a remarkable recovery as the cowslips bloomed and harvesting began, while the bogles took their attention elsewhere.

Years passed and the young girl became a woman. Naturally she attracted a suitor in the form of a young lad who passed by her garden. Presently, he plucked up the courage and presented her with a bunch of cowslips, but upon taking them the girl grew ill, sunken and white, and she passed away within a day. The malicious bogles had used the cowslips as a means of saving her life as a child, and they had then used them as a means to take her life as an adult.

The story of the bogles and the Green Mist is first mentioned by folklorist Mrs M.C. Balfour in her *Legends Of The Lincolnshire Carrs* (1891), and it was told to her by an old man from Kirton-in-Lindsey. She commented on such Lincolnshire folk, 'I may say, in spite of their receptiveness towards things marvellous, that they are otherwise practical and somewhat unimaginative, and accepted the tales they had heard from their fathers with respect, indeed, but were content not to ask themselves for absolute belief.'

Even more other-worldly is the tale of the Moon, who shone her light like a huge torch into the wetlands of the Carrs and forced into hiding all the evil creatures that dwelt there. But still the creatures of the dark managed to gather, so the Moon donned a cloak to hide her glowing hair and descended into Lincolnshire to root them out. In the vast, stinking marshland of the Carrs, however, things were worse than the Moon had imagined and an old gnarled living tree called the Black Snag attacked her. The tree wrapped its branches around her and held her fast. The poor Moon watched powerless as a will-o' the-wisp (also known as will o' the wykes in Lincolnshire) appeared and lured a lonely traveller off into the murk to his doom.

As she struggled, the Moon's cloak slipped from her head and for an instant the bogland was illuminated, saving the nearby traveller from a watery death. But now the bogles knew who the living tree's captive was and they threw the cloak back over her head, plunging everywhere into darkness again, before throwing her into the water and dumping a coffin-shaped rock on top of her.

For the next few nights, the local folk wondered apprehensively what had happened to the Moon. A man in a tavern suddenly announced that he had an idea where the Moon may be – for he was the traveller that had almost been tricked into drowning by the will-o' the-wisp the other night.

Bravely the locals formed a posse and ventured into the gloomy evil of the swamplands, fearful that if the Moon were not freed then the bogles, old hags and other night creatures would take over the area. The traveller had told them of the landmarks they were to look for – a coffin-shaped rock, a cross and a candle. Finding such a rock, they then located a bush twisted into a cross atop which a candle-like light flickered. The place in the boglands where the search party had ended up, it is said, was known as the Great Snag.

Silently the men heaved the coffin-shaped rock up and over, and released the Moon from underneath the waters. Each of the men had just enough time to catch a glimpse of the most beautiful face they had ever seen, before the Moon reappeared in the sky. The swamp was illuminated, and the bogles that had been creeping up on the rescue party were all forced to flee the light into the depths of the morass.

The story of the Moon is something of a classic folktale, somehow summarising all the aspects of belief and atmosphere of that part of Lincolnshire, with the familiar theme of a veiled warning to stay away from dangerous places. Like the Green Mist story, it first appeared in Mrs Balfour's *Legends Of The Lincolnshire Cars* (1891), an article for *Folk-Lore* which was actually written in the broad Lincolnshire dialect. The story was recounted to her by a crippled nine-year-old girl called Fanny, who had heard the story from her grandmother.

What bogles actually were is unclear, although in Lincolnshire they seem to have been a cover-all definition for apparitions, ghosts and hobgoblins of various types. On dark nights farmers would, according to folklore, take lighted candles and circle their houses while chanting strange incantations in an attempt to get bogles to leave them alone. They would also smear blood on their doorstep to frighten them away. And in order to procure a good harvest, free of interference from the bogles, farmers would place bread and salt on flat stones. It also seems likely that these practices reached southern Lincolnshire in days agone, as bogles were also greatly feared by the fenmen of East Anglia at one time.

By the time stories of the bogles became part of the folklore of the Lincolnshire Carrs, they had perhaps become a little more malicious than their cousins in other parts of Britain. However, the connections to all manner of natural environment factors perhaps indicate they were borne out of isolated, superstitious peasants relying on a good harvest to survive, and their fear of the murky, barely navigable marshland – and very little else. The old man to whom Mrs Balfour talked to at the end of the 1800s in Kirton-in-Lindsey about all this recalled that these superstitions were practised before his grandfather's time, and genuine terror of bogles seems to have begun to wane perhaps around the middle of the 18th century.

THE TIDDY PEOPLE

Before Cornelius Vermuyden's team of Dutch engineers came to drain it in the 17th century, the valley of the River Ancholme in North Lincolnshire was marshy and wet. The work was carried out in 1635 at the behest of Sir John Monson, a local landowner based further down the Ancholme at Owersby, and financed by Francis, Earl of Bedford. This intrusion was violently resented by the local people, who saw their way of life being destroyed.

But more sinisterly, the wetlands and the marshes were said to be the home of all manner of creatures, demons and fairy folk, but it was the wrath of a race of little people who dwelt in these inhospitable conditions that the locals were concerned about…the Yarthkin, who were a personification of the fertility of the ground and became angry when neglected. However, the Yarthkins were more familiarly known as the Tiddy People or Greencoaties, or more commonly the

Strangers. Although these 'fairies' lived in uneasy harmony with the locals of the wetlands, they became angry when they were not appeased. At Owmby-by-Spital (some distance south of the Ancholme Valley area) this merely meant leaving a basin of water out for them at the time of the full moon.

Nor were the Tiddy People, in description, much like the traditional image of a fairy. For they stood about the size of a six-month baby, yet had the features of wizened-up old folk, with long noses and wide mouths from which their large tongues flapped. They were not heard to talk – although they tended to keep to themselves – but some claimed that they yelped when angry, and when happy they made a sound like an excited budgerigar. Their little frames and thin arms were covered by green jackets (hence the name Greencoaties), and they had big feet to assist their hazardous way across the marshlands. Some wore yellow bonnets on their heads.

The strange story of these little folk was related to folklorist Mrs M.C. Balfour by an old marshwoman who lived in the Carrs at the end of the 1800s, a legend passed on through the years of how these Tiddy People lived – and how they died out. Mrs Balfour wrote the story in the Lincolnshire dialect for her article in *Folk-Lore*, and this now well-known legend runs something like this.

In the stagnant bogs and marshes there lived the leader of the Tiddy People, and his name was (the) Tiddy Mun. At night, this most secretive of all the Tiddy People would wrap himself in a grey blanket and emerge from his inhospitable conditions to take himself off into the gloom, his cloak hiding him among the thick, swirling mists that gathered in the Lincolnshire Carrs. As he hobbled along (he was lame), with the cloak masking his wizened features, long white hair and white beard, Tiddy Mun would direct the mists to follow him to ensure he was always shrouded – for, despite his aged countenance, he was in fact taller than the other Tiddy folk, being the height of a three-year-old human child. The local people of the Ancholme valley would sing a rhyme about him, which went something like,

> 'Tiddy Mun, wi-out a name;
> White heed, walkin' lame;
> While tha watter teems tha fen;
> Tiddy Mun'll harm nane'.

Clearly, then, the drainage project in the Ancholme Valley was going to annoy the Tiddy People. Although they were not malicious like the boggarts and demons that inhabited the wetlands, it was still wise to keep on the right side of the Greencoaties, for they had powers: they could, if offended, bring blights upon fields of crops, causing them to wither and die almost overnight. To this end, farmers would often steal out at night in the loneliness of the countryside and leave produce at the isolated boulders that dot northern Lincolnshire; an even better way of appeasing them was to pour a few drops of milk or beer in the fireplace of your dwelling, thus enticing them into your house. The act of spilling the liquid made the Strangers consider the local a generous person, so they would occasionally turn up at the farm – particularly in the winter months – to warm themselves by the fireplace. Once the Tiddy Mun had warmed himself, the generous human host would be treated to a display of dancing by his little guest. In the evenings at harvest time, they could sometimes be glimpsed dashing playfully through cornfields, pulling the stalks about, but the Tiddy People did not randomly destroy crops. In fact, if the crops were failing through a lack of rain, local farmers would enlist the aide of a Greencoatie by spilling a few drops of water in the four corners of his field. If it looked like farmland in the area was about to be flooded by encroaching waters from the River Ancholme, the farmer would take his family out to the edge of the rising waters and shout into the night, his Lincolnshire dialect echoing through the swampland, 'Tiddy Mun without a name, the water's rough!' In their swampland dwellings, the Tiddy folk would hear the plea and the following morning the farmer would find the waters had receded.

Similarly, if a human happened to do a Tiddy person a favour, then this would never be forgotten — the Stranger would always repay the favour, even if it took years. As such, the relationship between the human folk and the little people of the marshland was mostly harmonious and beneficial to all.

All that changed in 1635 when Sir John Monson's drainage specialists began their project in the area, designed to turn the swampy Carrs into useful farmland. Soon, ditches, funnels and dykes were appearing strategically throughout the Ancholme Valley as Vermuyden's Dutchmen got on with their work. As the waters receded, so the superstitious anger of the locals grew: they were enraging the Tiddy folk of the marshes, they pleaded, and the work must stop!

Within weeks of the work starting, strange things started happening. A Dutch engineer would be found dead, drowned in the water of the Carrs, or else they would be found suffocated face down in the mud holes. Some of the Dutch engineers simply vanished, spirited off into the night and never seen again, despite organised searches. Accidents and disappearances plagued the project, and the casualty list was high. The folk of the Ancholme Valley whispered that the Tiddy People were taking revenge. What is more likely, almost certainly, is that rebellion erupted among the primitive local people, and the drainage workers were abducted and murdered in an effort to prevent the violation of a way of life that was centuries old.

Monson and Vermuyden simply imported more Dutchmen, and eventually firm land replaced the marshy swampland of the Carrs.

Whether the Tiddy People resented their name being used as a scapegoat for murder, or whether they rebelled against the human race as a whole for what Monson did to the area, no one knows. But the disastrous times that followed the drainage were laid at the door of the Strangers,

The Old River Ancholme now, seen from Brandy Wharf.

and their reaction was terrifyingly awesome. The rains failed to come, and the crops started to wither and die. Milk curdled. Sheep stopped lambing, and livestock grew sick and died. Famine threatened the area – but worst of all, a large number of babies were dying in infancy. The local folk were in despair, for none believed the Tiddy People could be so vengeful against them.

Finally, in desperation, the peasants decided to appeal directly to the Strangers. They gathered en masse on the night of the next full moon, and in what must have been a sight to behold they all congregated near Brigg at a ditch called Crossdyke (that drained the swampland) where they each poured water as an offering while loudly imploring Tiddy Mun to stop the famine. Waiting silently, the folk of the Carr looked out to what had once been a vast swampland and prayed that the Tiddy folk, in their rapidly-diminishing homeland, had not abandoned the humans.

For some time nothing happened, and as the mists swirled lazily around those assembled it seemed the Strangers had ignored their pleas for help. Suddenly, the stillness was disturbed by the ghostly sound of whimpering babies. The mothers who had lost children claimed that the sounds were their little ones, begging Tiddy Mun to be kind again, and they claimed to feel cold embraces by the ghostly infants. Some claimed that tiny unseen hands tugged at their garments that night. Many thought they could feel the brush of tiny wings fluttering about them.

Suddenly the air was split by a sound, much like the screeching of a peewit, which the people took to be Tiddy Mun himself talking to them. It was his familiar, if odd, laugh, and the folk knew that their symbolic return of the drained water had appeased the little folk. Heartened, they returned to their farms and dwellings.

Soon after this ceremony the malaise that was plaguing the area began to reverse, and the weather turned again. Livestock diseases cleared up and the infants of the locals stopped falling victim to the terrible spell. For a long time afterwards the grateful peasants would take offerings of water out for the Strangers on the nights of the full moon, unwilling to risk a repeat of the near-famine that overtook them.

The Tiddy People were rarely seen afterwards, and it appears that man's desire for money and progression had robbed them of much of their homeland. Perhaps they gradually migrated. Perhaps they died out. For, in time, the reassuring, peewit-style cry of the Tiddy folk ceased to be heard.

Folklorist Mrs M.C. Balfour wrote of this story in 1891 that the old marshwoman, who had provided this tale, '…in her young days herself observed the rite she described, though she would not confess to it within the hearing of her grandchildren, whose indifference and disbelief shocked her greatly. To her, "Tiddy Mun" was a perfect reality, and one to be loved as well as feared.'

THE SHAG FOAL

In her volume *County Folklore Vol 5: Lincolnshire* (1908), Miss M.G.W. Peacock described a lingering belief in an entity called the Shag Foal in the region around Scunthorpe, notably Kirton-in-Lindsey to the south. Here, travellers had once told of a small, scruffy, rough-coated foal or donkey-like creature that haunted the marshlands and led unwary folk off the beaten track with its blazing, torch-like eyes. It would only show itself when the traveller had become hopelessly stuck in the bogs – upon which it would slowly drift away through the trees, making a sound not unlike half a horse's whinny and half human laughter. The Kirton-in-Lindsey Shag Foal was apparently last heard of around the mid-1840s, and there was a general consensus that it was not merely a 'ghost' but some kind of shape-shifting trickster goblin – 'shag' being another word in those days for goblin.

To the east of Scunthorpe, this creature took the form of a ghostly-white calf and was said to haunt a tunnel over a stream between Wrawby and Brigg. It became known as the Lackey Causey

Calf, for its reputed habit of trying to lure travellers into the waters of the causeway. Miss Peacock wrote that it was supposed to appear headless on some occasions.

North-east of Scunthorpe at Barton-upon-Humber, they called this malicious entity the Tatter Foal, or Tatter Colt, and it inhabited the surrounding marshlands in the form of a rough-coated horse with blazing red eyes. It too lured or tricked children and travellers into the dark wilderness of the boglands before leaving them trapped; as it vanished it did so accompanied by a frightening noise that sounded like a grating coffin lid, or iron chains clanking. One Eli Twigg described it to Miss Peacock thus, 'Why, he is a shagg'd-looking hoss, and given to all manner of goings-on, fra cluzzening hold of a body what is riding home half-screwed with bargain-drink, and pulling him out of the saddle, to scaring an old woman three parts out of her skin, and making her drop her shop-things in the blatter and blash, and run for it.' The Tatter Foal was reckoned to be no goblin, but the Devil himself. Along the banks of the River Trent there was a great fear of a creature called the Purpus-Pig, which appeared from the waters with a rope around its neck to drag those unfortunate enough to see it to a watery death. There is no suggestion that this monstrosity was a goblin, but it indicates a pattern of thinking at places near water.

Miss Peacock's investigations into the Shag Foal indicated a persistence of belief in the creature. One old lady described the entity as a phantom-like animal, which was a deep black colour. Miss Peacock related how she herself (and an acquaintance) had been attacked one night at midnight by a hound, and at this the old woman exclaimed, 'Had it any white about it?' Miss Peacock assured her that it had had a white chest, and the old woman, very relieved, commented, 'Ah! Then it was not the Shag Foal!' This took place at Barnoldby-le-Beck, south of Grimsby, and shows how far the myth of the sinister Shag Foal had spread.

In the 1830s a Shag Foal was reportedly being seen at Goosey Lane, or Boggart Lane, near Roxby, north of Scunthorpe. But Miss Peacock, in writing, noted that the Shag Foal was rarely heard of by 1891. However, as late as 1936 Ethel Rudkin wrote in her *Lincolnshire Folklore* that the Shag Foal was reputed to lurk underneath the railway bridge at Dorrington. This is south of Lincoln, and a long way from Scunthorpe; one can only wonder if, by the time Rudkin collected her volumes on county legends, the story of the Shag Foal was so widely known that even far-away Dorrington had accepted it as its own.

THE SPITTAL HILL TUT

In days gone by, so they say, there existed a creature not unlike a hobgoblin; in Lincolnshire, this fellow was called Tom-Tit, Tut or a Tut Gut. This sprite is noted in *County Folklore Vol 5: Lincolnshire* (1908) as lurking in the area of Spittal Hill (named after an old hospital) in Freiston.

Its behaviour was odd. It would take the form of a small rough-coated horse, and in this respect is similar to the Shag Foal of the Scunthorpe region – which was said by some to be a goblin in disguise. The Spittal Hill Tut, however, made no attempt to lure people to the waters, despite the fact that Freiston is within spitting distance of both the Wash and the River Haven. Its main concern seems to have been to hurry the traveller through Freiston as quickly as possible, and this it would do by mounting their horse (being in the form of a horse itself) and squeezing the life out of the rider with its hind legs. It accompanied the rider for some distance and then suddenly vanished. Miss Peacock wrote that its behaviour was down to either the fact that it was protecting buried treasure or that a crime had been committed on the spot at Spittal Hill.

Spittal Hill today.

GOBLINS AROUND THE HOUSE IN THE 19TH CENTURY

Other bogies, goblins and fairy creatures haunted Lincolnshire nurseries and homes, going by various names such as the Wryneck and the Fenodyree. Researching in 1891, folklorist Miss Mabel G.W. Peacock heard stories that this latter would 'befriend the house in which he dwells', i.e. one assumes that he would choose a human house as his locale. It seems the goblin spirit more commonly went by the name of the Hob-Thrush, or Hobthrust. Ultimately, they all may well be the same type of little folk.

The folklorist noted in 1897 a well-attested story of how a Hob-Thrush was supposed to have attached itself to a house in East Halton, North Lincolnshire, three or four years prior. It performed domestic tasks much in the manner of other sprites in Lincolnshire, but his behaviour had one idiosyncrasy. Apparently he could be made to 'walk' (appear) if the owner of the property stirred the contents of an iron pot that was kept in the cellar. This pot was supposed to contain 'children's thumb bones'. Miss Peacock identified the premises as Manor Farm, and it is clear at this point that it is the same Manor Farm which *still* allegedly houses the battered old 'cursed' pot noted in the previous chapter. Even Alfred Lord Tennyson himself, one of Lincolnshire's most famous sons, had been aware of the story of the East Halton Hob-Thrush, thanks to Mabel Peacock. She told him that the creature had hounded the family for generations, but when they tried to leave sometime around the early 19th century, the Hob-Thrush had smuggled itself into a splash-churn on the wagon. He stuck his head out and said to a neighbour, who had arrived to bid the family farewell, 'Aye! *We're* flitting!' Clearly it had intended to travel with them to their new destination. The family realised they were stuck with the Hob-Thrush and began to unload the wagon once more.

Miss Peacock later wrote in her 1908 volume on Lincolnshire folklore of an acquaintance of hers, who knew of a homestead in Goxhill (coincidentally just north of East Halton) that had held such a sprite. The woman related how 'better than 65 years since' she recalled hearing her grandmother relate tales about a race of these little fellows, who haunted farms and assisted in the indoor and outdoor work. The goblin at Goxhill, she recalled, had been 'a solitary specimen of the race', by which it is assumed that it had been the last one, the others having died out.

The lady could not remember the name of the race of sprites, but there is a likelihood they were the Hob-Thrush. It is worth noting that, as with the Shag Foal, the Spittal Hill Tut, the Wryneck and the Tiddy Mun, the Hob-Thrush was also said to dwell by water: both East Halton and Goxhill are villages near the banks of the River Humber in North Lincolnshire.

The Story of Yallery Brown

While the Tiddy Mun may have been a benevolent member of the Yarthkin race, his cousins just to the south were apparently more malicious. Although, then again, Yallery Brown may have been a different entity altogether, since he could talk. Folklorist Mrs Balfour, collecting tales of marshland folk at the end of the 19th century, was told by an old ex-labourer named Tom Tiver of an encounter he had had with one of these sinister creatures at Kirton-in-Lindsey. The story at the time caught the public imagination and, although recorded in the sometimes difficult-to-translate Lincolnshire dialect Mrs Balfour was prone to using, it has become a well-known staple of Lincolnshire folklore and follows these lines.

Tom claimed that, decades ago, when he was 18, he had been taking an evening walk one July night, his journey taking him through fields and past the allegedly haunted spinney. Suddenly, the stillness of the evening was broken by what sounded like a baby sobbing.

The young man began to search frantically through the long grass in the darkness, drifting in the direction of the crying. Suddenly, whoever it was that was crying began to speak. A little voice whimpered, 'Oh the stone, the great big stone on top!'

As he rooted around in the gloom, Tom came to a great slab hidden in the undergrowth and almost covered over by the elements. He knew that the folk of the marshes called these slabs 'Stranger's tables', on account of the rumour that the Tiddy folk danced (or had at one time) on them under the moon. Tom was somewhat fearful of the Strangers, but such was the plaintive cry that eventually he gave in and turned it over with much effort.

Underneath, he saw to his amazement a little creature about the size of a one-year-old baby. A little, wizened face peered out at him, and the Yarthkin's earth-coloured body was wrapped in a tangle of its long yellow hair and beard, which obscured any clothes it may have been wearing. It had bright, black eyes and, despite its size, appeared to be centuries old. The little fellow told the stunned youth its name was Yallery Brown.

When Tom asked the little person if it were a bogle or what, it retorted that he should not ask. But, because the lad had saved him, he would always be his friend. He would provide him one wish in acknowledgement of this. Tom, being somewhat idle, answered that he would like a helping hand at work, and then thanked the little creature.

At this, Yallery Brown flew into a rage and shouted that he did not want to be thanked! When he had calmed down, he told his rescuer that if he ever needed help, he need only say, 'Yallery Brown, come up from the ground! I want you!' and he would instantly appear. Then he vanished in front of the startled teenager.

Tom's job was that of a labourer at Hall Farm, and when he arrived at work the following day he was stunned to see that all his tasks and jobs had already been completed. This was great, so the youth spent the whole day with his feet up, and the next day, and the one after that.

Soon, problems began to present themselves. The other labourers were noticing how little Tom was doing, and they knew something was amiss. Some were spotting a little figure flitting about in the dead of night doing Tom's tasks. Worse still, Tom's jobs were being done at the detriment of their own, for as his tasks got done so theirs were undone! Eventually they complained to their employer.

Tom thought it was about time he showed willing, so he attempted to do his job, but every time he grabbed a broom it would whisk itself out of his hands, or else the plough would shoot away from him. In the end he was sacked.

In a fit of rage, the teenager shook his fist at the earth and shouted, 'Yallery Brown, come up from the ground! I want you!' The little creature appeared before him.

Tom told him that his assistance was no longer appreciated and thanked him to leave him alone. Yallery Brown smirked and cackled at this. He would no longer help the youth…but as he had been thanked yet again, he would never leave the boy alone and dog him throughout his life.

In retelling the story for Mrs Balfour, the old labourer made it clear that he put all the misfortunes in his adult life at the door of Yallery Brown. He frequently found himself looking for another job, and his disastrous marriage – including the deaths of his children – was laid at the Yarthkin's door. His attempt at farming was a failure as his livestock never grew fat. And all the time he heard the Yarthkin's mocking song ring in his ears,

> 'Wo'k as thou will, thou'll niver do well;
> wo'k as thou mayst, thou'll niver gain owt;
> for harm an' mischance an' Yallery Brown;
> thou's let oot thyself fro' unner th' sto'an'.

This tale was retold for posterity in Mrs Balfour's *Legends Of The Lincolnshire Fens* in an article for *Folk-Lore*, and it alleges to be a (relatively) modern first-hand account of an encounter with the little people – although she suggested that the eponymous narrator was retelling an old local tale with himself as the first person.

THE JINNY ON BOGGARD

At a sharp turn in the River Trent between Wildsworth and Owston Ferry, known locally as the Jean Yonde or Jenny Hurn bend, there reputedly dwelt a bizarre water-borne creature known as the Jinny On Boggard. There was occasionally spotted a little being with long hair and the face of a seal, which sped across the river from the east bank to the west. His transport was something that resembled a large pie dish and he propelled himself forcefully across the water with two tiny oars the size of teaspoons. When it had reached the western bank, it would cross the road and rummage around in the fields.

For all its banality, this final comment on the thing's behaviour lends credence to the possibility that people were at least seeing something. What it was, though, is impossible to say, although its name implies that the local folk linked it to the other-worldly, troll-like boggarts. It is said that a muddy short cut that developed had done so because people walking the path wouldn't follow the Trent and pass the fearsome Jenny Hurn bend. This short cut became known as the Half Part, and it used to be a common saying that there would have been no Half Part if it weren't for the Jinny On Boggard.

Ethel Rudkin noted in her *Lincolnshire Folklore* (1936) that strange stories had clung to this particular bend for generations, and the tale of the 'pygmy-being' was apparently common currency among riverside folk.

FAERIELAND

It used to be said that on a certain heath in Metheringham, there could be spotted fairies consorting in unusual company – the witches. Unexpected company indeed for the sprite-like fairy folk, but in keeping with their other-worldly status nonetheless. More traditional were the fairies, who, folklore tells us, aided the building of Lincoln Cathedral by carrying stones along the route from Stow.

Folklorist Miss Peacock noted in *County Folklore Vol 5: Lincolnshire* (1908) how one Eliza B, a young girl in her service at one time, knew a woman who claimed to have seen fairies dancing on Brumby

Common, southwest of Scunthorpe. Eliza had believed the woman's claim without question. Fairies were reckoned to have been seen larking about at Blyborough in the late 19th century, and between Somersby and Harrington, Miss Peacock noted, could be found a place known locally as Fairy Wood. Fairies were once said to have brought hot cakes out of the wood to farmers.

Nearer our own time, in 2004, the *Lincolnshire Echo* reported the appearance of a ring of fungi on the lawn of a house in Lancaster Drive, Scampton. The oddity caused something of a row between the residents and experts, with the residents claiming that fairies had planted the mushrooms and were living among them! It goes to show that belief in these little people did not end with the famous Cottingley fairy photos.

That conflict of belief was brought into sharp focus for one teenage girl, who sighted fairies one evening in Haxey. Recounting the story as an adult in an article on fairies in the *Daily Mail* in September 1997, she told how, while still a schoolgirl, she and her boyfriend had taken to relaxing by the shores of a little lake. One summer they noticed how the nights appeared to be filled with electrical charges in the atmosphere. Young love, perhaps...but one particular evening as the sun began to fade, the pair heard a tremendous sound like the beating of wings. There were no birds visible, and this noise was accompanied by a wind that rustled the bushes.

The sights and sounds pre-empted the coming of the fairies. Twilight was deepening, but the couple were still awake, and gradually they began to make out the forms of small figures dancing on the waters of the lake. The little figures were graceful, and the young pair formed the impression that they were silver, blue and grey; the girl and her boyfriend also formed the impression that the sprites were attempting to make contact with them through mental telepathy.

The teenagers felt that the fairy folk were twilight people in both senses of the word: both in the time they chose to appear, and the people that they appeared to. Who better to approach if you were a fairy than a young couple half asleep by the water's edge dreaming of love? This is one of the rare accounts of an appearance of the 'traditional' fairy that we are all so familiar with, as opposed to the wizened little goblin type of fellow.

What, then, to make of the strange experience of a man in Lincoln one balmy autumn evening in 2004? It was almost midnight, and the man opened his back door for a cigarette before bed. In the darkness, at the foot of his long garden he heard what appeared to be the giggling of small children: apparently a little girl of around three or four and an even younger boy. The sounds lasted only seconds before being drowned out by an articulated lorry that roared down a nearby bypass, and when the vehicle had passed the young man could not hear the sounds again.

The garden concerned backed on to nothing but rural countryside and apart from his immediate neighbours, the nearest sign of civilisation was the bypass beyond a field. Toddlers cavorting in a field in the middle of nowhere at midnight? Possibly, but the witness preferred to believe otherwise.

AND FINALLY...THE GNOME INVASION

In June 2003 the folk of Brattleby were invaded...by gnomes. Overnight, 14 properties in the village were covered with scores of garden gnomes. Normally it is the other way round, gnomes are swiped *out* of front gardens by drunken pranksters, but for some mysterious reason unknown culprits had staged a bizarre precision raid and deposited the little fellows all over. It was later suggested that the odd act was a swipe at the homeowners, who were said to live in a 'posh' part of Brattleby and would therefore resent their lawns being decorated with something 'common'.

But perhaps not. In June 2004 some Brattleby residents received letters asking them to find good homes for their gnomes – the letters were unsigned, and who wrote them remains a mystery. These lucky 13 recipients of the letters then found that glazed ceramic gnomes had been placed on the driveways of their homes. The mystery had returned.

Months passed, and in the meantime some residents displayed their gnomes – as requested – in their gardens. Others stored them away in their garages, where they collected cobwebs and dust.

Then, in June 2005, the enigma reappeared. Four garden gnomes were found sitting in a bed of pansies under the Brattleby village sign.

Later that year more gnomes put in a bizarre Christmas appearance. On the cold, foggy morning of 9 December 2005, some 20 brightly-coloured gnomes were found queuing at a bus stop at the side of the main B1398 road through Brattleby. For the first time the prankster had deposited the little fellows in December, not June, and he had also left the gnomes at the bus stop in broad daylight, somehow without being seen.

How many more gnomes are deposited in the village before the culprit is caught, where they come from and what motive lies behind this odd behaviour is impossible to tell. But in the words of parish council chairman councillor Mike Spencer, 'Who it is remains a mystery, but I suppose it does create a bit of fun each year.'

Gnomes: always welcome in the village of Brattleby.

CHAPTER 6

GHOST STORIES OF LINCOLNSHIRE

INTRODUCTION

Not surprisingly, one of the oldest instances of alleged ghostly activity concerns Lincoln Cathedral. A ghostly horn sounding on the premises, within the walls of the cathedral, is supposed to be that of Bishop Robert Bloet, the second Bishop of Lincoln Cathedral, and the great bells are also alleged to have been peeled by an unseen hand on occasion. Bloet died on 10 January 1123, collapsing into the arms of the king as they rode on horseback through woodland in Woodstock, Oxfordshire. His body was conveyed to Lincoln, where it was buried before St Mary's altar in the cathedral. The bishop had not earned himself a popular reputation in his lifetime, and one 'Bale, the foul-mouthed' asserted that the church keepers at Lincoln Cathedral were forced to perform a service of prayers to exorcise Bloet's spirit – which, they said, roamed the building along with 'other walking spretes'. This account is interesting as it is possibly one of the oldest documented accounts of a haunting in Lincolnshire, and it certainly predates the legend of the Lincoln Imp as well. Legend has it that another bishop appeared in ghostly form: Henry Burghersh, who had been bishop of Lincoln for 20 years when he died in Ghent in 1340. Yet he is said to have appeared after his death before the canons of Lincoln in hunting dress, ordering them to hand back parkland at Tinghurst, Buckinghamshire, which the bishop himself had enclosed in his lifetime.

Many ghost stories that are centuries old have passed into the folklore of Lincolnshire, with not much to evidence them other than a few historical facts and the basis of legend. Such was the case of the 'Irby Boggle', a ghost story with little foundation – yet even today people 'know' that the slain Rosamund Guy haunts Irby Dale Wood. The story goes that on 1 November 1455, Rosamund and her husband-to-be both disappeared while walking in the woods on the evening before their wedding. Locals from the nearby village of Irby Upon Humber heard screams from in the forest, but nothing was to be found.

Some two years later, the intended husband, a ploughboy called Neville Randall, turned up in the village and explained that on the night before the wedding he and Rosamund had quarrelled in the forest and gone their separate ways. He had assumed she had made her way back to the village. There were obviously strong suspicions that young Rosamund had been murdered by her intended, but nothing could be proved against him.

Some years later, workmen in the forest uncovered the skeleton of a young woman, and ever since Irby Dale Wood has been haunted by Rosamund's spectre who, according to legend, appears on each anniversary of her disappearance and is known as the Irby Boggle.

Given the folklore element of much of the content in this chapter, many of the stories are necessarily of this type. Yet first-hand accounts do exist of such supernatural encounters, as evidenced by this story in Gutch and Peacock's *County Folklore* (1908), which purports to be a reproduction of a true and sober account from about the year 1695. The witness was returning home by horse from Gainsborough when he espied by the road a sinister sight at about 10:00pm. Six men were carrying a corpse, and this so frightened the rider that he spurred on his horse. At this point he was perhaps more scared by the fact that he had come across a group of men disposing of a murder victim, but they appeared not to pay him any attention and were silent as to his passing.

Nonetheless, the horseman spurred on his mount towards Broughton, occasionally looking back over his shoulder. Every time he did so, no matter how far and how fast he had ridden, the group of men carrying the body were always the same distance behind him.

As he neared the outskirts of Broughton, he looked back once more and found that the spectral group had gone. But in their place was a horrendous phantom that looked like a bear, which had '...a great huge ugly thing sitting thereon'. This, one assumes, means a type of goblin creature was riding the bear. The whole, ghastly entity then vanished in a flash of fire that was so powerful that it made the witness' horse rear. The rider was thrown to the ground.

If this fantastical story is true, then it proves that these utterly bizarre encounters, terrifying in their meaninglessness and something apart from a folkloric story, are not merely a contemporary phenomenon. For example, one James Egar, a Trentsider, told folklorist Edward James Peacock of Bottesford Moors that he had witnessed a group of spectral horses around the year 1800. The horses, he alleged, had been glimpsed by moonlight (by himself, among others) walking on the still surface of the water of the River Trent at the junction with the River Humber. However, sober accounts of strange phenomena are perhaps best evidenced by the full chronicling of the Leasingham Poltergeist case, and in particular the story of the Epworth Poltergeist, Old Jeffrey. In the Victorian era, the *Stamford and Rutland Guardian* in particular delighted its readership with accounts of mysteries and haunted houses. So while some tales were so ingrained in folklore that they were poorly evidenced by the time they were finally written down, others were events in their time and were well recorded.

A SPANISH LADYE'S LOVE FOR AN ENGLISHMAN

A large manor house called Thorpe Hall sits nestled on the western edge of Louth, within the parish of South Elkington. Its present appearance is largely due to Charles Bolle, who rebuilt it in 1690, and there have been subsequent alterations and enlargements throughout the 18th, 19th and 20th centuries, but the manor was originally established in 1584 by Charles Bolle's great-grandfather, Sir John Bolle.

Sir John was a soldier of exceptional renown. During the administration of Ireland by the Earl of Essex, he commanded the taking of Donolong and Lifford Castles, and he was appointed Governor of Kinsale. He was knighted by Queen Elizabeth I for his conduct during the siege of Cadiz in July 1596, and it is during this raid, it is said, that he first encountered Donna Leonora Oviedo among his prisoners — 'a fair captive of great beauty, high rank and immense wealth'.

Donna Leonora became enamoured of her gallant captor, so much so that she pleaded with him to allow her to come back to England with him disguised as his page. Despite her entreaties, Sir John was forced to tell her that he already had a family back home. Thomas Percy's *Reliques Of Ancient English Poetry* (1765) contains a poem called *The Spanish Ladye's Love For An Englishman*, which describes the incident thus, 'Courteous lady, leave this fancy; Here comes all that breeds the strife; I in England have already; A sweet woman to my wife. I will not falsify my vow for gold or gain; Nor yet for all the fairest dames that live in Spain.'

Donna Leonora resolved to take herself away to a nunnery, but before she did so she presented Sir John with her jewels and valuable knick-knacks, including her own portrait drawn in green, which continued to hang at Thorpe Hall long after the Bolle family had been forgotten. The portrait was eventually sold *c*.1760, and this may have been the inspiration for Percy's poem.

Many versions of this legend persist. Some say Donna Leonora followed Sir John back to England, hoping to make him love her. But as she approached Thorpe Hall, she heard the merriment of her former captor and his family from within and, realising it could never be, stabbed herself. Sir John

Bolle died at Thorpe Hall on 3 November 1606, aged 46, and with him died the truth as to most of these events.

Thorpe Hall has long been said to be haunted by the ghost of a woman in a green dress, with most stories saying she appears beneath a particular tree close to the mansion. She is also held to glide across the South Elkington to Louth road (the A631), and she is reputed to haunt Thorpe Hall itself. During the lifetime of Sir John's son, it is famously said that a place was habitually prepared at mealtimes in memoriam of Donna Leonora, a superstition which apparently continued well into the 20th century. The story of the Green Lady of Thorpe Hall is one that countless generations have grown up with around Louth, and even today there are people that recall being told the story for the first time – and how many people 'are supposed to have seen her'...

The Green Lady is held to drift the countryside approach to Thorpe Hall.

THE HOLBEACH GAMBLERS

In the late 17th century a party of four would often be found at the Chequers Inn (now the Chequers Hotel) on High Street, Holbeach, where they would gamble and drink their evenings away. The notorious party of young tearaways comprised of Dr Jonathan Watson, Abraham Tegerdine, Mr William Slater and farmer John Guymer.

The death of the farmer, however, split up the quartet, and the eve of his burial found the remaining three drowning their sorrows at the Chequers. Eventually, Tegerdine suggested that they should go to nearby All Saints Church and keep their dead friend company for one last evening, before he was laid to rest. Fuelled by alcohol and bravado, the three got up and staggered up the road and into the churchyard. After managing to open the church door the trio sought out their friend's coffin in the gloom at the altar, using a lamp they had brought.

After much toasting and drinking they began to grow bored and cold. So it was suggested that they play a game of cards by lamplight using the coffin lid as a table.

All agreed that their deceased friend should be allowed to sit in on the game, so they prised off the lid of the farmer's coffin, hauled the corpse out and propped it up. The cards were dealt and the three gamesters took it in turns to play the corpse's hand. More beer was consumed and everyone congratulated the body on playing a much better game of cards as a dead man than he had done as a live one.

Suddenly, the putty-coloured face of the corpse began to move. The head turned and the face leered at the three gamblers. Then there came 'from the depths of the vault an ear-piercing shriek and three ghastly spectres burst through the floor. Each seized a partner, threw his grisly arms round him and vanished with his prey.'

The following day villagers steeled themselves to enter the church. They had heard the commotion of the night before, and a sinister sight met their eyes within All Saints Church. The coffin was upturned and the deck of cards lay scattered across the stone floor. The body of farmer Guymer – a self-satisfied smirk on his dead face – sat propped up against the altar rails. Of the three gamesters there was no sign, and they were never heard of again...well, not in earthly form anyway.

It is said that they were spirited off by the wraiths; some even claimed that Satan himself had appeared and taken them. For years afterwards the spectral outlines of the four men were glimpsed in the porch of the church, beckoning all drunkards into the churchyard so as to share their fate.

In an investigation into the old legend for *Lincolnshire Life* magazine in 1994, R.A. Cooper noted that all the participants in this legend were real, or at least their surnames were a matter of fact on local registers of the era. Those who wish to believe the old tale, or who are looking for an explanation for the disappearances of the three gamesters, might speculate that they were killed by grave robbers or thieves whom they happened upon at the church that night in Holbeach.

THE CROWLAND DROVERS

Some time in the early 1700s a traveller named Isaac Kirton was forced to seek shelter and accommodation during his journey, thanks to an angry storm that was gathering overhead. He approached an inn near Crowland as the rain started to fall, but was a little put out when the landlady attempted to dissuade him from staying there. After much wrangling she agreed to let him sleep over in a room that was 'never used', but which was the only one free.

That night a knocking at the bedroom door interrupted Kirton's slumber. The rapping persisted, so eventually he roused himself and threw open the door...merely to find an empty passage yawning at him. Upon closing the door the gentle knocking again sounded, so Kirton once more opened the door. Again the passage stood empty and silent.

When the knocking began again, Kirton shouted out that whoever the perpetrator of the sounds was should identify themselves. At this, three ghostly apparitions floated into the bedroom.

The spectres informed the startled traveller that they were the spirits of three drovers, who had been on their way home from a livestock market and had stopped off at the inn for refreshments. They had made no secret of the fact that they had money on them, and the landlord, on finding this out, had murdered them and buried their bodies. The drovers were engaged in the long-distance sale of livestock and were not local, merely following a drover's route via Crowland. Who would know if they disappeared en route? The ghosts beckoned Kirton to follow them, and they led him outside into the back yard where they pointed at a spot on the ground: that, they said, was where they were buried.

Kirton placed his whip at the spot indicated and returned to his bedroom, but his strange encounter played on his mind and he got no sleep. The following day Kirton approached a nearby cottage and offered the owner monies if he would dig up the back yard of the tavern at the spot the ghosts had indicated. The grim excavation uncovered the badly-decomposed bodies of the three murdered drovers.

The landlord of the tavern was placed under arrest, and upon hearing of how the three corpses had been located he confessed in a state of shocked disbelief. He was subsequently executed after his trial.

This story turned up among the archive papers of the Huddleston family of Sawston Hall, Cambridgeshire, a prominent Catholic family of whom copious amounts of manorial records, title deeds, estate papers and family correspondence exist at the Cambridgeshire County Record Office, dating from the 14th century. From this, there is some suggestion that 'Isaac Kirton' was, in fact, a pseudonym used by one of the Huddleston line themselves – who had experienced the supernatural encounter first hand.

THE GIRSBY FIREBALL

Between Market Rasen and Louth lies Girsby, a little place north of Burgh-on-Bain. Girsby Hall has a brutal tale of horror attached to it. It is said that in the late 18th century, a young servant lad was abducted by a band of brigands and forced to promise that he would unlock the front door of Girsby Hall for them at midnight so they could rob the place. As soon as he got back to the manor, the boy told his employer, Mr Pindar, what was going to happen. The result was that when the robbers assaulted the property they were met by a party of well-armed men, who opened fire on them with muskets. Those who survived were carted off to Lincoln Castle, and after a trial the four brigands were hanged and gibbeted at a crossroads a mile from Girsby Hall.

A few months after the trial the teenage servant travelled to Horncastle on an errand for his employer. His route took him past the crossroads where the four corpses swung and after that he was never seen alive again. The poor boy was found dead some time later in woodland off the road, the skin flayed from his body.

It is said that no one was ever convicted of the lad's murder. But the local magistrate was of the opinion that he was killed as an act of retribution by the executed robbers' friends. Locally, they were not so sure. For they said he had been killed from beyond the grave…by the ghosts of the four men he had helped to execute. In the years afterwards, a legend claimed that the boy's body had been torched and at the site of the crime a screaming ball of fire was sometimes seen to tear across the road, which became known as the 'Girsby Fireball'.

STUART AND GEORGIAN POLTERGEISTS

The experiences of the York family were chronicled in a piece entitled '*A true and faithful Narrative of the disturbance which was in the House of Sir William York, in the parish of Lessingham, in Lincolnshire.*'

By Lessingham it is meant Leasingham, north of Sleaford, and the uncanny events began in May 1679 with the latch of the outer door somehow repeatedly lifting itself very quickly for between two and three hours. In July it was recorded that the doors were slamming shut on their own, and, weirdly, that the chairs of the house held a 'gathering' in the hall of the house before mysteriously returning to their proper places in various rooms throughout the building. By August the manifestation had taken the form of phantom knockings at the door. In September thumps sounded throughout the house as though someone on stilts were walking about the place.

Perhaps the most curious feature of this phenomena is that at the time, Sir William had a plumber and a carpenter working on the premises, and it could be assumed that the bangs, thumps and knocks were somehow linked to all this. But it is noted beyond doubt that all the poltergeist activity occurred in the evening *after* the workmen had left. Moreover, often the sounds were made against the iron and lead that the plumber had installed – almost as if the entity were copying the din that the plumber had made during the daytime.

The poltergeist would also copy the sounds that the other workmen made as well, such as the noises of wood being chopped which emanated from the deserted yard. The entity also imitated the sounds of servants breaking coals in the coal yard and in general appears to have had a strange habit of copying the noises made by humans at the house.

It is written that the noises came three or four times a week, in the evening, and the family chased the sounds as they bashed at the doors of the outhouse, the wash house, the brew house and the stable. It is indicated that the noises would lead the pursuers to one part of the premises and then instantly be heard rapping at another part of the building.

It is also interesting to note that this poltergeist *appears* not to have had an affinity to pre-pubescent teenagers, particularly girls, as is often reported. Although there were children in the house, their ages are not specified, and the phenomena ceased entirely in October when Sir William had to leave Lincolnshire for London, to attend Parliament.

On the other side of Lincoln, far to the north in the Isle of Axholme, Epworth Old Rectory still stands on Rectory Street, Epworth. In 1716 the parsonage was invaded by a frightening supernatural force, the details of which would later be chronicled by a son of the house – none other than John Wesley, the founding father of Methodism.

At the time of the phenomenon, the parsonage at Epworth was occupied by the Revd Samuel Wesley, his wife Susanna and their daughters Emily (about 22), Mary (21), Nancy (20), Sukey (19), Hetty (whose age is unclear, but may have been aged between 12 and 19), Patty (aged 9) and little Keziah. There were three servants: Robert Brown, Betty Massey and Nancy Marshall. Then there were the family pets: a mastiff and a cat. At the time of the incident, the three sons of the house (Sam, Charles and young John himself) were away.

The first sign of the coming events were strange sounds heard within the parsonage: 'several dismal groans' followed by strange knocking, and a sinister cackling noise was also reported. This probably occurred on 1 December 1716. The following night the servant Brown was repeatedly roused from his bed to answer furious knockings on the front door, only to find no one there. He would later claim that this was the night that the 'thing' had gotten into the rectory, for he heard an unseen entity moving about the room making a noise that sounded like the gobbling of a chicken. The following morning Brown mentioned the night's bizarre events to one of the maids, who chided him; however, later that day, persistent hammering at the door as the maid tried to write her diary so scared her that she fled the room. About a week after this Emily and Sukey Wesley had been locking up when both had heard the sound of 'a large piece of coal' being smashed and splintered as though for fuel somewhere in the kitchen. Mystified, they searched the ground floor of Epworth Rectory and found the dog asleep and the cat at the other end of the building – and nothing to account for the noises. At 9:45pm every night, footsteps were now being heard plodding down from the north-east corner of the rectory, and Emily Wesley christened the invisible force 'Old Jeffrey', after an old man who was said to have passed away in the place before the Wesley's time there.

At first, Samuel Wesley refused to believe that the manifestation was a supernatural presence. It is said that he first considered the activity to be caused by rats, and so he employed a Scottish horn blower to play his bagpipes within the rectory. The theory behind this was that the drone would eventually drive the rats out, but in time 'Old Jeffrey' learned to imitate the noise as it was being played. Samuel himself had been among the last at the rectory to report the entity, and it appears his wife Susanna tried to keep the reports of other members of the household from him, lest he would think them '…a warning against his own death, which, indeed, we all apprehended'. Indeed, Samuel himself did not experience anything until 21 December, when furious knockings from his bedroom wall led him to attempt to seek out the manifestation with the mastiff. Apparently the search for the entity quickly depressed the animal, and henceforth it took to nightly barking at thin air before slinking off to a hiding place beneath the stairs, cowed and whining. This became the sign that the thumping and knockings were to begin.

For some two months the household was hounded nightly by 'Old Jeffrey', as the manifestation grew increasingly bolder and more violent. Doors opening on their own and phantom noises, like silken dresses rustling or cradles being forcefully rocked, were superseded in intensity by other, more disturbing poltergeist activity. Brown, the servant, was tormented on two occasions by a phantom white rabbit, which had vanished when he chased it with a candle. Mrs Wesley saw what looked like a white badger, without a head, snuffling around underneath one of her daughters' beds, which then vanished amidst daughter Emily's petticoats.

While the children apparently chased the entity from room to room almost as if it were a game, for the adults it was a truly disturbing time. The thing appeared to hold a particular enmity towards Revd Wesley. Typically, on 26 December he suffered a noise like '…the quick winding up of a jack, at the corner of the room by my bed head'. The knocks that followed were '…hollow and loud, such as none of us could ever imitate'. There is also the suggestion that Samuel thought the entity a Jacobite goblin, since it made much noise 'over our heads constantly, when we came to the prayers for King George and the prince'.

The closest thing 'Old Jeffrey' displayed to the archetypal image of a 'ghost' was the strange figure in a white gown – 'something like a man' – which had terrified young Hetty by drifting down the stairs. She was so frightened that she fled, chased into the nursery by a sound as of an old man with a gown loosely trailing behind him. But the manifestation's true form is almost beyond description. Samuel Wesley is famously held to have drawn his pistol and challenged the entity to face him in his study; in his quest, he followed the poltergeist into virtually every room in the parsonage during the outbreak, and he would often sit alone, door closed, and try to talk to it. Disturbingly, he never heard what he could discern as an articulate human voice – only two or three pathetic squeaks. He described its attempts to communicate as '…a little louder than the chirping of a bird, but not like the noise of rats, which I have often heard'. The sign that the thing was in a room at any given time was the 'dead hollow note' which marked its presence.

Sometimes, however, other noises reached a thunderous crescendo. Susanna Wesley recorded, 'One night it made such a noise in the room over our head as if several people were walking; then… running up and down stairs, and was so outrageous that we thought the children would be frightened

Epworth Old Rectory is now a major tourist attraction.

so your father and I rose and went down in the dark to light a candle. Just as we came to the bedroom at the bottom of the broad stairs, having hold of each other, on my side there seemed as if somebody had emptied a bag of money at my feet, and on his as if all the bottles under the stairs (which were many) had been dashed to a thousand pieces...'

During a visit on 28 December, a clergyman from Haxey, Mr Hole, independently verified the phenomena with these words, 'The noises were very boisterous and disturbing this night.' The thing's animosity towards clergymen apparently also extended towards Mr Hole, for he was also roughly shoved as Samuel had himself been on occasion. Despite fears for the persecuted family, Samuel is alleged to have roared, 'Let the Devil flee from me; I will not flee from the Devil!' But there was a strange aspect to this statement. On 28 December, the night Mr Hole had stayed, Samuel had been due to leave the rectory for a visit, but the noises had been so terrific that he had thought better of it. However, he did make his journey on 30 December, and – bizarrely – reported, 'I January 1717. My family have had no disturbances since I went away.'

The malicious force that plagued the family had all but subsided by the end of January 1717. Many are the theories put forward as to this mystery: Wesley was hated by Dissenters, as well as the local 'cunning folk', or wizards, whom he frequently preached against, and there has been speculation that the whole episode was manipulated by the Wesley's political enemies. The finger of suspicion has also, slightly unfairly, been pointed at one of the daughters, Hetty, whom the entity appeared to attach itself. During the phenomenon, John Wesley (at that time 13-and-a-half) had been absent from the rectory, but in later years he drew upon his family's written accounts of the event to chronicle *An Account of noises and disturbances in my house at Epworth, Lincolnshire in December and January 1716*. John was utterly convinced that 'Old Jeffrey' was supernatural in nature, perhaps born out of trauma within the family after Samuel threatened to desert Susanna unless she recognised the Prince of Orange as the rightful King of England during those strife-torn times. It is noteworthy that for some weeks after the phenomenon began at the start of December 1716, several family members feared that it foretold bad news – Susanna drove herself mad with worry that one of the boys, away at the time, had somehow been killed, and it has to be wondered how far this 'negative' energy 'fed' the poltergeist before the family learned that all the boys were well. John's accounts in *The Arminian Magazine* of The Epworth Phenomenon so fascinated the British public that it prompted one reader, a doctor and legal expert called Fitchett, to comment '...the evidence, if it were given in a court of law, and in a trial for murder, would suffice to hang any man.'

A HAUNT OF ANCIENT PEACE...

Like Thorpe Hall, many of Lincolnshire's well-established ghost stories are attached to the county's stately homes.

The plum-bricked 'dolls house' that is Gunby Hall was built in 1700 by Sir William Massingberd at Gunby, between Candlesby and Burgh-le-Marsh. The Massingberd family had previously lived at Bratoft Hall, but their residency was tarnished by an act of brutal violence carried out by Sir William himself. He is said to have shot to death a postilion whom his daughter intended to elope with, and for this act was sentenced to appear annually in London where his family coat of arms was smeared with blood. This was not as preposterous as it sounds: Sir William was a Tory MP, and the third baronet of an old county family, and this was an age when the law in such cases favoured peers rather than commoners. Still, the stigma took its toll on Sir William and in 1698 Bratoft Hall was demolished, with the family eventually moving into Gunby Hall.

Gunby Hall, near Burgh-le-Marsh.

Within the 1,500-acre estate, beyond Gunby Church, the shaded path leads to the Ghost Walk and the pond. It is in this pond that the postilion's body is held to have been thrown, and for generations afterwards it was claimed that the ghostly outlines of the murdered servant and Sir William's lovelorn daughter haunted what is now Ghost Walk. A deathly-cold sensation would chill those who saw the ghosts, but it lifted when the spirits faded from view.

As Alfred Lord Tennyson wrote with Gunby in mind:

> 'And one, an English home – gray twilight pour'd
> On dewy pastures, dewy trees
> Softer than sleep – all things in order stored,
> A haunt of ancient Peace.'

Perhaps this is literally so for the two ghosts who are still believed to haunt the estate.

THE GREY LADY OF GAINSBOROUGH OLD HALL

In the centre of Gainsborough can be found the unmistakable mediaeval manor house called Gainsborough Old Hall. The original mansion was built by Sir Thomas Burgh, but was burnt down by Lancastrian forces in 1470; Sir Thomas rebuilt it in red brickwork, adding the famous three-floored polygonal tower in 1483, but architecturally very little has changed over the centuries. The hall still presents the striking, timber-framed appearance of a seat of mediaeval power.

Within the tower, at the north-east corner of Gainsborough Old Hall, a spectral woman is held to still linger. The popular story behind the Grey Lady is as follows. She was the daughter of a Lord

Gainsborough Old Hall.

of the Manor, who, one night, attempted to elope with the heir to the Talbot family of Torksey, further south along the River Trent. Talbot was a soldier considered not a good enough match for the young noblewoman, so, with the help of a maid, they arranged for a boat on the Trent to secretly collect her. Unfortunately, the Lord of the Manor found out about the planned elopement and thwarted it. His heartbroken daughter took herself off to the tower where she spent the rest of her days, although some versions claim she was exiled there by her enraged father. Legend has it that the poor child pined away and died a lonely death in the tower, and centuries later the girl's unhappy spirit was said to haunt the tower and the hall itself.

The most shocking account of an encounter with the Grey Lady is said to have occurred in the early 19th century, when the story of a semi-delirious tradesman employed as a painter was pieced together after he was found sprawled in the hallway leading to the tower, repeating in terror, 'She is there!' It transpired that a mysterious phantom lady dressed in white had suddenly appeared before him, smiling and beckoning him to follow her. The painter had merely stood there in stunned silence, before slipping into a stupor as the Grey Lady appeared to grow increasingly angry with him. He had passed out, and it seems it took some time for his delirium to clear.

This legend is a classic ghostly anecdote and has no doubt provided the foundation for the ongoing belief in the Grey Lady – she has allegedly been heard and glimpsed well into the 20th century. A certain part of the Old Hall is now known as Ghost Corridor. So famous is the Grey Lady's association with the hall that these days, Gainsborough's famous Ghost Trail Experience begins and ends there.

GHOST STORIES OF THE 19TH CENTURY

Antiquarian and columnist for the *Stamford and Rutland Guardian* Adam Stark recorded an instance of a strange entity that plagued the tenants of a small cottage at the south end of Gainsborough around August 1823. It announced its presence with a sinister tapping at the window pane, door or bedpost, and when it took on a 'physical form' it apparently chose to move around in the form of a black dog or cat. But apart from the knockings, Stark recorded what would later come to be recognised as atypical poltergeist behaviour, 'Indeed the principal object of the attack seems to be a poor harmless girl…' who '…readily abandons herself a prey to this aerial nocturnal visitant'. Various attempts were made to rid the cottage of '…the spirit from the vasty deep' without success.

There appears to be little in the way of substance to this report, but the style of writing speaks to an appetite for sinister stories of the spiritual, which the *Guardian* columnist readily fulfilled. There is certainly no shortage of ghostly tales from this era.

Tom Otter (whose real name may have been Temporell, or Temple) was sentenced to death on 12 March 1806 for the murder of his bride of a mere day, Mary Kirkham. Otter, a 28-year-old Nottinghamshire navvy, had been forced into a shotgun wedding with the heavily-pregnant Mary on 3 November 1805 – and that very evening he battered the poor girl to death with a hedge stake near Drinsey Nook at (what is now) the B1190, also known as Tom Otter's Lane. After being hanged in Lincoln, Otter's body was suspended 30-feet off the ground in a steel gibbet cage at a spot near the crime, still known as Gibbet Wood.

Even before Otter had been hanged, strange stories had attached themselves to the brutal event. Mary's body had been recovered from a ditch and placed on a cart to be transported to the Sun Inn, Saxilby. The cart was not bedded with straw, and, as such, a gruesome trail of blood was left from the crime scene all the way to the public house; legend has it that the drops of blood on the stone steps of the inn could not be washed away. In years to come, they later said, the Sun Inn echoed with the pathetic crying of Mary's unborn infant.

On 20 March 1806 enormous crowds swarmed to Drinsey Nook to see the gibbet hoisted. The day was jinxed from the start: the drawbridge over the Fossdyke Canal collapsed when the cart transporting Otter's corpse clattered over it. The gibbet was put up in high gales, and three times the contraption collapsed – the third time fatally injuring someone in the crowd. Others were crushed as the mob surged forward to see the gibbeting.

The bloodied hedge stake Otter had used in the murder was put on display at the Sun Inn, and within a year odd rumours began to circulate that the curiosity had somehow supernaturally wrenched itself off the wall of the pub on the anniversary of Mary's death, only to be located at the site of her murder. Whether there *was* supernatural intervention or not, the landlord of the Sun Inn was clearly on to a good thing, as the crowds are said to have swelled at the hostelry as the anniversary of the crime approached yearly. They whispered that whenever the hedge stake was recovered, it was wet with fresh blood...at this the Bishop of Lincoln is said to have had the murder weapon confiscated and burned secretly in the Minster Yard at Lincoln Cathedral, as a relic of superstition.

The gibbet containing Otter's body swung for decades, the skeletal jawbone providing a habitat for a bird and a nest of chicks. The gibbet eventually collapsed in 1850, but a century after the killing on that dark, lonely Lincolnshire lane, some could still recite a rhyme about the birds that nested in the corpse: 'There were nine tongues within one head; The tenth went out to seek for bread; To feed the living within the dead.' The remains of Tom Otter were buried near to the gibbet, and presumably are still there somewhere in the vicinity of Gibbet Wood.

The Old Rectory is sited at Fulletby, north of Horncastle, isolated and almost hidden by tree cover in a remote part of the southern Lincolnshire Wolds. The building has its origins in the 16th century and these days is approached by an immensely-long copse-shrouded drive. The current owner (2005) is aware the place is supposed to be haunted, but the following story was first noted by local poet Henry Winn in the 1880s, in his volumes on village history.

During renovations in the early 1800s a human skull was discovered and buried in the churchyard. The following morning it was found disinterred and among the rubble generated by the building work. So the diligent labourers scratched their heads and had it reburied in the churchyard. The next morning it was found yet again among the debris on the site. The workers were beginning to think that the skull was cursed, and so they walled it up in the chimney of the new building.

What followed was a series of poltergeist-like outbreaks that terrified the servants and even led to some of them quitting their jobs. The entity seemed to prefer a particular passageway in the building, but the most commotion was caused in the kitchen, where violent smashing sounds led the household to think that someone was breaking all the crockery. When the servants ventured into the kitchen the following morning they found everything orderly and undisturbed. The thing also invaded bedrooms, and sometimes servants would wake up cold and shivering in the middle of the night to find that their bed linen had been mysteriously thrown off the bed and across the room.

In 1840 the building became a rectory and 14 years later, the first rector, the Revd John Jackson, had the place almost rebuilt. This involved the supposedly haunted passage being closed up and, more significantly, the chimney said to house the accursed skull being torn down. After this the inhabitants were no longer troubled by the poltergeist. One wonders how much of the good reverend's decision to renovate and rebuild was due to the poltergeist activity that plagued the property.

Another skull is supposed to have been bricked up within the Great Hall, near Edward King House, Lincoln. The skull had once stood on display, but one owner had found it distressing and disposed of it. It began screaming, and it only stopped when it was brought back into the Great Hall. It was subsequently decided to brick it into the superstructure so it could never be accidentally thrown out in the future. As with the Tom Otter legend, it has to be wondered how much of the details of such stories were common parlance locally at the time of the event, and what was elaborated on by hearsay and subsequent generations to make the tales the versions they are today. There are many ghostly legends that appear to have little or no foundation beyond local assurance that it is so; in Digby, they said that if one were to run backwards round the great tomb of Squire Robert Cooke in St Thomas' Church 12 times, then you would chance to hear the phantom echoes of the lavish parties the squire was famous for. The squire died in 1814 and his tomb bears the inscription: *Robert Cooke, Gentleman.*

A legend from further south is even more indicative of hearsay. In Elsea Wood, a small area of ancient woodland to the south of Bourne, it is not just the fallow deer, the bluebells and all the other creatures of the forest that dwell there. Elsea Wood has historically been haunted by Nanny Rutt. In life she was said to have been Nancy Rutter, a 19th-century serving girl who fell pregnant by her employer at Northorpe. Ashamed, disgraced and abandoned, she took herself off into Elsea Wood to give birth in private. But the child died and the woodland became Nancy's refuge from the outside world. Over the years she gained a reputation as a 'wise woman' and a witch, towards the end of her life inspiring more fear and fascination than the kind of scorn she had suffered in her youth. Elsea Wood adjoins Math Wood, and it is said that in subsequent years a young girl went into the wood, to a spring now called Nanny Rutt's well, where she vanished. Lore has it that she was 'taken' by the ghost of Nanny Rutt. This very early Lincolnshire predecessor to *The Blair Witch Project* is very likely to have been a cautionary tale against wandering off into the wood; there is also a veiled sexual message as well, and apparently the tale was popular in the conservative Victorian and Edwardian eras.

However, contemporary reporting of events as they happened did occur. On 26 March 1897 the *Stamford and Rutland Guardian* carried a report on a haunted house in St Mary's Place, Stamford, that was attracting considerable attention locally.

The haunting had first come to light when a tenant moved into the property in 1893, whereupon he was troubled by 'strange, unaccountable and unpleasant noises'. The disturbances generally occurred between the hours of 11:00pm and 4:00am in the morning and so perturbed the resident that, shortly before the paper carried the story, he had moved his family and his furniture to another house. The newspaper reported that the noises took the form of footsteps sounding repeatedly on the stairs and – more distressingly – human voices were sometimes heard. They sounded like an angry man scolding someone and a woman moaning. In the week following the family's departure, excitable crowds were reported to have gathered outside the house in the evening in the hope of seeing something weird. On the Tuesday morning a man reportedly witnessed a mysterious apparition pass by twice in front of an upstairs window. The man dashed into the house and found that the only people in the building were a servant girl and a washerwoman, both of whom were busily engaged downstairs. A search was made upstairs but nothing was found to account for the strange apparition witnessed from the street.

MARATHON RUNNER STILL GOING

It is perhaps no surprise that ghostly stumbling footsteps are heard at the 18th-century Abbey Hotel in Crowland. But these are not phantom echoes of a staggering drunk, more a supernatural reminder of a very famous event in Crowland history. For the footsteps are said to be those of Henry Girdlestone, a local farmer who boasted in 1844 that he could walk 1,000 miles in 1,000 hours. On a February morning he set out on his marathon challenge.

After a month's marching Henry appeared to be going into some sort of trance, and his chums offered to cancel the wager: but Henry refused. Forty days later he staggered back into the Abbey Hotel, and he had covered some 1,025 miles – but in 1,176 hours.

Grave in Lincoln Castle of an executed poacher, whose lurcher dog allegedly haunted the nearby Strugglers' Inn, Westgate in Victorian times.

After this astonishing feat, Henry sat down at the Abbey and scoffed a huge meal before sleeping for three days. Henry's walk became so well known that the *Lincoln, Stamford and Rutland Mercury* celebrated the 50th anniversary of it in 1894.

It is unknown whether his friends actually paid up the cash. Perhaps his frustration at narrowly losing the bet is the reason why his footsteps were, for decades after, heard echoing from an attic in the night. Tradition holds that the footsteps also clumped along corridors.

In October 2002 the hotel manager told the *Spalding Guardian* that Henry still did his rounds in the old building. Brian Berchielli claimed that at 3:30am every morning, he was awoken by 'Henry' coming into his bedroom and shaking his feet to waken him. One wonders if this was perhaps Henry's old bedroom, and his ghost wished to rouse someone whom he found sleeping in his sorely-needed bed!

The Abbey Hotel is also reputed to be home to the ghost of a woman who was murdered in one of the rooms. Mr Berchielli claimed that several patrons had apparently witnessed a ghost, which took the form of a little old lady with 'wispy grey hair', who haunted the function room above the bar on the first floor.

LOOKING BACK – CHRONICLING 19TH-CENTURY GHOSTS

Victorian urban legends and excitable contemporary newspaper accounts aside, some of the most fascinating ghost stories of the 19th century did not come to light until well into the following century, thanks in the main part to thorough chronicling of local lore that had not been previously written down. Although many of the alleged incidents had taken place decades earlier, they were nonetheless related first hand to collectors of the curious such as Eliza Gutch and Mabel Peacock, the Revd James Alpass Penny and famously Ms Ethel H. Rudkin. It is thanks to them that we know of many Victorian Lincolnshire curiosities, among them the Shag Foal and Hairy Jack, the phantom black hound as big as a calf with blazing eyes, who was long held to haunt the country lanes of northern Lincolnshire. Rudkin in particular was fascinated with Hairy Jack, otherwise known as the Black Shuck or the Bargest. As late as 1938 she wrote of the legendary phantom hound, 'The Black Dog walks in Lincolnshire still; and there are a number of living people who have seen him, heard him and even felt him.'

She also noted this curious story. Around the year 1862 a party of poachers had crossed the River Trent to hunt the area to the south of Wildsworth, which is on the east side of the river just south of the Jenny Hurn Bend, of sinister repute. Off Carr Lane can still be found Whoofer Lane, and the party of armed men who hunted game in the darkness of this remote area of Lincolnshire were aware of an entity said to haunt the landscape called the Whoofer Boggard, but they paid little heed to the stories. However, after the nets had been laid it became clear the men were not alone. A strange noise in the distance caused all to pause, and one of the party gave a whistle: a well-understood signal between local poachers but one which would not be responded to by gamekeepers, farmers or policemen.

What responded to the call sign, however, was not the whistle of a fellow group of poachers somewhere else in the darkness. It was a horrendous, awful shriek of mocking laughter which met their ears, and at this most of the party fled in terror, convinced it was the Devil himself.

One of the poachers, however, refused to leave the nets, and he said aloud that he would flee neither man nor Devil; a sudden blood-curdling shriek met his ears and at this he too fled. It seemed the screaming laugh was coming at him from just above his head, and as he turned and ran after his friends the sinister laughter followed him, hard on his heels.

When talking about the incident around the fire the men would remind each other that the incident had taken place early on a Sunday morning, just after midnight. The poacher who had been the last to flee had been Ms Rudkin's uncle, from whom she had heard the story first hand, but she had also heard at least two others who had been there talk of the encounter. Such stories contain the curious ring of truth that some of the more established myths do not appear to.

Phantom ladies in white, grey or green have long been a part of Lincolnshire folklore. Locals would say that at Morton there was a bottomless pit, and if one peered into it you would see the White Lady who haunted the area. It has been suggested that perhaps the 'ghost' was the reflection of the moon in the water misleading people into thinking there was a spirit behind them. Nonetheless, locals believed the White Lady would rise out of the pit and float around the surrounding countryside. Ethel Rudkin, writing in the 1930s, discovered that the haunted pit lay near a road on the east side of the River Trent. Far away to the south, legend had it that The White Lady of Ringstone appeared on moonlit nights in a spectral carriage drawn by four horses. The carriage would draw up at the site of a now vanished village called Ringstone, at Rippingale, near the foundations of the long-lost mansion. Even further removed in the Lincolnshire Fens is Wrangle, north-east of Boston. Gutch & Peacock's *County Folklore Vol. 5: Lincolnshire* (1908) mentions tantalisingly how the rectory here was said to have been haunted by a Green Lady in the 19th century, and it noted that after her appearance the Green Lady would leave behind a physical memento of her visit: a peculiar ring, 'Surely a singular, if not a very irregular thing to do.' But one rare first-hand account of a White Lady provides compelling evidence that such legends may have had more than a grain of truth.

In his book *Folklore Round Horncastle* (1915), the Revd James Alpass Penny wrote of a mysterious White Lady that haunted Duckpool Lane in the village of Stixwould. According to the stories, this ghost had neither face, hands nor feet. She always kept the same distance from those who saw her,

The Abbey Hotel, Crowland. In the background is Crowland Abbey.

whether they sped up or slowed down, and would glide into the yard of the Abbey Farm at the top of the hill where she would vanish.

In 1912 the Revd Penny had spoken to a man called Fisher, who claimed to have seen the White Lady himself when a youth. As he walked home from a gala at Woodhall Spa with his brother one August evening at about 11 o'clock, Mr Fisher had become aware of a presence behind them. The two boys ran and caught up with their father, who was walking up ahead in the lane with another man.

Upon drawing his father's attention to their pursuer, all four as a group stopped and turned round. Some 30 yards behind them was a woman dressed in white. Mr Fisher Snr called out to her, 'Come on, let us have your company.'

The woman in white had halted in the lane, and so the group of four started off again and left her standing. The group were headed in the direction of Bucknall, and they had passed the entrance to Abbey Farm in Duckpool Lane into which the White Lady was traditionally said to drift.

Mr Fisher stated that 'at the gate of the bridle road that leads to Campeney Lane, past Lady Hole Bridge, where the great lady was drowned...' his father noticed that the lady was still following them, still some 30 feet away. At this his father took it upon himself to see who she was and started towards her. All watched in amazement while she vanished as he approached her in the lane. Upon returning to the group Mr Fisher stated that he had seen the lady's face, but it was no one he knew or even recognised.

This phantom clearly had a face, unlike the ghost of legend. But the Revd Penny intelligently suggested that perhaps she was the ghost of a Cistercian nun, a Cistercian nunnery having once stood in Stixwould. In her uniform of white, with black headdress, it might have appeared to some who saw her that she had neither head, hands nor feet depending on one's vantage point and the time she was seen.

Whoofer Lane, Wildsworth.

CHAPTER 7

GHOSTS OF THE 20TH CENTURY

INTRODUCTION

Well into the 20th century there were still accounts of 'traditional' ghosts of the type that haunted our stately homes. For example, just west of Lincoln can be found Doddington, famous for the splendid Doddington Hall which was built between 1593 and 1600. Despite its Elizabethan origins, massive alterations to it in the 19th century have given Doddington Hall an almost Victorian look. During that century, the hall was said to be haunted by a screaming wraith which threw itself off the roof every autumn. This was supposed to be a spectral re-enactment of a brutal incident in which a girl fell to her death while being pursued by a lustful squire. However, by the 20th century the phantom most commonly reported to haunt the hall was the Brown Lady, who appeared to new brides. The Brown Lady would materialise in one of the bedrooms and smile at the new bride as though giving them her blessing before disappearing. She was described as an old lady wearing an old-fashioned stiff, long brown dress. She was also seen smiling on the first floor landing, and she was never perceived by those who saw her as a threat: in fact, she appeared to be most warm and sincere. However, when witnessed, she was never seen for longer than a few seconds. During the English Civil War the hall was the home of Sir Edward Hussey, a Royalist, whose son died fighting at Gainsborough in 1643. But since there were marriage connections with a Parliamentarian general called Lord Fairfax, Doddington Hall was spared the devastation that might perhaps have befallen it. It is also fascinating to note that in 1829–30, the hall became the property of Mr George Jarvis after it was willed to him by Sarah Gunman, a lady friend whom was due to inherit the estate. One wonders if the hall's association with love under duress is perhaps what leads the Brown Lady to make her benevolent appearances, or indeed what links such a spectre to the hall in the common mind.

True or not, first-hand accounts of such 'traditional' ghosts are very hard to come by, and there appears to be a folkloric aspect to them – there is a *reason* for the Brown Lady to appear. This is as opposed to some first-hand accounts of alleged ghostly encounters, which perhaps provide more convincing evidence for the proof of spectres simply by their mere pointlessness, if not making quite such a good story. Evidencing this are the far-more believable anecdotes concerning the imposing building that stands on the corner of West Street and St Peter's Road, Bourne. Founded in 1896, the building used to be known as the Bourne Institute and served as a fashionable gentleman's club. I understand that footsteps are said to have been heard clumping through the building in the first half of the 20th century, which were even chased from room to room without success, and that is all there is to it. Today this proud Victorian building is The Pyramid Club, and it mainly functions as a snooker hall. Similar is the anecdote submitted by a serviceman, who noted an experience he had had during night time manoeuvres in woodland between Louth and Alford in 1942. As he walked in the semi-darkness of the country lane, he heard distinct footsteps crunching behind him, although the road was totally empty. The footsteps had a peculiar lurching gait and the road was enveloped by an oppressive silence, as though the place had suddenly come under a spell. In instances such as this, the total lack of any other element to the tale almost somehow lends credence to the story.

With a more sophisticated media in the first half of the 20th century, many 'traditional' ghostly stories stayed just that: legends, for the most part. But with folklorists like Ethel Rudkin in the 1930s chronicling contemporary accounts of ghosts from living witnesses, and local newspapers sending reporters out to investigate hitherto unheard of ghostly mysteries, however, recording spooky anecdotes as they happened meant information was being garnered which would be a source of material for future generations to study: written down as it happened, with the testament of witnesses, photographs...all of it a move away from the oft-unsubstantiated lore of bygone years. In 1932, for example, the *Lincolnshire Echo* sent a reporter to investigate claims that a phantom bugler could be heard playing 'The Last Post' at the terraced home of the Foster family in Kingsley Street, off Burton Road in Lincoln. The mysterious sounds apparently presaged the death of a crippled aunt, one Lucy Winter. On 10 February 1933 the *Lincolnshire Chronicle* carried an investigative report into a 17th-century house in Brigg that had once served as a Catholic church. Phantoms had been seen and tales abounded of hidden staircases and underground passageways, indicating that this was a 'secret' Catholic church in the days when one's religion could get you killed in Lincolnshire. Indeed, there was an old story of a murdered priest and indelible blood stains in the dust on the floor at the spot...

In the 20th century the Lincolnshire landscape changed forever as RAF bases developed during World War One and then, on a greater scale, during World War Two. A new generation of urban legends and ghostly tales were born out of these dramatic times, and although many of the old runways are now grassed over, their control towers derelict and battered by the elements, it is hardly surprising that stories of spectral airmen and other echoes of wartime activity are common fare nowadays.

Doddington Hall.

SMUGGLER'S TALES

Smuggling and shipwrecking are generally practices associated with south-west England, so it is perhaps little known that in Lincolnshire, as in all coastal areas, there was a thriving trade in such nefarious activities. In 1629 the sexton of St Peter and Paul's Church at Burgh-le-Marsh died from exhaustion as he rang the church bells in an effort to warn the *Mary Rose* away from the coast; he did this even as a mob outside attempted to break in to stop him, since if the ship changed course then they could not loot whatever might wash up on the beach. The hamlets and villages of the marshes on the east coast were for centuries 'warehouses' for contraband landed among the Lincolnshire sand dunes, and violence sometimes went hand-in-hand with these activities: the infamous Skegness smuggler Thomas Hewson – a tailor by trade – was suspected of robbing and murdering a young man at Sloothby but never convicted as no corpse was ever found. Presumably the unfortunate victim ended his days somewhere at the bottom of the North Sea.

The task of preventing smuggling fell to riding officers from Boston, and often they would be distracted and entertained in hostels such as the Vine Hotel in Skegness while other rogues would beach and unload smuggled goods.

Some time in centuries past this tactic of distracting a customs officer must have gone terribly wrong. The Vine Hotel is situated in Vine Road, a cul-de-sac off Drummond Road; it dates back to at least 1770 and for years was said to be haunted by the ghost of a customs man, who vanished in the nest of vipers that drank there in the early days when it was the Vine Inn. Around 1902, builders working in (what is now) the Grill Room came accross a skeleton while demolishing part of a wall to put in a display cabinet. The skeleton was still dressed in the rotting, tattered remains of a blue uniform with brass buttons carrying the royal crest. Various accounts of this story confuse the question of how old this skeleton is said to have been, but since smuggling tobacco persisted in Lincolnshire until well into the 19th century, it can be guessed that it had been bricked up in the Vine at least 100 years earlier. Neither did the skeleton's uncovering put an end to the wanderings of the ghostly customs man: well into the 20th century visitors in room eight were still being startled by the appearance of a figure in centuries-old uniform standing by the bed, who vanished before their eyes. And in 2006 a visitor from Windsor to the Vine claimed that his partner's sister had refused to stay another evening at the place. She had left, spooked by the stories that the place was haunted by smugglers and claiming enigmatically that the ghostly rogues had tried to steal the rings off her fingers while she slept!

'INCREDIBLE STORIES OF WITCHERY AT BINBROOK'

In December 1904, something out of a nightmare apparently transferred its attentions to Walk Farm, high and isolated in the Lincolnshire Wolds near Binbrook. The farm was owned by William Drakes of nearby Tealby but was worked by the White family, and the *Louth And North Lincs News* of 28 January 1905 carried an interview with Mr White in which he ascertained the reality of the disturbing sequence of events.

The first signs that something was wrong at the farm was atypical poltergeist activity: some objects unaccountably toppled from level shelves, including two dozen bottles containing paraffin or oil which were smashed on the floor. A dish of milk set for cream was mysteriously overturned on 30 December 1904, as was a large pot of cream ready for the churn. A dozen large dinner plates were said to have lifted themselves into the air and then to have landed – unbroken – in a big earthenware dish. A large flat-bottomed tub in the storehouse emptied itself and flooded the kitchen, but with much more water than the tub itself could ever have held. Fantastic accounts also held that a dead rabbit hung on a hook had detached itself, only to run around the kitchen before throwing itself back on to the hook to hang lifeless once more, although a simpler version of the event says that the rabbit was merely moved by an unknown force to another room, where it was deposited next to a beer barrel.

Whatever had invaded the farmstead, it brought violence with it. The *Louth And North Lincs News* told its readership of how a guard had to be posted at the fowl house, as chickens were being found slaughtered during the night, all killed in the same way: 'The skin around the neck, from the head to the breast, had been pulled off, and the windpipe drawn from its place and snapped.' The killings continued, however, and by the end of it all some 226 chickens had been butchered by a soundless, unseen perpetrator.

Disturbingly, small fires were also breaking out. The *Liverpool Echo* of 25 January published a letter from a school teacher in Binbrook, who claimed he was aware of an instance when a blanket had been found ablaze in a room where there was no fireplace. But the most serious incident concerned a servant girl, someone 'taken from the workhouse', who was found sweeping the kitchen floor unaware that fire was bursting forth from the dress on her back. Mr White, the farm tenant and foreman, came into the kitchen and shouted in alarm, and in the confusion he managed to throw some wet sacks over the screaming girl. She was critically injured, and when a reporter from the *Louth And North Lincs News* went to visit her in Louth Hospital she reinforced Mr White's claim that the fire on her back had started spontaneously.

The final straw came one day when a crowd of fascinated workers began to notice that a team of six horses were straining and struggling to pull a wagon out of a shed, as though something extremely heavy – yet invisible – was weighing it down. Mr White had perched himself upon a wheelbarrow which promptly took off on its own, with no one at the handles, and carrying the luckless farmer across the yard with it.

The Vine Hotel.

Charles Fort, the compiler of all things supernatural and out of place, was greatly fascinated by the Binbrook case. His book *LO!* (1936) also makes mention of a mysterious fire at a chicken house at nearby Market Rasen on 16 January 1905. The mysterious blaze had killed some 57 chickens and Charles Fort noted with interest, 'Perhaps a fire in a chicken house is not much of a circumstance to record, but I note that it is said that how this fire started could not be found out.'

Quite what was happening at Walk Farm can now never be known; one contemporary report is colourfully titled *Incredible Stories Of Witchery At Binbrook*, but today the activity would surely be recognised as that of a poltergeist. This is assuming, of course, that there was not a culture of abuse at the farm and a conspiracy of silence, or that the whole thing was an invention.

Evidence against this last point is in the form of an interesting letter submitted to the *Lincolnshire Echo* 75 years later by a Timberland resident called Ted White, whose grandfather and father had both worked at Walk Farm. In fact, his grandfather had been the man carted away in the wheelbarrow all those years ago, he maintained, and over the decades his grandfather had never deviated from the version of events he had given at the time. Ted White's father, over the subsequent years, had seen stable doors open and close by themselves and sacks of animal feed open by themselves, but this was little compared to the nightmarish visitation of 1905.

ECHOES OF THE PAST AT HAVERHOLME PRIORY

At Haverholme, three miles north-east of Sleaford, we come to the remains of Haverholme Priory. The building was founded in 1139 by monks from Fountains Abbey, York, but suffered 400 years later under the Dissolution. Much of the romantic building was pulled down in 1927, but the windswept shell that is left standing offers enough evidence to see why it was the inspiration for Chesney Wold in Charles Dickens's *Bleak House*.

The bridge over the River Slea.

Walkers in the grounds of Haverholme Priory have reported that they appear to be being followed by phantom footsteps. In the early part of World War One a lady acting as a nursemaid to the Winchelsea family was put up in a small room at the top of the tower. She was continually awoken in the middle of the night by the sounds of a woman sobbing and it was eventually pointed out to her that she was hearing the ghost of a Gilbertine nun – whose portrait hung on the landing at the top of the staircase. The nursemaid was not at all unnerved by the ghostly crying – when she left it was ultimately because of the behaviour towards her by the Winchelsea family. Perhaps the sobbing heard was that of Alice Everingham, who fled Haverholme in 1360. This broke her vow, so she was hunted down and returned. She in turn complained to the Bishop that she had never taken vows and so was being held as a prisoner, and so the Bishop ordered her to be freed.

The ruins are haunted, as depicted in *Lord Halifax's Ghost Book* by Charles Lindley, Viscount Halifax (1936), in which he claims the priory to be the most haunted place in England. Haverholme Priory lies off the A153 on an unclassified road from Anwick to Ewerby. At the stone bridge over the River Slea within the grounds, dated 1893, there is a more traditional ghost. A female figure has been seen leaning on the parapet, looking up the stream. But the strangest manifestation is one that allegedly terrifies dogs at the stone bridge – a kind of violent whizzing noise that whips up out of nowhere.

SINISTER CYCLISTS

North of Horncastle, the A153 takes the driver through the little village of West Ashby. Decades ago, when the pace of life was slower, a man making his way home on his horse and cart claimed that a cyclist on the wrong side of the road had caused the horse to panic and rear. When the frightened animal was brought under control the man scanned the road for the sinister cyclist…but there was no sign of anyone.

A remarkably similar story was told to ghost hunter Andrew Devereux by a Mr Andrew Lucas concerning his grandfather, Mr W.H. Lucas. The elder Lucas had been a bus driver during World War One, and one night, as he made his way along a lane near Mablethorpe, the shrouded beam of his wartime headlamps picked up a young woman on a bicycle up ahead of him. The road was narrow, and the bus driver could not get past. It seems the woman cyclist sensed this, for she suddenly speeded up and then, equally suddenly, veered off the lane into a roadside hedge before being lost in the evening gloom. Lucas stopped the bus, and with a handful of passengers he searched the lane – but of the woman and her bike, there was no sign.

LEGENDS OF WORLD WAR ONE

At almost midday on 7 December 1918, Lieutenant David McConnell – a newly-qualified aviator at Scampton aerodrome – departed from the base to deliver an aircraft to Tadcaster in North Yorkshire, such were the routine duties of Scampton in those days. The aerodrome had opened in late 1916 as Home Defence Flight Station Brattleby, for 33 Sqn RFC to defend against the zeppelin threat. The base had then developed into a Royal Flying Corps training aerodrome and been renamed Scampton in 1917, supporting 60 Training Sqn. But now World War One hostilities were at an end, frustrating the 18-year-old McConnell of his desire to defend Britain and dogfight the enemy.

The young Lt McConnell said a cheery goodbye to his roommate, Lt J.J. Larkin, and stated that he hoped to be back later that day after his routine flight to Tadcaster.

Later that day at 3:25pm, Larkin was interrupted from his pipe and book in his quarters by the sound of footsteps and then McConnell's unmistakable voice saying his cheery greeting, 'Hello boy!'

Larkin looked up, surprised at his friend's speedy return from North Yorkshire, and he asked, 'Back already?' McConnell stood in the doorway of their quarters, dressed in his flying gear and a naval cap – a Royal Naval Air Service cap he persisted in wearing despite the fact that the RNAS didn't exist any more as such, since it had merged with the Royal Flying Corps to form the Royal Air Force. The teenage flyer replied, 'Yes. Got through all right. Had a good trip.' McConnell then added, 'Well, cheerio,' before going out and closing the door.

Some 20 minutes later, Lt Larkin was interrupted in his musings a second time, this time by Lt Garner Smith, who came into the room and said he hoped young McConnell would be back in time for a planned night out in Lincoln that evening. Larkin told him the boy was already back from North Yorkshire, he had seen him just a few minutes ago.

Later that evening news reached the camp that Lt McConnell would not be returning.

During his trip, McConnell and the pilot of a second plane, a little two-seater (accompanying McConnell to bring him back from Tadcaster), had hit heavy fog. McConnell's fellow pilot thought the weather too bad and put his aircraft down…but the headstrong novice flyer persevered, flying his own aircraft into the atrocious conditions. His landing at RAF Tadcaster was botched, and McConnell had been killed in a tragic crash landing. His wristwatch was smashed and stopped at 3:25pm, testifying to the exact time of the unfortunate young man's death.

The time of McConnell's death was the exact time that his roommate, Lt Larkin, claimed he had been conversing with the young man in their quarters at Brattleby.

Larkin was dragged before his superiors and quizzed about his claims to have talked with a dead airman who had never returned from his mission. Larkin stuck to his story, and his complete lack of reason to lie about such an encounter left the whole affair as a frustrating, baffling puzzle.

The incident was subsequently investigated by the Physical Research Society and has earned a niche nowadays as a classic Lincolnshire mystery. However, like World War Two, two decades later, such an atmosphere was fertile ground for such strange allegations. For example, after World War One ended a band of doomed men were said to still walk along Wrawby Street in Brigg, a spectral retracing of the march that took them to war in 1914.

In 1919 a post-World War One group photograph was taken of the members of the Maintenance Group of HMS *Daedalus* on the runway of the airbase at Cranwell. This very famous image was taken by a photographic concern called Bassano's Photographic Company and shows a faded, opaque face among the line up, at the back and almost hidden. The photograph ended up in the possession of the widow of Air Vice Marshall Arthur Capel. Bobbie Capel was adamant that the mysterious face was positively identifiable as that of a mechanic named Freddy Jackson, who had died in a horrific accident on the runway two or three days *before* the photograph was taken. This claim is at odds, however, with research by archivists attempting to identify 'Freddy Jackson' – who have met with little evidence that such a person served at Cranwell in World War One.

QUEEN MAUDE

There are very few ghosts of 'famous' souls in Lincolnshire. Only Boudica, Alfred Lord Tennyson (at the Vine Hotel, Skegness) and Guy Gibson (at the Petwood Hotel, Woodhall Spa) spring immediately to mind. But the tiny hamlet of Santon in North Lincolnshire has a unique claim to supernatural fame: it boasts the only known 'royal ghost' anywhere in Lincolnshire.

Ethel Rudkin, in her *Lincolnshire Folklore* (1936), noted that the locals believed that a spectre named Queen Maud rose from a hole in a road at midnight to dumfound and terrify travellers. Rudkin felt the likeliest candidate for the ghost would be Empress Matilda, also known as Maude, whose forces fought King Stephen of England for the crown in a bitter civil war in the 1140s. King Stephen was actually captured in battle in Lincoln on 2 February 1141.

Quite what Empress Maude's connection with Santon is remains unclear. But north of the village of Broughton on the west side of Ermine Street there could be found, as late as the 1930s, a large depression close to the road called 'Maude's Hole'. Here it is said that during the struggle Maude was successfully hidden on one occasion.

The royal ghost would always appear at midnight, every night, and walked near the depression. Rudkin received numerous indications that many living people (in the 1930s) had seen this apparition, and one person referred to her as 'Queen Mab'.

The incident is noteworthy for several reasons. It is a typical, rural example of folk belief that must have survived for centuries if 'Queen Maude' was indeed the notorious Empress Matilda. Equally fascinating is the assertion that she was still 'being seen'. And legends like this have a history of repeating themselves: in March 1976 the *Lincolnshire Echo* ran the story of a 'head' seen rolling away down a slope near Lincoln Cathedral. This object is held to have tripped people up and sent them diving out the way, and it is sometimes said to be either the head of Empress Matilda or Queen Isabella – although neither were beheaded, and as at Santon, the connections are unclear.

HUNTING BORIS

More than one person who, in their earlier years, attended Spalding High School, on Stonegate, Cowbit, has told me that the place was supposed to be haunted by an entity nicknamed 'Boris'. The school is a girls' school and I understand that in the 1920s it was common practice for the older girls to organise what were known as 'Boris Hunts', a kind of game where the younger girls chased the 'ghost' from room to room at Christmas. Although the idea was meant to be a bit of Christmas fun, the tradition did not survive very long, and it had long since died out by the time anyone I have talked to attended the school.

The reason was, apparently, that some of the teachers became disturbed by the game. Some of the rooms at Spalding High School were reputed to contain an extremely threatening supernatural presence, and the frivolity of the Boris Hunt unnerved the staff. Some of the elder girls would cover themselves in white sheets and leap out to scare the younger girls.

In a former life the Georgian building had been Welland Hall. The building stands near the banks of the River Welland and rumours persist that at one time the master of the house killed his wife and then committed suicide when he discovered she was cheating on him. Perhaps the old story of the murder, coupled with the fact that the girls were 'hunting' the murderer's ghost, is what unnerved the faculty so much. For had not the ghost of the killer been said to haunt the building for as long as anyone could remember?

THE CAMMERINGHAM LIGHT

The popular version of the story of the Cammeringham Light, which haunted (what is now) the B1398, runs something like this. One such witness to the phenomenon is alleged to have been a postman who saw the ghost in late spring one year in the early 1920s. He said that it first caught his attention in the form of a bright light that gleamed for a second through the frost and mist of early morning; as he leant against a tree there were more flashes of light, above head level this time but closer to him. At this, an apparition swept out of the fog that resembled someone riding a chariot drawn by horses, and the postman realised that the flashes of light in the sky had been the sunlight catching the ghost's metal-clad arm as it raised the whip time and again to spur on the beasts. It travelled on the grass parallel to the main road and despite its impressiveness it made no sound whatsoever.

Folklore has attributed other details to this apparition: it has also taken the form of a warrior queen from ancient days gone by. She rode a chariot, which was pulled by two mighty horses – one white and one black – and her long hair and gown billowed out behind her. She was reportedly adorned with fine jewellery...the popular myth is that this is the ghost of Boudica, legendary queen of the Iceni tribe. In the year AD60 it is thought that, following the massacre at Colchester by Boudica's supporters, 5,000 soldiers of the Roman IXth Legion were ordered from Lincoln to go south to Colchester to contain the situation. However, the soldiers were ambushed in the fen country, and those that were not massacred fled back to Lincoln. Boudica and her army pursued the fleeing soldiers almost to Lincoln itself. It is thought that her route might have taken her along the Roman Ermine Street (the A15) – but why her apparition would appear at nearby Cammeringham is unclear.

It has been pointed out that the Boudica theory coincided with a resurgence of the ancient warrior queen's legend. But another explanation is likely, for it is clear that the landscape which the B1398 traverses was, or is still, the focal point of mysterious earthlights, or Will o' the Wisps. They were regularly seen at Cammeringham, Blyton, Harpswell and especially Willoughton in the early years of the 20th century, and eminent folklorist Ethel H. Rudkin also noted in her diary on 17 September 1931 that it had been witnessed towards the end of the summer. She indicated that she felt it was a natural phenomenon, adding that it had been a very wet summer – an observation she would not have bothered to make if she thought the light were a ghost.

Writing for *Lincolnshire Life* magazine in 1974, one G.F. Garner told how he heard of the Cammeringham Light when he stayed at his uncle's house in Sturton-by-Stow one summer in the 1920s. Mr Garner's grandfather, Richard Garner, had gone on a hunt for the phenomenon years before with a man named Taylor. They encountered the light and Taylor had seen it clearly, insisting it was there, but Garner simply had not been able to see it. Apparently Taylor was a deeply religious man and he had fallen to his knees in frightened prayer, at which point the light had begun to approach him. But then his dog barked at the apparition and it disappeared.

Today, the Cammeringham Light is a well-known local legend. Boudica or Will o' the Wisp, people seem to have grown up with it and there are those who can indicate fields where the light is supposed to appear, even these days in the early 21st century. One resident has claimed that on numerous occasions while walking her dog, there appeared to be a field which the dog simply would not allow itself to be taken on to. It would run, agitated, and strain at the lead until it was taken away from the field; it can be no coincidence that this woman 'knew' that this was one of the fields where villagers had encountered the Cammeringham Light in the past.

CURSE OF THE CAUL

Just for the record, it was not *always* thought that 'ghosts' were goblins, sprites or the result of forgotten murder victims unable to accept that they had died. In fact, ancient folk belief can sometimes rubbish the theories that phantoms are only the result of those who died under tragic or premature circumstances being unable to rest in peace, or the trauma of the event somehow meaning that it is destined to forever be repeated in meaningless phantom appearances.

Sometimes there were other superstitious reasons for the phenomena of ghosts. Upon birth, some babies will have what is known as a caul — a thin, filmy membrane which is the remnants of the amniotic sac and which covers the head and face. It is entirely harmless and easily removed upon birth by the doctor, and in mediaeval times it was thought that a child born with the caul was destined for greatness.

However, Edwin Radford, writing in the 1940s, noted that, in Horncastle at least, if the person born with a caul was not *buried* with it then they would be destined to wander the earth after death looking for it. A Horncastle undertaker had actually been presented with a caul by a woman so it could be kept safe for her eventual death and burial. The reason was that her mother and grandmother had been born with cauls and not buried with them, and they had 'walked dreadfully after death' because of this fact.

RAF SCAMPTON

RAF Scampton reopened in August 1936, on the site of the World War One landing field of the former Flight Station Brattleby. These days it is the home of the world-famous Royal Air Force Aerobatic Team — better known as the Red Arrows — but it is also perhaps equally famous as the setting for the formation of 617 Sqn on 15 March 1943 — the legendary Dambusters, led by Wing Commander Guy Gibson.

Those who take the atmospheric guided tour around the base are no doubt enthralled by the tales of wartime heroism and conflict, quite simply by virtue of the fact that the evidence of such a famous event is all around them. But Scampton is a place rich in a variety of supernatural phenomena, already noteworthy for the legend of Lt McConnell.

A disembodied voice is held to have mouthed, 'Hello...' at a man walking through an empty hangar, and ghostly chatting has also been heard to emanate from the old crew room (opposite the RAF Scampton Historical Museum) when the place is empty. Out beyond the built-up complex of RAF Scampton the land is given over to the control tower and a huge runway, which seems to go on forever on a foggy day. This runway stretches parallel with the A15, the old Roman Road, and a lost Roman soldier is still held to wander the runway on those misty days. Within the control tower itself, a ghostly airman wearing a lifejacket has been glimpsed.

At the other extremity of the runway, in the stretch of land between Gibson's old quarters and the runway itself, can currently be found the well-tended grave of Nigger, Guy Gibson's pet dog, who had accompanied the flying ace when he had served at Digby and Coningsby. The grave is surrounded by railings to deter souvenir hunters, and the commemorative stone displays the sombre inscription, *Nigger. The grave of a black Labrador dog, Mascot of 617 Squadron. Owned by Wing Commander Guy Gibson. Nigger was killed by a car on the 16th May 1943. Buried at midnight as his owner was leading the Squadron on the attack against the Mohne and Eder Dams.*

Within the RAF Scampton Historical Museum a photograph of Nigger can be seen, one of the few in the public forum. It depicts the men of 617 Sqn crowded around the big black Labrador with Gibson himself teasing the animal with a pipe; it is part of Dambusters folklore that the dog trotted around after its master and was indeed treated to the occasional halves of bitter or a puff on Gibson's pipe in the run up to the endeavour.

Nigger was indeed killed on the eve of the raid on Germany's industrial heartland of the Ruhr. He was run over outside Scampton's main gate, and Gibson was sombrely informed of the accident as he was finishing a final debriefing session with his flight commanders and bomb aimers. Gibson became seriously depressed at the death of his old companion, and he naturally tried to keep Nigger's

RAF Scampton.

death a secret from the crew and personnel at Scampton. It could hardly bode well for the mission if the team's mascot had been killed the very evening before the crucial and dangerous attack on the Ruhr.

Nevertheless 19 Lancasters alighted from the grassy runways of Scampton the following evening on their mission and in waves pounded four of their six targets in the Ruhr with giant drum-shaped 'bouncing bombs'. The bombs ripped huge holes in the Mohne and Eder dams and released millions of gallons of vital water that the industrial Ruhr depended on. The raid was a spectacular success – but eight of the Lancasters were lost, along with 53 of the 133 crew.

In January 1944 617 Sqn were relocated to RAF Woodhall Spa. Gibson himself was killed on 19–20 September 1944 when his Mosquito crashed in the village of Steenbergen in the Netherlands, in circumstances that are still unclear. It is thought that his aircraft either developed engine failure or was shot down by *flak*, and he was flying too low for either him or his navigator to parachute out.

In the aftermath of the war, strange stories circulated around RAF Scampton concerning a mysterious black dog that was being seen. In the early 1950s it was observed looking up at the top floor windows of the officer's mess building, and it was completely motionless. Later the mysterious animal somehow managed to invade the building and when confronted raced up some stairs to the first floor. It was hotly pursued, but somehow it performed a vanishing trick, despite all the doors being closed and its only escape route being back past its pursuers. It was also seen bounding through the airbase after a light snowfall, yet somehow it managed not to leave any tracks; and when on the night of 16–17 May 1953 an NCO and his wife witnessed a black Labrador-type dog run soundlessly past the main gate at dusk and out on to the road, personnel were beginning to speculate that it was the ghost of Nigger which was being seen...

It is alleged that when filming of the classic British war movie *The Dambusters* (1954) was taking place at Scampton, the dog that 'played' Nigger would cower and whine when it was anywhere near the dog's grave. There is also a Hollywood urban myth which claims that in the movie, a mysterious dog can be seen running through a tree line at the end of the film in a scene where Gibson is talking to Wallis at RAF Scampton. As no dogs were on the airbase at the time, the strange dog that eagle-eyed viewers can spot is unaccounted for: could it be the ghost of Nigger?

The big black Labrador was already a legend in his own lifetime for the personnel of Scampton, but the cult of Hollywood and some truly bizarre allegations concerning the dog's ghost have propelled the hound to the status of a modern Lincolnshire legend. For example, in 1987, during a commemorative photograph-taking following the unveiling of the Dambusters memorial in Woodhall Spa, a mysterious black Labrador calmly trotted into the photographer's view. It took its place among the choir from St Hugh's school and could not be coaxed away. So in the end, the official photograph of the scarlet-cassocked children next to the Dambusters memorial also included a big black Labrador, looking directly at the cameraman...

Such an incident is beyond mere coincidence, but whether this be for supernatural reasons or more tangible human factors is down to one's own beliefs. Nevertheless, such incidents have only added to the mythology of this famous animal, and with *Lord Of The Rings* director Peter Jackson's remake of the Dambusters movie announced on 31 August 2006, such a mythology can only grow.

In Times of Conflict

As with the story of Guy Gibson's faithful pet hound at RAF Scampton, there are a wealth of strange stories that have attached themselves to the many RAF bases that sprang up across the length and breadth of Lincolnshire at the onset of World War Two. For the squadrons stationed there, with their high casualty figures from dangerous missions and ground accidents, and where action, celebration and tragedy jostled for space, it is hardly surprising that a new generation of urban legends were born around such locations – some of which have persisted well into the 21st century, especially given the spooky, derelict conditions of some of the heroic old airbases.

An updated version of the McConnell legend was told by comedian and author Michael Bentine from personal experience in his autobiography. Bentine had served as an intelligence officer stationed at RAF Wickenby, a bomber base constructed between 1942–43. It was just after midnight and Bentine was walking through a snowfall towards his hut, having just returned from a week's leave in London. In the moonlight he saw the tall, unmistakable frame of his friend 'Pop' heading towards his own hut, and he called out, 'Hi Pop, I've had a great leave.' The other man raised his hand in acknowledgement. Some six hours later Bentine was woken by his batman and was shocked to learn that 'Pop' was in fact dead: he had perished two days earlier when a Lancaster he was navigating had crashed disastrously on the Lincolnshire Wolds, killing everyone on board.

Such weird stories were, unsurprisingly, repeated in various forms at other airbases. Even in the midst of war there were accounts of mysterious phantom airmen who rudely ignored those who challenged them in secure complexes, only to vanish as they walked away. However, it was after the war finished that urban legends began to attach themselves to airfields.

By 1945 the number of Royal Air Force bases in Lincolnshire exceeded 46. A number still remain active to this day, such as Cranwell and Scampton, while some retain the echoes of their former glory in other ways, such as RAF East Kirkby – which is now home to the famous Lincolnshire Aviation Heritage Centre. For the most part, however, one by one these places of action and extreme heroism were abandoned and left to the elements as life moved on in Lincolnshire. Over the years, some have

The memorial by the rain-lashed runway of former RAF Fiskerton.

all but vanished entirely: RAF Skellingthorpe, on the western edge of Lincoln, closed in 1952 and gradually developed into the vast, sprawling Birchwood housing estate, its former life only visible in the form of an attractive memorial that faces proudly out on to Birchwood Avenue.

Others are rather more atmospheric, such as the plaintive memorial that stands by the sad remains of what was once RAF Fiskerton, in the gloomy countryside east of Lincoln.

Places such as this are scattered across Lincolnshire. Where overgrown, rain-lashed tarmac runways stretch on to private land now owned by local farmers, and local teenagers take driving lessons; where lonely, windowless, graffiti-scrawled control towers look out over fields and crumbling concrete bunkers…there is scarcely an abandoned airfield that does not harbour urban legends about guilt-ridden spectral RAF officers, or the ghostly drone of a phantom bomber doomed to crash. Some of the deserted control towers echo with inexplicable Morse code tapping or sinister footsteps, while mysterious flyers with the pallor of death dragging ripped parachutes behind them are the very stuff that lore and legend are made of. Phantom pipers are sometimes reported by baffled drivers playing sad laments at lonely war memorials. Unfortunate cyclists decapitated by the propellers of taxiing bombers are also rumoured to be witnessed in ethereal form. Legends of ghostly WAAF's, perhaps endlessly awaiting the return of a dead fiancé by the perimeter of some near-forgotten airfield on freezing nights, are also typical.

Typical, yes, but in some cases so fascinatingly credulous as to make almost any tale believable, as anyone who has visited an isolated, deserted control tower will tell you.

THE POLTERGEIST AT THE GEORGE HOTEL

Back in February 1952 it was reported that the 200-year-old George Hotel in Market Rasen (now the George Inn) was badly haunted. There had been paranormal activity at the hotel for weeks according to Mrs Carwithen (whose position is not recorded, but was presumably the proprietor). The mischievous sprite appeared to have a liking for hiding small objects, such as handkerchiefs, in peculiar places; it also seemed to have something against lightbulbs, as it would throw them about and misplace them. An electrician who was brought in to reattach the light fitting to the Jacobean-design chandelier professed himself puzzled by how the light fitting had come detached. There had been no evidence of wear on the wires. On another occasion a bulb flew out of a wall fitting and some crackers were flipped off a mantelpiece by the entity. The two cats and one dog were sensitive to some kind of presence in the hotel, becoming agitated sometimes for no reason, according to Mrs Carwithen.

There was other poltergeist activity as well. Doors would be found mysteriously opened and on one occasion a Mrs Dickinson, an employee, had left the kitchen with the lights switched on – only to find them unaccountably switched off when she returned. All this sounds like typical poltergeist pranks, but this entity apparently had an actual 'presence'. A guest had recently complained that he had not managed to get a wink of sleep because there had been footsteps thumping outside the door as someone continuously walked past his room all night.

But Mrs Carwithen herself could provide an actual description of the ghost, for it had been seen…although the report does not clarify who had actually seen the wraith. The presence behind all the trouble was a woman in a red dress of the fashion worn 150-odd years ago. She was of medium height and somewhat stout, and she appeared to have a white mobcap on her head. But what the cause was behind her mischief, the staff could only speculate.

WALLY OF WRAWBY STREET

Among the numerous ghost walks that take place in the region these days, the one at Brigg, North Lincolnshire, begins in a very apt location: Wrawby Street. The street has quite a haunted heritage. Brigg's version of World War One's 'Grimsby Chums' are supposed to walk the street in spectral form (accompanied by eerie brass band music), and on the Brigg ghost walk they will tell you how the old Congregational Chapel is long held to be haunted by a strange dark figure wearing a hat and a cloak. In nearby Queen Street, another staple of Lincolnshire folklore – phantom horses – are allegedly heard clip-clopping. An old woman who pitifully harasses passers-by is held to be the ghost of an octogenarian who froze to death while begging on Christmas Eve in the town many decades ago.

But no.56 Wrawby Street was more familiarly the haunt of perhaps Lincolnshire's most famous ghost of the early 1960s. In its previous life, no.56 was a fishmongers; by the early 1960s it was a fish and chip shop. However, the two-storey house above it was plagued by thumps, bangs and general poltergeist behaviour…and the mysterious appearance of a little old man who manifested on the stairs in dark-coloured clothing. The apparition seemed to be hunch-backed, and folklore claims that the spirit, in life, cut his own throat at the premises. The poltergeist activity has also spread next door to no.57, a building formerly home to the *Lincolnshire Times* weekly newspaper. Here, the spirit was nicknamed 'Wally' and thought to be the ghost of a long-dead doctor. Despite the confusion, the paranormal entity is likely to be a collective, as opposed to two separate ghosts; although seemingly harmless, the *Scunthorpe Telegraph* noted in 2007 that the ghost(s) have nonetheless 'terrified people down the decades' at the two premises.

CHAPTER 8

MODERN GHOSTLY ENCOUNTERS

INTRODUCTION

These days, in the early 21st century, very little has changed. Despite the advance of technology and civilisation, people still claim to see ghosts just as they have always done. Or if not that, then they will 'know' for a fact that a certain building is haunted. In Osgodby, it is commonly said that a former Catholic chapel that fronts on to Main Street is haunted by a ghostly Grey Lady. South-east of Lincoln, following the B1191, will take the driver through the village of Martin, and as the road rises prior to the Timberland junction it is reported that the clanking of irons and chains can be heard. Locally they speculate that this is a phantom echo of prisoners, perhaps from the mediaeval era, being marched through Martin. Further south, Kate's Bridge on the A15 at Thurlby takes one over the River Glen and is locally 'known' to be haunted by a woman who hanged herself there. Furthermore, if one should spot the wraith in their rear view mirror while driving over Kate's Bridge then a family member will die within a week. Ghostly Roman soldiers are said to march along Mill Drove in nearby Bourne, while out on the eastern coast Oliver Cromwell's army is still held to march along Main Road in Saltfleet.

Quite what the basis is for these oft-unsubstantiated legends isn't always clear: it has just always been so. But this repetition of folklore is more than fascinating, particularly when it concerns a modern report of a ghost at a building or place which has been said to be haunted for as long as anyone can remember. There are a wealth of such tales noted in this chapter, which bring this anthology of Lincolnshire's ghosts full circle.

Nowadays, ghosts are a major industry in Lincolnshire. New ghost-hunting concerns are appearing all the time, notably among them the Bassettlaw Ghost Research Group (BGRG), whose investigations in October 2003 into the haunting of a picturesque 200-year-old cottage in Market Rasen highlighted a terrifying sequence of events that centred around the eight-year-old son of the house. The boy claimed to have an invisible 'friend' who could zoom all over the house, including up the walls and across the ceilings. Poltergeist activity plagued the household and the boy was physically attacked by a nasty little girl he encountered, who shook him and banged his head against a wall. At the conclusion of the BGRG's investigation, one member was thrown down the stairs by an almighty shove, as though the entity was delivering a final 'parting shot'.

Also notable in this field is the Lincolnshire Paranormal Research Team, whose numerous visits beginning in November 2004 to the allegedly haunted Woodcocks Inn, at Burton Waters Marina near Saxilby, produced some occasionally surprising results. Not least among these was a feeling of extreme nausea suffered by one member, something not unlike being given dentist's gas. This event took place outside the main gates, and the team were told by the owner that some years previously a man had gassed himself to death in his car at the spot. Could this have been the same 'man' who was occasionally seen outside walking up to the front door – only for him to have vanished when staff opened it for him?

There are others: in Grimsby the local medium group Spirit Searchers have conducted a number of investigations at haunted public houses in the town. On 8 February 2005 they arrived at the spacious Market Hotel on Yarborough Road, after word got around that management had encountered a spirit which stood behind the bar. Security alarms had also been mysteriously triggered and CCTV footage had picked up unaccountable noises emanating from the office. But ghostly goings-on are now such a sure-fire winner with the Lincolnshire public, as elsewhere, that serious study competes hand in glove with ghosts as entertainment. Ghost walks are common events, particularly in the city of Lincoln itself, where the Original Lincoln Ghost Walk is now such a fixture that guide Margaret Green took Hollywood actor Tom Hanks and his family on a personalised ghost tour during the filming of *The Da Vinci Code* in 2005.

But this desire for all things spooky has not been borne out of mere jumping on the commercial bandwagon. Jenny Bright and Dr David Cross's *Ghosts Of Lincoln* (1995) conjectured that ghosts were 'real' – and generated the sensation that wherever one lived in the city of Lincoln they were not far from a haunted place. From the Theatre Royal on Clasketgate, where, in 1974, a portly, moustachioed gentleman smoking a cigar famously vanished in The Circle as a staff member approached him (leaving the seat in the 'down' position), to nine dark, faceless human-shaped entities appearing before a horse rider in the Bunker's Hill fields in the mid-1980s, Lincoln was a city full of lost souls. Perhaps best illustrating this point is the 14th-century White Hart Hotel in Lincoln's Bailgate, its 48 suites and corridors haunted by numerous ghosts: that of a slain highwayman hiding his burnt face; the famous cowering 'mob-capped girl'; the gent in the cravat hunting his 'ginger jar'; and giggling, mischievous children among them. A concentration of ghosts, in an area of Lincoln where there is already a haunting on every corner.

These days it now seems as though almost everywhere in Lincoln has some kind of ghostly story attached to it...a veritable industry indeed. But then, perhaps it has always been so.

By their very nature, most stories in this chapter are anecdotes, but it serves as a reminder of the prevalence of ghostly lore in the county. Most of all, it illustrates that, in Lincolnshire, some things never change, and love of ghostly tales seems to be one of them.

The famous White Hart Hotel in Lincoln's Bailgate.

GHOSTS OF HISTORIC LINCOLN

There is a well-known legend of a phantom horseman who has been seen thundering through the central arch of Exchequergate from the direction of Lincoln Cathedral. The horse is a black stallion and the horseman, his cloak billowing behind him, shouts, 'Open the gates' as they gallop across the cobbles of Castle Hill toward the gates of Lincoln Castle. In life he is held to have been attempting to deliver a pardon for a man due to be hanged for murder – but he never made it in time.

This popular story was given new life in April 2006 when Dawn Scargill, aged 37, took a distinctly-intriguing photograph at the top of Greestone Stairs, an exhausting, atmospheric climb which brings one out before the immense south-east corner of the cathedral. It was 9:30pm, and within the swirling mists caught on camera can be made out the simulacrum of a galloping horse. Its neck and head are turned to the right, almost as though the animal is looking at the photographer, and once spotted it is tempting to also make out the form of a man with a billowing cloak riding atop the beast. Moreover, the form would appear to be 'running' a few feet off the ground, and its direction would be leading it to Exchequergate.

Such an event is bound to ensure the legend of the ghostly horseman never dies, but his is not the only ghost haunting this part of Lincoln. Perhaps it is only to be expected that such an area, drenched in history, has collected a concentration of ghosts to shock and excite the tourists. But it is the occasional resurfacing of such ancient ghost stories via a modern encounter that is particularly fascinating.

The aforementioned Greestone Stairs are a case in point. The stairs are traditionally the haunt of a 17th-century cleric, who hanged himself from the archway that is a feature of the stairs, and the supposed shade of this unfortunate has been seen to disappear into adjacent brickwork. In early February 2006 a strange thing happened during the ghost walk concerning the Greestone Stairs ghost. The tour had reached the archway, and those assembled took photographs of the spooky spot. One of the party's cameras failed totally – not that strange, but somewhat suggestive in light of what followed. A woman took a photograph of her mother standing underneath the arch: nothing was seen, but upon viewing the image (taken with a mobile phone camera) a strange, vague misty shape was clearly visible standing behind the woman's shoulder. No arms or legs could be discerned, but the shape was definitely 'human-like', and as one witness who had seen it commented, 'I would not ever have believed it if I had not seen it with my own eyes.'

Near the apex of Greestone Stairs, in a courtyard opposite Greestone Terrace, can be found the pre-mediaeval building known as Tithe Barn. These days it houses art students and is used by Lincoln University, but it is said that within its sturdy brick walls a White Lady has been seen next to a blocked-off stairway, and the place also suffers arbitrary poltergeist outbreaks. In the upper half of Tithe Barn they say a phantom monk has been spotted within the lecture theatre, in the corner of the room watching the students as they sit studying. All of this would appear to stem from recent renovations – which follows the familiar pattern of poltergeist outbreaks at refurbished pubs in this part of Lincoln.

It is another phantom monk (or perhaps the same one?) that is said to have been occasionally glimpsed turning and wandering back up the steps and through the door of the west front of Lincoln Cathedral. And in October 1964 the Sub-Dean, Peter Binnell, was forced to totally dismiss a story that was bringing crowds of schoolchildren to the cathedral, where they stared up at the towers in the hope of seeing a 'ghost'. The apparition apparently took the form of a small white mass or, as some had it, white lightning that flashed from one of the towers to the ground.

On 3 March 2006 Margaret Green, who leads the Lincoln Ghost Walk, told the *Lincolnshire Echo* a curious tale. On three separate occasions when she had been taking tourists around this haunted site, people had reported that the group had been joined by a mysterious White Lady. On each occasion, she joined the group in Exchequergate and trailed them to the Judgement Porch at Lincoln Cathedral. At this point the tour is about halfway through, and here the strange woman dolefully shakes her head as though she cannot go any further 'and disappears'. She apparently brings with her a smell of particular perfumes, which can be detected at certain points.

Through Exchequergate, and facing Lincoln Cathedral on the other side of Castle Hill, is the impressive, imposing entrance to Lincoln Castle. In 1068 William the Conqueror ordered that work begin on building the castle under the supervision of one Coleswain, or Coleswegen, and what remains today is still one of the finest examples of Norman castle building in the UK. The strategic location of the Lincoln Castle took important trade routes into consideration, and it also took into account the northern rebellion and potential invasions from across the North Sea. These days, as tourists and visitors walk around the immense 12th-century battlements, they are afforded a magnificent, breathtaking view of Lincoln and the surrounding county.

Cobb Hall is a defensive tower built around 1233–34 in the north-east corner of the castle, which has spawned a modern urban legend. In Victorian times the gallows had been erected on top of Cobb Hall — a public hanging, visible to all the townsfolk.

Two centuries earlier in 1642, a letter from Parliament to prison keeper Smith at Lincoln Castle referred to a dungeon within the castle as a 'nasty stinking place' called the Witch Hole. This may refer to the dungeons that are found underneath the grim fortification that is Cobb Hall. It is said that during a family visit to the hall, a strange lady in a long black dress suddenly appeared in the tower and tried to push the young son down the steeply-inclined ladder into the dungeon. As the father wrestled to stop the boy falling, the woman in black vanished. Subsequently, the little boy's mother would hear a 'voice' as she walked to work via the towering exterior of Cobb Hall, which came from within and told her to come back, only this time on her own...

Such is the stuff of modern folklore. At the south-east end of the castle, however, there are modern accounts of strange occurrences within the Observatory Tower. The top of the tower is reached via a very narrow, winding spiral staircase, and there are stories of how one can look upwards and see figures on the stairs nearer the apex. But when one reaches the windy, exposed top, they find themselves alone. On Good Friday 2004 a couple alighting the stairwell with their two children were overcome by sensations of fear and nausea; a photograph taken before they descended shows a misty, ill-defined white shape with them in the confines of the stairwell.

MISSING BITS

There can be no more 'traditional' an image of a ghost than that of the headless spirit. Quite why some locations in Lincolnshire attracted rumours of such impossible entities is unknown, but they did. For instance, at a little place south of Grimsby called East Ravendale there is a piece of folklore which tells how St Martin's Church is haunted by a headless man, who leaves the building and staggers off into the night into the adjacent valley. Apparently he returns some time later with a laughing head now tucked under his arm. There, he sits on the ruined wall and continues to laugh out loud. A traditional spectre if ever there was one, which a labourer is even held to have opened the gate for on one occasion. In a similar vein is the phantom coachman, who was said to haunt a place called Ostler's Lane in Maidenwell, a small village to the south of Louth. The driver of the ghostly coach and horses was headless — his head rested in a box beside him as he whipped the horse's reins. In Dorrington, folklore had it that the area was haunted by another traditional spectre: that of a wraith carrying its own head, who appeared near Fen House. Then again, it is alleged that the manifestation of a headless

The entrance to Lincoln Castle: Observatory Tower on the left.

woman wandered the village of Westwoodside, North Lincolnshire. She appeared 'at certain times of the year' and was held to haunt the approach to the Carpenter's Arms public house in Brethergate.

There are many other instances of incomplete spectres from folklore, but what is fascinating are their modern counterparts. On several occasions, notably in the mid-1960s, a fair-haired woman, carrying something resembling a picnic basket, was seen making her way through cornfields on the western edge of Scunthorpe. She wore a blue dress with a ruffed neck, and two children played around in front of her with innocent glee – but she ignored cheery hellos and, worse still, her body faded away below the waist. She had no legs whatsoever, and shocked witnesses were always very clear as to this point. Two teenage boys saw the ghostly trio, led by the drifting woman, from about 50 yards in 1963 and the encounter still haunted one of them, Stephen Bowman, over 40 years later, when his story appeared in the *Scunthorpe Evening Telegraph*.

WHO ARE THE PHANTOM HORSEMEN?

There has long been a tradition that mysterious, ghostly horsemen roam Lincolnshire's byways and country lanes. Maybe the spectre that patrolled the roads of Frodingham, on the northern outskirts of Scunthorpe, was pure folklore, but he was terrifying enough. Travellers were warned that this entity would appear out of nowhere and leap on to the back of their own mount as they travelled if they were not careful. This dark, cowled creature was reputed to be headless...although some said that the cowl partly concealed the grinning, skull-like face of a most dreadful harbinger of doom.

To the south of Louth can be found Tathwell, and a similar legend tells of how, in days gone by, a phantom horseman would appear before other riders at Orgarth Hill. Apparently the phantom horseman's mount was a scruffy-looking beast, and the apparition (both man and beast) would often vanish as it rode alongside carriages and such like on the road. The Orgarth Hill encounters were recorded to have taken place *c.*1870.

Folklore or not, such apparitions have their modern counterparts. On a winter's night towards the end of January 1967, a motorist taking part in a rally event, along with two passengers, was following a route which had taken them eastwards via Belvoir Castle. As the trio rounded a bend in a road just south of Denton, the driver was forced to jam on the brakes in an emergency stop to avoid colliding with a man on a horse, who was about to cross the road. In the headlights, he was astonished to see that the man riding the beast wore a cloak and tricorn hat, and for all the world looked like a traditional 18th-century highwayman, but the vision had appeared to vanish as he slammed on the breaks of his car. The abrupt halt alerted the attention of the man's driving companions, who claimed that they had not seen the curious figure in the road, and he must have been left with the sensation that he had been the victim of driver fatigue – were it not for the fact that he later heard testimony from a fellow driver who had himself suffered a near-collision with the man on horseback, under almost exactly the same circumstances and at the same point in the road.

The story of the Horseman of Denton was originally noted by ghost hunter Andrew Mackenzie decades ago, but – surprisingly – there are people locally who are vaguely familiar with this ghost, although whether this is from oral tradition or the incident in 1967 I cannot say. I was assured that this phantom horseman was 'supposed' to haunt the road between Denton and Hungerton, and had done since as long as anyone could remember. I have been similarly assured that a phantom horseman haunts the village of Canwick, and also Canwick Hill. More recently, the *Grimsby Evening Telegraph* noted how, *c.*2002, a lorry driver was supposed to have skidded to an emergency stop on the A18 south of Grimsby one night, utterly convinced his vehicle had slammed into a horseman that had swept out of nowhere into his path in the darkness. A fellow motorist had found the lorry driver sitting in shock at the steering wheel, petrified and repeating that he had just killed someone. He managed to coax the detail that it was a horseman, but a subsequent search found absolutely no evidence of a collision. Such stories, clearly, are popular folk tales, which, despite the passing of time, refuse to go away.

THE THING OUTSIDE NETTLETON MANOR

In about 1974 Ms M, of Nettleton Manor, Nettleton, near Caistor, was awoken at midnight by her five-year-old daughter. The little girl was frightened and said that she could not sleep because of a large black object in the shape of a floating sack that kept coming up to the window, as though looking in, every 10 minutes.

The concerned mother followed her daughter into her bedroom where she saw the thing for herself, drifting to and fro outside, past the window. It continued its weird behaviour until about 3:00am, when it vanished with the onset of dawn.

The night had been perfectly still and the following morning, upon inspection, there were found to be no clues in the garden as to what the thing might have been. But the following day a neighbour six houses away was found dead, having apparently died at around the time the strange entity was spotted outside the manor.

Nettleton Manor is on Moortown Road, and these days it is a care home for the elderly.

THE URBAN LEGEND OF THE HAUNTED HOUSING ESTATE

There remains today little evidence that the great Birchwood housing estate was once the site of RAF Skellingthorpe. Like all of Lincolnshire's airbases there had been tragedy there: a total of 208 bombers that took off from 'Skelly' either failed to return or crashed upon returning to the UK. In May 1944 two airmen died when an explosion ripped a hangar, caused by three bombs becoming dislodged from a tractor-towed bomb trolley train. However, even before the Birchwood housing estate was developed, a visit to the site of former RAF Skellingthorpe in 1970 had famously revealed visions of the past to a woman who had spent the war years there as a WAAF. Walking the perimeter tracks, she saw a scenario as of a fully-working RAF base – she even espied her former fiancé, a man at the base she had been briefly engaged to, among all the spectral activity.

A 1948 proposal to turn RAF Skellingthorpe into a civil airport had come to nothing, and in the 1970s–80s the site caught the attention of developers. As a result, the Birchwood housing estate sprung up and spread, and there are persistent rumours that several of the houses were plagued by poltergeist activity in the early days. One wonders how much of this is urban legend; however, if it is true then local clergymen must have been kept extremely busy, for several exorcisms are reputed to have been carried out in various houses.

The phenomenon was far reaching. Birchwood is adjoined by the Doddington Park housing estate, which also falls within the perimeter of what was once RAF Skellingthorpe. In the mid-1980s a woman claimed that she encountered an airman within her home, off Abingdon Avenue, who simply faded away before her eyes.

One wonders if it is all linked. And more to the point, why the death of the airbase and the development of the estate brought such ghostly activity with it. I have heard that there were graves on the site of RAF men and personnel, which became disturbed, but I suspect this to be an urban legend.

On 11 February 2006 a Lincoln resident submitted to the *Lincolnshire Echo* a curious story that seems comparatively recent, and it perhaps indicates that something is still going on at the Birchwood estate. At one time, a family member, a brother, had lived in an unnamed house on the Birchwood estate. The four-year-old son had repeatedly talked of encountering a man called 'Darryl' within the house, but this was just put down to the 'imaginary friend' syndrome. Then, one day, the boy's father saw 'Darryl' for himself...a man of around 50 or 60 years old, who was at the top of the stairs and simply vanished through a wall.

PLANES, TRAINS AND AUTOMOBILES

Whether one accepts ghosts as 'real' or not, it is clear that the phenomenon takes a variety of forms. A poltergeist is clearly a different manifestation to an apparition. And an apparition which appears to 'interact' with human beings (warning them, assaulting them, smiling at them, etc.) is clearly different from an apparition that merely shows itself apparently performing the same routines as it did when alive. If we accept these as 'real', and by association phantom cats, dogs and horses in the same theme, do we then accept that such ghostly reappearances extend to non-living objects such as ships, boats and planes?

There are numerous stories of phantom aeroplanes, most linked to the remnants of World War Two RAF bases. Such a place is RAF Blyton, which fell into decay after the end of the war. One legend tells of how a doomed bomber, crewed by Polish airmen, clipped a tree as it plunged towards the Trent, and to this day that particular tree will not grow properly. Locally they say that the damaged tree can be found on the eastern (Lincolnshire) side of the Trent at the bend known as Jenny Hurn, south of East Ferry. In the decades after the war there were rumours that a ghostly airman wandered the remote Isle of Axholme, even after the crashed bomber full of corpses had been recovered while dredging a ditch near the Trent in the mid-1960s. The airman, they said, was either deathly silent, or else asked for directions in a foreign tongue. But maybe the bomber itself still makes that last fateful flight: there are stories in Blyton village of how a great, old-fashioned bomber swooping silently over the roofs of the houses and heading west in the direction of the Trent has been seen. These kind of stories are typical at abandoned RAF bases and, indeed, active ones, where one might speculate that perhaps aircraft are being brought in for air shows. There is a suggestion that sometimes pilots will conserve fuel by switching the engines off and risk 'gliding', perhaps accounting for the silence of these 'ghost aircraft'. That, coupled with the witness' realisation that the plane is from a different era, may explain some of the encounters.

In the mid-1990s a driver and his passenger were motoring at night along the eerie and winding stretch of the B1190 between Tom Otter's Lane and Doddington Hall. The couple were heading in the direction of the hall itself, approaching the bridge over the railway lines. Twin headlights of an approaching car were visible through the trees, bracken and brambles, and were growing closer, but upon rounding the bend, crossing the bridge and dipping over the other side, the motorists found themselves suddenly driving alone on the B1190. The twin headlamps of the oncoming car had been mysteriously extinguished, and furthermore there was nowhere that the approaching vehicle could have turned off and parked. The whole incident happened in seconds.

Could they have seen a ghost car? It is perhaps possible in view of the story told to the *Lincolnshire Echo* in 2006 by 64-year-old nurse Judy Meakins. The incident had happened around 1986. It had been 10:30pm and Ms Meakins was driving back towards Lissington along the B1399 via the old RAF Wickenby airfield in the direction of Holton-cum-Beckering. The stretch of road was very straight, and coming directly towards her Ms Meakins saw an 'old fashioned single-decker bus with a very long bonnet'. The vehicle was full of bright light and as she drove past the bus she saw several strangely-dressed passengers wearing what seemed like 1940s-style uniforms and hats. The two vehicles passed each other in the road, and a slightly unsettled Ms Meakins looked in her rear view mirror. Although the road was straight, and she should have been able to see the tail lights of the bus disappearing into the night, there was nothing.

The small railway station at Hallington, west of Louth, was closed to passengers on 5 November 1951, and although the station house still stands (it is a private dwelling), the tracks were eventually ripped up after 1956. For many years afterwards people claimed that a 'phantom steam locomotive' could be heard passing by Hallington in the dead of night. The abandoned stretch of track continues away from Hallington in a south-westerly direction. Its course takes it through a disused railway tunnel at Withcall, and, in the 1970s, a man claimed that he was in the tunnel when the phantom train suddenly appeared, bearing down on him in the semi-gloom. He screamed in terror and pressed himself against the damp interior wall of the tunnel, and he watched as it thundered past him. He heard the hissing of the steam and the roar of the engines. The ground shook beneath his feet, and acrid smoke burnt his lungs and eyes. As the locomotive swept past and disappeared down the tunnel, the man noticed how the windows of the carriages glowed strangely.

Preposterous? Possibly, but such allegations are not new. Some half-a-century earlier, Ethel Rudkin had noted a report of a man who was walking along the 'dip' in the Scawby to Broughton Road, north of Scawby, when he saw a legendary phantom coach and horses long held to haunt the road. He followed the spectacle as it crashed into a nearby lake in the grounds of Scawby Hall. Rudkin related that the manic laughter of the coachman was also held to be heard on dark nights. A similar legend is attached to Burton Road on the north-western edge of Lincoln. A stagecoach is said to have crashed into a hay cart stuck in mud during a thunderstorm, and on certain windy nights the clatter of furious hooves can be heard near Burton Road, followed by terrible screams that are carried away on the wind.

THE SILENT AIRMAN

In the mid-1990s, N, then in her very early 20s, claimed that on two occasions she awoke at a house where she was staying the night and found that the bedroom had been invaded by a phantom RAF officer. The house in question was called Ossington at Saltfleetby-St-Peter, east of Louth, and on the first occasion N unaccountably awoke bleary-eyed in the middle of the night. As she focussed, her eyes fell upon an RAF officer in full uniform, including hat, who simply stood and stared silently out of the bedroom window. After this experience had happened a second time, N questioned the owner of the house and was told that the previous occupants had had a son. The son had been an airman who had died young, killed in an accident. After this incident, N became so frightened of the bedroom that she refused to stay the night in that room ever again.

MODERN HORROR STORIES

In February 1998 one Kevin Whelan, of Sleaford, contacted the daytime television show *This Morning*, which was chairing a debate on the supernatural. Mr Whelan told the programme that in mid-January he had been driving southwards along the A15 at two o'clock in the morning. As he drove up the slope towards the left turn-off to Ruskington, he saw on the horizon what looked like a white shadow, and before any of it had registered a face appeared in the windscreen from the driver's side. Mr Whelan chillingly described the apparition thus, 'It had dark hair. It was like a Greek-looking person. The skin was olivey-green, it had a pitted face…I could see the teeth. I could see everything. One hand was up. From the neck down was like a sort of…on a photograph when you photograph someone with a flash on, it's too bright, you get that white fluorescent sort of look.'

Mr Whelan was travelling at about 60 miles an hour, and for some 40–50 seconds the thing looked in at him while he, frightened and irrational, could think about little else other than trying to stop the tape machine which was playing music loudly. The apparition faded away down the side of the car and Mr Whelan had arrived home in Sleaford in a state of extreme distress. The call opened the floodgates for a number of reports of variations on this phenomena on the A15, which dated back decades. The creature's raised hand – as though in warning – appeared a particularly repetitive detail.

The so-called 'Ruskington Horror' has become a classic modern tale of ghostly terror: well-attested by many witnesses after Mr Whelan's initial account, and subsequently investigated by the *This Morning* team and a fascinated local media. Seemingly not linked to this, however, is a phenomenon known as 'phantom strangulation', which is held to afflict drivers in the vicinity of Ruskington, who believe that something invisible is throttling them after they have pulled over, perhaps to get their bearings.

There are also widespread rumours of a similar affliction alleged to immobilise people at Belmont (Bellmount) Tower, an arched tower on a hill on the outskirts of an area of woodland known as Belton Park, which can be found north of Grantham. I have heard that one stricken rambler recently was found to have vicious red handprints about his throat after such an invisible assault. There are also rumours of a strange, unearthly screaming that seems to be of a young girl in distress, repeatedly being heard from deep within the woodland of the Deer Park, which shocks dog walkers and the like.

It is an interesting point that the nearby stately home named Belton House, which dates from *c.*1688, also experienced a curious phenomenon when a portrait of Lady Alice Sherald was removed for professional cleaning in 1980. A spontaneous image formed on the underside of the protective glass of the family tree, which had hung nearby and in the vicinity of Lady Alice's bedroom. The image resembled nothing so much as a lady in period costume, with an elegant neck adorned with a fine necklace…and although shoulders and hands also appeared, the manifestation remained headless. Lady Alice herself haunts Belton House and is known as Belton's Bright Lady, but she is certainly not suspected of being the sinister entity that lurks in the woodland of Belton Park.

THE CRYING GIRL

In *c.*1998, R was living in flats in Station Road, Sleaford. She had fallen asleep in the bedroom with the television on, and sometime later she found that something had awoken her. As she lay in bed her eyes gradually focussed on a 'tiny little girl' aged about five, who stood silhouetted in the night time gloom in the doorway. The little girl wore a black and white Victorian-style petticoat; she was very pretty and her hair was in pigtails – but she sobbed uncontrollably and seemed very upset.

R asked of the strange child, 'What's wrong? Are you alright?' but this only seemed to upset the little girl further. The more that R tried to comfort the child the more agitated she became, until gradually she faded away from view.

R is adamant that the incident was not a dream. The television was still playing the end of a film that she had started watching before she fell asleep and it is worth considering that this kind of encounter appears a distinct category again from other types of 'ghostly' encounters, such as poltergeist outbreaks, 'tape recording'-type ghosts, etc. The incident appears almost cross-dimensional. Possibly, then, at some point decades ago, a little girl had opened a familiar door and somehow found herself looking at a woman sleeping in a bed in an unfamiliar room from the future, while a strange magic box in the corner appeared to contain moving pictures. Perhaps this is why she became so upset when R tried to talk to her. If a diary entry from 100 years ago were found noting such a strange incident, then perhaps we would be better placed to understand this incident.

The flats on Station Road are a relatively new development project. Since the start of the century, the area had been worked by employees of Charles Sharpe and Co. Ltd, a seed merchant, and warehouses had once stood on the site that now houses the flats. Around the same time as R's experience, a friend and neighbour had awoken in the night to see what appeared to be the phantoms of four workmen stood at the foot of the bed: more strange echoes of the past within a modern development in this part of Sleaford.

HAUNTED HARLAXTON MANOR

There are said to be many ghosts at Harlaxton Manor. This gigantic mansion at Harlaxton, south-west of Grantham, was built c.1837, although its mixture of styles – Elizabethan, Baroque and Jacobean – presents possibly one of the most visually-impressive buildings of its type in Britain. In 1937 the by-then abandoned manor was purchased by the eccentric Violet Van der Elst, who had electricity installed; there are some that say she used Harlaxton's famous grand library as a seance room to contact her husband after he died. Perhaps his is the spirit that is held to materialise very early in the morning in the library, although a vision in white that has been seen in the clock room is purported to be Violet herself. It is also said that the manor echoes with the pathetic crying of an infant, who slipped on to the open fire in the clock room when the nursemaid cradling the child fell asleep. It is unclear when this happened, but perhaps it took place during Harlaxton Manor's previous life. The 'first' Harlaxton Manor was built on a different site in the 14th century and pulled down around 1857.

Harlaxton is now owned by the University of Evansville, Indiana. One balmy July night around 1999, a security guard patrolling the vast, empty grounds of the manor began to feel distinctly uneasy, as if he was not alone. The college was empty at this time of year and as he walked the empty corridors, past locked doors, he thought he sensed movement at the top of the staircase, as though someone was darting out of sight.

He dashed up the staircase but found the area empty. But as he stood at the top of the stairs in the night time gloom he turned and looked back down the staircase – and saw something that turned his blood cold. At the foot of the stairs stood three very dark male human forms, apparently watching him. In fright, he switched on his torch and shone it at the three figures – the light fell on nothing, for they had vanished.

The security guard ran down the stairs and found the spot where the figures had stood to be as cold as ice. In the brightly-lit canteen he called for security back up from the main gate a mile away, claiming that intruders had gotten into the manor, even though he didn't see how this was possible. When the backup arrived the spooked young security guard handed in his resignation on the spot.

THE LINCOLNSHIRE COUNTY PAUPER LUNATIC ASYLUM

On high ground south of Lincoln at Bracebridge Heath, there opened in 1852 the grandiosely-titled Lincolnshire County Pauper Lunatic Asylum. By 1854 the equally-grandiose Italian-style building

The deserted and allegedly haunted Victorian asylum at Bracebridge Heath.

itself, together with all its wings and outbuildings, occupied seven acres of land and was home to some 250 patients. This was almost as many actual locals who lived in the village of Bracebridge, which at that time was on the opposite side of (what is now) the A15. The patients were both men and women, and typical of the inmates was the wretched Ann Bryan, of whom the asylum records note in 1874, '...mentally usually very quiet, and harmless; but if in anyway interfered with she becomes suddenly excited and violent – or if she sees any patient being removed in consequence of excitement, she will often take the part of the patient, acts then violently on the nurses. Bodily health weakly, looks pale and rather thin. Sits idly in the ward doing nothing – has had one fit since last note – bread and cheese and beer for lunch.'

In time the sprawling asylum became the Bracebridge Mental Hospital, then St John's Hospital. By the time St John's closed down in December 1989 the village of Bracebridge Heath had much expanded, and nowadays a housing estate envelopes the shell of the old asylum. Today, the vast building stands as an out-of-place relic from another era in overgrown scrubland, its windows smashed and boarded up. Much of the asylum is fenced off from the general public and it is easy to see why such a sad, eerie building has very quickly earned a reputation for being one of the most haunted places in Lincolnshire: I have been told that *c*.1990 two removal men employed to empty the place of furniture were put to flight by horrific screaming that they heard coming from another part of the building. Today, there can be few who have walked past it using the shortcut to the A15 path who would not at once concede that it is the epitome of a haunted building.

When my own parents, who are well versed in the history of the village, moved to the housing estate that now surrounds the south-eastern side of the asylum, there were some raised eyebrows at the choice. Even by the 1990s it was well-known locally that mournful wailing and screams echoed through the sturdy walls of the place. A friend of theirs in the fire brigade told them that it was not unknown for the fire brigade to be called out to the ruins at night after local residents had reported what they thought were small fires burning within the building. Although the building was repeatedly attacked by vandals, there were never any fires to put out and it seems that some of the firemen may themselves have seen the strange lights drifting within the gloomy corridors and halls of the former asylum.

Unmarked graves, with remains indicating that inmates had at one time been buried seven-deep, which were found by the A15 at a location known locally as 'the cemetery', have only added to the sensation that the place should be avoided. Within this grassed-over and hidden-away area (just beyond the southern edge of the housing estate), it is still possible to see the outlines of a giant 'rectangle' in the grass – which I am told is the area that was excavated by surveyors and where the skeletons were unearthed. It is a spot that sends the blood cold, particularly when told the local supposition that the skeletons were put back and covered over once more. There are no headstones anywhere.

The western edge of the old Lincolnshire County Pauper Lunatic Asylum is now the Homestead public house. Bracebridge Heath is a commuter village and there are perhaps many people driving between Lincoln and Sleaford who stop there who do not realise that behind the attractive façade of the Homestead can be found the cavernous shell of such a notorious building. But locally the reputation of the place is well known: I have been told of rumours that phantom nurses and distressed inmates from long ago haunt the pub, which have been seen by staff and, occasionally, customers as well.

STRANGE ENCOUNTERS AT THE ROADSIDE

Accounts of strange figures glimpsed at the side of the road go back well before the motor car took over Lincolnshire's roads. In October 2002 one Ralph Skeef told the *Spalding Guardian* of a terrifying encounter his own grandfather had had in the early years of the 20th century. Skeef senior had been cycling along a road at Beggar's Bush, Weston, just north of Spalding, when something had appeared in the middle of the road. The entity had been wearing a steeple hat and a long black cloak, and it had drifted right through the shocked cyclist.

But it is truly with the advent of the automobile age that the urban legend of 'mysterious entities' seen fleetingly from the safety of the car interior has taken off. The 'thing at the roadside' can take many forms: in Ludford in the early 1960s it was reckoned locally that a strange white figure haunted Girsby Lane which would occasionally sweep out in front of oncoming vehicles, glancing in their direction, before vanishing through the trees on the other side of the road. In 1992 it was reported that motorists were spotting what appeared to be the shade of a black-robed figure at the roadside as they drove along the B1210 between Great Coates and Stallingborough. One wonders if this is the same dark figure that is reputed to lurk along the A180, which runs parallel to the B1210: this entity is said to be almost seven feet tall.

Such encounters are not far removed from that other staple classic of urban legend: the phantom hitch-hiker. It has been claimed that in a lay-by near the King George V Bridge at Keadby, west of Scunthorpe, in the early 21st century, a taxi driver supposedly picked up a fare – a young girl who asked to be dropped off near the Glanford Park football ground. As they neared their destination, the taxi driver was shaken to discover his passenger had vanished en route. Near Greetwell, along the lonely B1398 to southern Scunthorpe, there are rumours that another female phantom hitch-hiker will flag down motorists and play much the same vanishing trick as the woman at Keadby Bridge. One wonders if the spectres are not one and the same. This girl will ask for a lift to Kirton-in-Lindsey and ask to sit in the back seat. After the car has set off, the driver gradually becomes aware that his passenger has somehow vanished en route.

More driver fatigue? Pure urban myth? Or has our ever-shrinking planet and ever-increasing reliance on the automobile occasionally allowed us to experience for ourselves what we only assumed was folklore?

WATCHING OVER

In 2002 Ms S's husband died very young, in his mid 30s, leaving her to bring up their daughter M on her own. In order to help ease the pain she took M to live in a new house in Skellingthorpe, and it was here that strange things happened.

At the time of the events, little M was just one-and-a-half years old, and one day she suddenly startled her mother by running up the stairs as fast as her legs would take her, very upset. Trying to comfort her daughter, Ms S asked what was wrong and received the reply that, 'Dada, dada there.' M was, at this moment, pointing to a corner in the hall and was very frightened, until her mother – who could see nothing – managed to calm her down.

The fact that her daughter was able to see something that she could not unnerved Ms S somewhat, but perhaps it did not surprise her. For not long after her husband's death she too had experienced odd events in the house the family had shared together before she had taken her daughter to Skellingthorpe. This house was at Cherry Willingham.

In the aftermath of the family's tragedy, Ms S had seen what she called 'a shadow' come through the hall and into the back porch. The door creaked as it passed, and she remembered that this was the usual routine of her husband when he had gone outside for a cigarette.

Even stranger was the incident when she had heard her phone ring, but by the time she had reached it she had missed the call. Seeing who had called, she was astonished to see her phone tell her the call had come from her deceased husband's mobile phone...a phone which naturally was no longer used and was currently shut away in a drawer in the kitchen.

How could this have happened? Ms S is unsure, but perhaps in this instance the tearing apart of the young family was not only horrendously painful for her but also for her husband, who, although deceased, could not bring himself to depart from his loved ones. These experiences prompted Ms S to visit a medium, and although she remains tight-lipped about what she was told by the woman behind closed doors it has apparently put her mind at ease. Furthermore, the presence is no longer felt, but little M still has a recurring dream where her daddy will take her to the park, and she is the age she was when he passed over. The family currently reside in Saxilby.

GHOSTS OF GRIMSBY

For some reason Grimsby seems an unlikely place to go ghost hunting. Perhaps it is Grimsby's association with development and expansion in the Victorian era (that led to it being the largest and busiest fishing port in the world by the 1950s). The feeling one is left with is that Grimsby is too 'new' to have ghosts, unlike ancient Lincoln or Boston for example.

The truth is that Grimsby has existed since at least the 9th century, when the Danes settled in the area, and there may even have been a small town for Roman workers sited there some 700 years before that. In mediaeval times Grimsby had two parish churches, although the only one that remains now is St James' Church. At Nuns Corner, where Scartho Road (A16) joins Laceby Road (A46), there also once stood a mediaeval nunnery, St Leonards – and it is quite astonishing how many of the ghosts are reckoned to be monks or nuns, which is somehow strange for such a great fishing port as Grimsby.

A century ago, *County Folklore Vol 5: Lincolnshire* (1908) made allusions to 'curious anecdotes' concerning ghostly nuns that were said to haunt the St Leonard Priory, but it did not elaborate. Nearer the present time ghost hunter Robin Furman reported an undated encounter with an eerie apparition at his then house at Nun's Corner. He was alighting the stairs and upon reaching the top he saw the form of a tall nun wearing an old-style head dress. The nun had looked completely real to Mr Furman, but she had no face…just a kind of strange glowing light where her face should have been. The nun then drifted away, the whole encounter leaving Mr Furman mystified but not scared – there had been no time to be scared. Perhaps the most unnerving incident, however, concerned the Barningham family. There had been a rash of unexplained phenomena within their Newton Grove home, so a television camera was rigged up in a bedroom upstairs where much of the disturbances had occurred. After a few hours, a group of six people watching the footage being relayed to a television set downstairs watched in amazement as the face of a hideous old man in a monk's habit materialised on the screen. For the Barningham family this was the last straw, and they left the place in September 1967.

The town has many other ghosts. The Corporation Arms in Freeman Street has been reported haunted in the present day by a shy spirit. The ghost is believed to be that of Mrs Drayton, a former landlady who died in 1918, but, although her presence is strongly 'felt', somehow she has not actually been seen. And in November 2000 the *Grimsby Evening Telegraph* ran a story that the Asda supermarket on Holles Street was plagued by a mischievous poltergeist. Next it was the turn of the Index Store in Freshney Place, also troubled by a poltergeist. In May 2005 investigators descended on Beagles Lighting on Cleethorpes Road after reports that *another* poltergeist had invaded the premises and was causing much havoc.

The National Fishing Heritage Centre, Alexandra Dock, Grimsby: said to be haunted by a former skipper of the Ross Tiger.

It is the mundane settings that seem to mark Grimsby's ghosts apart from others: council houses, shops and supermarkets. What all this evidences is an added dimension of reality for ghosts and poltergeists. Why should spirits merely confine themselves to ancient castles, cathedrals, churches and stately homes? If they are part of our shared existence then it is only right that sometimes they will find their way into a shopping complex such as Freshney Place.

GHOSTLY LADIES OF AYSCOUGHFEE HALL

Ayscoughfee Hall was built by the River Welland, Spalding, for a local wool tycoon named Richard Aldwyn (or Ailwyn). It was completed *c*.1451, and so little has changed that it would, in fact, be recognisable as it is to someone from the 15th century. In the 17th century the hall passed to the Johnson family before becoming a school. During World War One it housed Belgian refugees displaced by the fighting. The hall is now a museum/tourist information centre, and over the years staff have reported a ghostly sensation in the rooms and galleries; there is a ghostly White Lady said to wander around Ayscoughfee Hall and up to Church Gate, before going down Love Lane and then back again to the hall. Who she is isn't clear. However, pipe smoke detected downstairs is alleged to be the result of the ghost of Maurice Johnson – who died in the 1700s – lighting up again.

On 10 May 2006 Helen Grant (aged 34) was strolling around the gardens of the hall with her partner David Nicholls when she glanced at the building and, through the window, saw a strange woman in period costume within the hall. Helen, of Stonegate, told the *Spalding Guardian*, 'It didn't look like a ghostly figure. It looked like a normal person.'

The sighting lasted only a matter of seconds. The woman that Helen saw was in her 30s or 40s and in period costume; she wore a cream dress with blue flowers and a high neckline with a scallop effect. She had long, dark hair and wore an Alice band. David ran to the window to see the person for himself, but by the time he got there the mysterious woman had vanished.

The museum staff were baffled by the sighting, and they confirmed that no one fitting the description of the woman had been in Ayscoughfee Hall at that time. Furthermore, there was an interesting coincidence. A week or so before Helen's sighting a painting of the late Isabella Johnson was taken from storage, dusted off and hung in the very room where the mysterious figure was spotted.

Could Helen have sighted the legendary White Lady? Or has the reintroduction of Isabella Johnson's portrait disturbed a new spook at the hall?

THE GREY LADY OF THE BOSTON STUMP

On certain autumn evenings a distressing ghostly re-enactment has been witnessed. The vague figure of a woman in white is seen to throw herself off the top of the Boston Stump, the 272ft-high octagonal tower of St Botolph's Church. More disturbing is that the phantom woman is holding an infant baby. She hurtles towards the ground, but disappears before she hits the earth.

Anyone who has climbed the 365 steps of the tower, past the centuries of graffiti scrawled on the inner walls, to the summit, knows what a daunting expedition this can be at the best of times. Wind buffets the balconies and it is difficult not to feel totally exposed to the elements; on a clear day the tiny dot on the north-western horizon that is Lincoln Cathedral can just be seen.

Locally this wraith is known as the Grey Lady, and to this day people will tell you that she patrols the Boston Stump. Folklore has it that if you walk three times around St Botolph's Church at midnight and look upwards you will see her. One assumes that the Grey Lady and the phantom suicide are one and the same, and even today there are reports of her. Upon visiting Boston in October 2005 I found that there were very few people who were not familiar with the story. I was even told that the Grey Lady had been seen recently, in the early 21st century, on the first balcony of the tower. Whether this is true or not, it certainly indicates that the myth of the Grey Lady of the Boston Stump endures to this day.

Quite who the Grey Lady was in life is not clear. There were two recorded suicides in the 19th century, one a woman who died when she crash-landed on an unfortunate pedestrian below. It has also been suggested that it is the ghost of Sarah Preston, a promiscuous wife blamed for spreading the plague in the town in August 1585. Folklore has it that she climbed the tower and jumped. However, the most likely contender is thought to have been a young mother who lost her husband sometime in the 17th century and decided to end her grief by killing both herself and her newborn baby.

In the main part of the church below there has been another ghost sighting. The organist has reported that a mysterious figure walks along the central aisle, and it has been witnessed by him when he has been alone in the church.

THE NATURE OF GHOSTS

A last selection of miscellaneous, well-attested hauntings in Lincolnshire serves to illustrate, if such were needed, just how far-reaching the phenomenon of belief in ghosts is in the county.

In 1984, during a parish meeting at Epworth Town Hall of The Epworth Society (engaged in compiling the historical *Town Trail*), society chairman Stanley Houghton told the gathering that in 1960 he had taken one of the new bungalows on Burnham Road. The area was still very much a building site, but on numerous occasions footsteps had been heard as though something invisible were running past the bedroom window. He was baffled, but the house was near (what is now) the A161-Blow Row junction in Epworth; this was where one Poll Pilsworth had been interred around 1791, after being chased by a mob who suspected her of murdering five villagers. Poll, a nurse, poisoned herself before she could be caught.

In January 1967 the vicar of St Peter and St Paul's Church in Caistor, attempting to lay stories that the place was haunted to rest as superstitious folklore, left a tape recorder in the church overnight which recorded echoing footsteps and loud, clear notes from the pipes of the church organ.

In the 14th century the abbot of Thornton Abbey, Thomas de Gretham, had been walled up by his brethren, possibly as part of a conspiracy. His remains were not uncovered until *c.*1830, when workmen broke down a hidden door and found a secret dungeon in which stood a table and chair. On the table stood a candlestick, a breviary and a crucifix, all thickly coated in dust. Then, in the gloom of the chamber, their eyes fell upon something laid out on the equally dusty floor – a skeleton, dressed in the tattered garb of a monk's habit. In the early 1970s a Grimsby businessman and his wife, touring the impressive, atmospheric ruins of the 12th-century abbey at East Halton, were alerted to a strange, plaintive sound of faint organ music that floated across the grounds. They were completely alone, and a search revealed no explanation, so they stood perfectly still in order to catch the weird melody as clearly as possible, whereupon it faded away in the wind.

Jenny Bright's *Ghosts Of Lincoln* (1995) noted how a relief landlord at the 15th-century Lion and Snake public house in Bailgate left the bathroom one afternoon, clad in a towel, and encountered a ghost, sometime in the 1980s. He actually pressed his back against the corridor to allow a solid-looking, stooped-over old woman, her hair tied back in a bun, to pass him in the narrow confines. Bemused by the woman's appearance, he later learned this curious old lady had been witnessed many times and was the pub's 'resident ghost'.

The Lion and Snake, on Christmas morning 2006.

This tiny portion of Sleaford Castle remains among the earth mounds.

The September 2004 edition of *Lincolnshire Life* featured an article on the White Lady of the Angel and Royal Hotel, Grantham, who had appeared so frequently to staff by 2001 that it was possible to provide an excellent description of her: slim, average height, her long plaited hair tied back into a bun. She was dressed in a full-length white, or cream, fitted bodice, and her full skirt appears to have a kind of fitted 'framework' to keep it stiff, and the whole ensemble presents an image of an 18th century lady.

In early 2005 the *Scunthorpe Evening Telegraph* carried a piece about a legendary 'angel of mercy', who, in decades past, was rumoured to haunt Scunthorpe General Hospital. The ghost, they said, appeared when children were desperately ill, and it seemed to be a nurse who wore a long skirt, covered with a long white apron. She left in her wake a scent of old-fashioned, violet-smelling perfume, and she had earned the nickname 'MacPeace'. The story prompted an excited response from readers, including former nurses who verified the legend. Piece by piece the story was put together, it being eventually established that 'MacPeace' had been Bertha Peace (née MacHarry) who had died in the early 1960s, leaving the strange legacy at the hospital where she had worked.

On 1 April 2006 the *Lincolnshire Echo* established that Brown's Pie Shop on Steep Hill, Lincoln, famously haunted by a poltergeist nicknamed Humphrey, was still plagued by the entity. In fact, Humphrey appeared impossible to get rid of. His antics have been recorded at Brown's for years (if not decades), and he even withstood an attempt to exorcise him by celebrity ghost hunter Derek Acorah in February. By the time the *Echo* visited, Humphrey was back to his usual attention seeking, although there is some suggestion that the entity is linked to a mysterious little boy occasionally seen on the premises.

RAF Coleby Grange, battered and haunted.

At Christmas 2006 while visiting a friend in Sleaford, I was told a story that was doing the rounds in the town. Apparently people were saying that a ghostly cavalier fighter could be seen battling an invisible opponent by the copse-enshrouded remains of Sleaford Castle, on the north-east corner of the ancient earthworks. Where this rumour had started, my friend could not say...

And so it goes on. It would be possible for this chapter to continue indefinitely. Currently attracting the attention of ghost hunters and the curious alike is the abandoned Control Tower which still stands on private land on the remains of RAF Coleby Grange, to the east of the village of Coleby. The place is the embodiment of a haunted site: lonely, overgrown and deserted, and for years there have been rumours of a phantom airman filled with remorse who gazes out over the overgrown runway from the top floor. Some kind of malicious spirit is also held to throw stones at visitors to the site.

One is left feeling that ghosts are, quite literally, all around us. These, however, are not merely superstitious folkloric stories that have been told for generations. There are real, living witnesses who are risking ridicule by going on record and relating what they swear is true. Some are just modern incarnations of stories that have existed in one form or another at a particular location for decades, if not centuries. So does the sheer wealth of stories indicate that the supernatural is real? What all this says about the paranormal is open to interpretation; with such a wide variety of ghostly goings on, what they say about the nature of human belief is perhaps just as pertinent a question.

LAYING OF SPIRITS

Closely linked with the phenomena of 'ghosts' is the practice of exorcism. It is an ancient ritual aimed at ridding a place or person of demonic spirits, typically performed by a priest acting as an exorcist who rids haunted properties by invoking God. Exorcism in its various forms has been performed worldwide since at least the time of Christ and in Britain is generally considered a mediaeval practice, as evidenced by the exorcism of Lincoln Cathedral in the 12th century. In the Lincolnshire Wolds, in the 17th century, money that changed hands was exorcised to rid it of the malaise of the Black Death sweeping the nation. Exorcism was further linked to such superstitious practices as 'trapping' evil spirits, or witches, in bottles, such as is believed to have taken place at Pilford Bridge over the River Ancholme. However, the ritual is still a recognised practice of many religions, and it may surprise some to know that exorcisms are not unknown to have been performed in the modern era in Lincolnshire. Many of the ghost-hunting concerns in the county now employ professional mediums to assist the transition of spirits from this world to the next. Regarding this trend, perhaps a typical sign of the times is the exorcism performed at a house in Woodhall Spa by a television psychic. The *Lincolnshire Echo* reported in February 2007 how Mia Dolan had performed the 'cleansing' ritual at a badly-haunted house that had in the 1940s been an RAF billet. Strange shadows had been witnessed on the staircase, and 'soldiers voices and footsteps' had been linked to a number of letters, penned in the 1940s, which were found hidden under floorboards.

Such events are hardly unique in Lincolnshire, and of course are somewhat removed from exorcisms involving the clergy. But it should be noted that there are a myriad of sites in the county held to have been the subject of secret, 'traditional' exorcisms: notably at the Birchwood Housing Estate and the Black Horse Chambers Bistro in Lincoln – all of which took place before the current fad for ghosts began, and which perhaps lend some small support for the existence of ghosts by mere virtue of their having taken place at all.

CHAPTER 9

THE WEIRD ANIMAL KINGDOM

INTRODUCTION

Although not currently a pet owner myself, I have witnessed first hand the strange, almost psychic, ability of pets, notably dogs, in certain situations. On several occasions in the early 21st century while with friends at their home on a housing estate in north Lincoln, I observed their pet English bull terrier, Boca, display a fascinating pattern of behaviour. Whenever the master of the house would leave to collect food, beer or a film, Boca – a proud, attractive and very powerful dog – would generally either snooze warily with one eye open (looking at me) or else play 'tug' with rags in the back garden, waiting for her master to return.

Generally, the following would happen. Boca would suddenly become alert and dart into the living room, where she would leap on to the sofa and stare out of the living-room window at the driveway. She could not be distracted and would remain in this position for some minutes, while those in the house would try to get her to play. It was to no avail; she would keep her watch until eventually – usually two, three or four minutes later – the owner of the house would pull up in the driveway. At this she would bound to the front door, tail wagging, and leap up at him to see what he had brought home. In short, the dog apparently knew – several minutes before the event – that her master was on his way home and would soon arrive. Although this behaviour might not surprise dog owners, it is nonetheless extremely strange to a non-pet owner.

Rupert Sheldrake's *Dogs That Know When Their Owners Are Coming Home: And Other Unexplained Powers Of Animals* (2000) cites an interesting example of animal clairvoyance in Grimsby. This particular owner was frequently warned of an impending epileptic fit he was about to suffer by the behaviour of his mixed-breed dog Jip. Normally Jip would follow his master around when an attack was due and would stay very close, or if his master was sat down Jip would jump up on him. But stranger still was the fact that Jip appeared to sense when his owner was about to suffer an attack even when both master and dog were in *separate* rooms. In such instances Jip would come bounding up to his owner from the kitchen and pin him to a chair. Jip's owner was adamant that his pet's behaviour under such circumstances was different to the normal playful larking of dogs; it was protective, worried and somehow specifically linked to the impending epileptic seizure. Sheldrake wrote, 'So whatever signals Jip is reacting to can be felt in a different room.'

It is not just dogs either. On 20 April 2006 Jane Overton appealed in *The Scunthorpe Evening Telegraph* for information on the whereabouts of the family's two lost cats, Lady and Baby. Mrs Overton told the newspaper that the family were particularly concerned, as the two pets had exerted a 'calming effect' on her 18-year-old epileptic daughter Selina at the family home in Oriole Road, Scunthorpe. Both cats had disappeared in the last month; since then Selina had had more seizures than ever before, as the teenager was particularly distressed about the loss. Lady in particular was missed, as she had had a habit of sticking by Selina when she was having a seizure. Lady, a six-and-a-half-year-old white cat with black patches on her head, would always stay by the teenager, laying with her and 'kissing her until she woke up'. And stranger still, the feisty feline had even come and alerted Mrs Overton to the fact that her daughter was having a fit on one occasion, when there was no one else around. Jane Overton told the newspaper, 'She is more like a dog in that way – you wouldn't expect it from a cat really.'

Tales of curious animal behaviour always delight us, and there is a never-ending source of such stories in Lincolnshire. Noteworthy is the instance in December 1848, when a young farmer called Copeman had his throat cut by a drinking partner one night on Low Road, between Kirton-in-Lindsey and Grayingham. The ground was soaked in blood and so a bloodhound named Herod was employed: the animal sniffed the blood, and then he instantly led the party across hill and dale, through woodland and over fences, right to the very front door of the farmhouse where the murderer lived.

Stories of dogs that protect their masters and even save their lives are standard fare in folklore the world over. Lincolnshire's own version of this concerns a farmer called Henry Stone, who found himself in the middle of a violent thunderstorm as he worked the fields in Skellingthorpe in 1690. Lightning flashed and rain poured, so Henry took shelter underneath a great oak tree. His pet hound inexplicably grabbed his coat sleeve and pulled him away, back out into the lashing rain.

The farmer shook the mad animal off and retreated once again to his shelter under the tree. But once again, his dog grabbed his coat and dragged him away.

By now he was losing patience with his pet, and when the dog roughly dragged him away from the tree a third time he was about ready to strike the animal; however, at that moment a bolt of lightning flashed and struck the tree, levelling it to a smouldering stump and killing a pheasant that had also sought shelter in the branches.

Henry Stone had a painting done of his dog, the tree and the pheasant to commemorate the event, and this painting can now be seen in the blue drawing room of Doddington Hall. Henry died in 1693, and he was outlived by his faithful pet.

It is perhaps worth pointing out that animals have always been thought to have a *certain* degree of extra-sensory or heightened perception. There are certain places where horses have been known to become stubbornly immovable, frightened by something they alone can sense: a particular field off Washdyke Lane, Osgodby, is one such place. Bottesford Beck, south of Scunthorpe, and Pilford Bridge, Normanby-by-Spital, are others.

Even stranger is the story of a possible mass migration of animals, experienced by a 22-year-old man on a fog-enshrouded lane near Grantham late one night in 1972. He had stopped his car on the lane when a distant howl prompted a flock of birds to take off from the trees. Following this, two distinct herds of animals – unseen in the fog – moved past his car, accompanied by thundering hoof beats, and general grunting and snuffling. The young man to whom this happened was inclined to class the encounter as a phantom one, but the fact is he claims that his car rocked and moved as though it was 'stuck in a flock of sheep', and the whole incident remains a weird enigma.

But this chapter is concerned with other animal oddities: such as the animals of folklore and legend, out of place beasts – and the panthers that prowl the countryside.

TREE GEESE

Perhaps the most outlandish of all claims pertaining to the natural world is that there once existed a species of tree from which birds were produced. These trees were recorded in 1597 as existing in the northern parts of Scotland, and they produced 'Shell-Fishes' called (in Scotland) the Barnakle instead of acorns, etc, which then fell into the water and gradually developed into a kind of fowl. These unbelievable trees also grew in northern England and produced a bird called Brant Geese. The trees were observed in Lincolnshire too, where they produced – much in the same manner as elsewhere – a bird called the 'Tree Goose'. This claim is truly outrageous, as any natural historian will verify, and it is hard to believe that anyone who had seen a barnacle attached to a wet rock or ship's hull could think it would, when free-floating in water, develop into a breed of goose. One wonders what combination of rumour, misidentification, strange coincidence or odd occurrence could have produced such a tale, yet it was widely believed. The noted 16th-century chronicler Raphael Holinshed, of Cheshire, once wrote – apparently in all seriousness – that he had seen the Tree Goose develop with his own eyes: he witnessed a barnacle that had sprouted feathers, which '...hang out of the shell at least two inches'.

ELIZABETHAN AVIAN CURIOSITIES

Around 1600, a scandalous pen and ink drawing satirised Queen Elizabeth I as a 'strange, vain fowl, supposedly caught at Crowley in Lincolnshire in 1588'. The insult was in a piece entitled *Queen Elizabeth Allegorized* which went unpublished for centuries, probably due to the risk the authors faced of imprisonment and torture as possible traitors. Assuming that such a strange bird was indeed caught, and that the incident was not made up for the purposes of insulting the monarch, the authors probably meant Crowle, in North Lincolnshire. The title phrase *Allegorized* suggests that the satire was based on the actual capture of a strange bird in Crowle. It is suggestive that, if the authors wished to satirically *invent* a strange bird being discovered and placed on the throne, they did not say it was caught in 1558 – the year Elizabeth came to the throne. *The Oxford Illustrated History Of English Literature* (2001) provides the illustration of the bird – spindly-legged, with massive and ridiculous-looking plumage covering its head and neck – and one can only wonder if this bird was, indeed, really caught and what it was.

Ben Jonson's *The Alchemist* contains the following quotation:

> 'Avoid Satan.
> Thou art not of the light. That Ruff of pride,
> About thy Neck, betrays thee: 'and is the same
> With that which the unclean Birds, in seventy-seven,
> Were seen to prank it with, on divers Coasts.
> Thou look'st like Antichrist, in that lewd Hat.'

The Alchemist was written in 1610, and the above quote possibly refers to strange birds with ruffs around their necks which were found on the Lincolnshire coast in 1586, rather than in 1577. Puritans apparently took these mysterious birds to be portents: they were the 'unclean bird' of Revelation 18:2. Their neck feathers and quills were compared by wags at the time to the elaborate collars and frizzled hairstyles of 'gallant dames' and fops of the era. But exactly what kind of bird they were is unclear, although there is certainly the possibility of a connection with the odd bird allegedly caught at Crowle two years later. Then, just as now, one would assume locals were familiar with all local birds...but these Lincolnshire birds, apparently, caused quite a stir. If the sightings were based on reality, they were apparently complete strangers to our shores and cryptozoological oddities.

SWARMS

An apparently unremarkable fly once graced the collection of curiosities owned by the Yorkshire antiquarian and collector Ralph Thoresby (1658–1725). It had been sent to him by the Revd Mr Hall, of Fishlake, South Yorkshire, in 1699 together with an account of its remarkable heritage. Mr Hall reported that earlier that year, in May, the folk of 'Kerton in Lincolnshire' (Kirton) had looked in a north-west direction with growing trepidation as the sky and the horizon grew dark. It appeared as though a thunderstorm, or other extremely bad weather, were heading their way.

However, as it grew nearer the townsfolk realised this was no weather front. Kirton was literally swept by a huge swarm of flies that turned day into night and caused those caught in it to turn their backs towards the onslaught. The immense swarm swept through Kirton in a south-easterly direction; the Revd Hall managed to obtain the fly as a bizarre souvenir of this episode.

In his third giant compilation of all things weird and wonderful, *LO!* (1931), Charles Fort recorded almost what sounded like plagues off the east coast of Lincolnshire. Drawing on an article in the September 1869 publication of *Zoologist*, Fort recorded that, off Lincolnshire, belts of water – some a few yards wide, some hundreds of yards wide – were thick and pea-souper in appearance due to millions of floating, drowned aphides, i.e. small bugs such as greenfly and blackfly. Off the coast of Norfolk, a veritable island of drowned ladybirds, about 10-feet wide and two or three-miles long, was witnessed. Fort mused that wherever these gigantic swarms emanated from, there was no record of them having passed over anywhere in Europe.

On 26 July great columns of bugs were seen to come down from the sky 'at Bury St Edmunds, about 60-miles south of the coast of Lincolnshire', where the swarms enveloped those caught up in it so thoroughly that they almost could not breathe. That same day, Chelmsford, in Essex, was similarly affected by the mysterious plague.

In early September 2002 residents of Donington-on-Bain were stung by giant mystery wasps of an unknown variety. One resident of the village described the insects as largely black with some yellow markings, and over twice the size of a normal wasp or hornet. They were also exceptionally aggressive, and they delivered a powerful sting. One woman who was stung found that her arm '…came up like a balloon'. The mystery wasps were perhaps a variety from south and central Europe called Dolichovespula Media, which had migrated towards the British Isles, but one is nonetheless reminded of the *X-Files* episodes where bee husbandry was used to create lethal bees by unknown conspirators.

WATER BULLS AND WOLVES

Mabel Peacock mentioned in 1891 another peculiar animal oddity – the so-called Water Bull that made its home in Lincolnshire streams. By the early 20th century this enigma no longer haunted the county – but Peacock claimed that the deep pools formed in downwards-flowing becks and streams were still known as bull holes, after this mysterious thing that had once dwelt there.

In the Middle Ages, the people of the Fens believed there existed a giant animal called the Water Wolf, although it is unclear whether this was a real animal or a local variant on the various 'water animals' of folklore – such as the Shag Foal, the Water Bull and the Lackey Causey Calf. H.C. Darby's *The Mediaeval Fenland* (1940) notes the *belief* in 'large water wolves', which suggests they may have been spiritual creatures, perhaps in the same vein as the great white wolf supposedly sent by St Peter to aid Hereward the Wake when he became lost in Rockingham Forest during his uprising against William the Conqueror. However, cryptozoologist Richard Muirhead has suggested that maybe Water Wolves were real creatures, perhaps misidentifications of a species of seal that were able to live much further inland in those days before drainage.

CURIOUS ANIMAL BEHAVIOUR IN TEALBY

On the lighter side of things came a story in 1924 reported in the *Market Rasen Mail,* about an incredible white wyandotte hen owned by a Mr W. Horton of Tealby. The hen would confine itself from the other birds in the chicken house, almost as if they were not good enough for it. This aloof hen refused to go anywhere near the chicken house when she was due to start laying – opting instead to sneak into the farmhouse and awkwardly climb the stairs, one at a time. At the top of the stairs, the hen would lay her eggs – and nowhere else was good enough. In the winter, when the back door was closed, the hen would perch itself on a table outside the window and peck the pane with her beak repeatedly until the Hortons gave in and allowed her inside. Two weeks before the report appeared in the *Mail* the hen had been due to lay, but wherever she was put she would get up and make for the stairs of the farmhouse. Finally the Horton's gave up, and they placed her hay-lined box at the top of the stairs where the hen then contentedly nestled and produced her eggs.

Staying in Tealby, the villagers in 1929 and 1930 followed the fortunes of their own little local star – a cat called Katie who was owned by the postmaster, Mr H. Lee. Katie would amaze Mr Lee by letting herself in the house for her bowl of milk: she would spring up at the back door, grab the latch with her paws and push down, opening the door. She would also open other doors in the house the same way. This act can only have been learned by seeing how humans opened the door and copying it. The fact that she habitually performed the feat shows that it was something she had learned and remembered, rather than an accident. Little Katie became quite a celebrity, and in due course the media got hold of the tale. London newspapers became interested in the story, and so did the Gaumont British Film Co, who decided that they wished Katie to feature in a newsreel. Sadly for Mr Lee though, Katie was killed in a scrap with another cat that Christmas.

TOADMEN

The so-called 'Cunning Folk' of centuries gone by – herbalists, wise women and men, conjurers, wizards and magicians – have long since vanished from the Lincolnshire landscape, their dubious skills no longer required in such a technological age. However, some may note that a more modern incarnation of the 'Cunning Folk' could be found in eastern England between the two world wars. Their abilities bridged the gap between witchcraft and the so-called 'Cunning Folk', and modern-day Lincolnshire psychics like the late Doris Stokes *et al.* They were the Toadmen, and, quite simply, they possessed the ability to control the animals.

To become a Toadman, one had to carry out a peculiar ritual. The would-be psychic took a toad and buried it in an ant's nest. When the toad's body had been picked clean, the man could recover the bones and toss them into a running stream at midnight. All the bones were swept away downstream – except one, which was key shaped and could easily be recovered from the water. A certain ritual – of which the details are unspecified – was then performed and the left-over bone empowered the Toadman with the ability to psychically control animals, particularly horses. To tire out the horse, all the Toadman had to do was touch its shoulder; to get it moving again, all he had to do was touch its rump. It was also rumoured that those possessed of this gift were also able to exert their influence over unwary women...

Adrian Morgan's *Toads And Toadstools: The Natural History, Folklore, And Cultural Oddities Of A Strange Association* (1995) tells us that if a toad could not be procured then a frog may do; however, this empowered the psychic with gifts that were not as strong as if he had used a toad. Nevertheless, Morgan states that Toadmen were widely sought after by those who owned farmsteads in eastern England during the inter-war years: no doubt there are those still alive in Lincolnshire who can recall such characters locally.

GIANT HORSE OF SKEGNESS

In February 2004 *Fortean Times*, a journal of strange phenomena, published a letter from a reader in Loughborough, Leicestershire, that ran as follows:

Many years previously, when he had been a child of four or five, the witness had been taken to Skegness on a day trip by his grandma. During the journey he had gazed out of the coach window at the fields and observed sheep and horses. He vividly recalls that as he gazed absently out the window, the coach passed a field in which, apart from regular-sized horses, there trotted a truly immense horse – possibly three times as big as all the others in the field. The enormity of the animal frightened the life out of the boy, and no one else on the coach appeared to see this beast, yet he maintained in his letter to the magazine that the sighting was not down to youthful imagination and even today his recollection of the animal – and his fright – were as clear as when he had looked upon it as a child.

This story is somewhat reminiscent of a curious experience related to me by a man concerning an occasion when he had been on his way to school with friends in the late 1970s. He had been about seven and walking along Brant Road, Lincoln, with his mother and the other children. Falling behind, his eyes fell upon a group of insects in the grass by the fences of Broughton Gardens. Looking closer, the boy saw how there was a caterpillar, a worm and what may have been a maggot – all of which terrified the boy, as they were fat, grotesque and immense, four or five times bigger than normal. The boy stood there, wondering why no one else had seen these monstrosities. He looked away, then back, and they were still there. This was no trick of the imagination, but before he could stammer anything his mother caught him by the arm and dragged him away.

This incident sounds like a light-hearted reminiscence of an adult who had perhaps just read *James And The Giant Peach* as a boy, but I am assured that there were what looked like many normal-sized insects about the three giants. As with the witness to the giant horse of Skegness, these monstrous creatures frightened the boy so much that the memory of the incident remained clear into adulthood.

BIG GAME HUNTING IN LINCOLNSHIRE

On 26 July 2002 *The Lincolnshire Echo* published yet another account of a sighting of the mysterious creature known as the Lindsey Leopard. Thirty-two-year-old Charles Till, a Royal Navy chef from West Butterwick, had taken a ride out to Laughton Forest, which partly surrounds the village of Laughton, north of Gainsborough. He was some 100 metres deep in the woods, and as he walked along the track with his dog, Rusty, he spotted something about 15 metres in front of him.

Mr Till described what he had seen as a large cat resembling a cougar: it was something like a metre long and light brown in colour. As he watched it slink across his path, Mr Till felt no fear of the beast – merely stunned curiosity. The animal disappeared into the thick of the trees, and although Mr Till attempted to follow it he found it had vanished without trace.

The Lindsey Leopard is part of Lincolnshire folklore, and there can be few who live in the county who have not at least heard of the rumours that ABCs – Alien Big Cats – lurk in the more wild and remote areas of the county. The Lindsey Leopard – and creatures like him – have been reported for decades in Lincolnshire, and, as it is with all cryptozoological creatures, this raises the notion that there is not one single big cat, rather a colony – or colonies – of them. There have been sightings of out-of-place big cats in Lincolnshire since the 1950s, but among the first of the 'modern' reported sightings to be given credit was the experience in 1976 of a police surgeon called Dr Alec Jamieson. On 20 September he was startled to glimpse a large, sandy-coloured cat that he thought was a cougar wandering the grounds of a convalescent home called Seely House, on the seafront at Skegness. The enigmatic animal was about five feet in length, and it was also spotted by a colleague, PC Gartshore, who was called in. PC Gartshore described the beast as a big, Labrador-sized cat. The incident had taken place late in the afternoon.

A police search of the grounds of Seely House turned up several paw prints that measured two and a half inches by three inches, but local media never followed up on whether they belonged to a cougar or some other wild animal.

Interviews with staff at Seely House produced the information that in the weeks preceding the 20 September encounter, they had repeatedly seen the same animal but had assumed, perhaps naturally, that it was some sort of dog. The mystified police brought in an inspector from the RSPCA, who, together with local naturalist John Yeadon, hid among the grounds of Seely House hoping the animal would return. It didn't, and it was never seen again.

Doubtless the impressive nature of the witnesses helped this sighting stand up in court, as it were, but it is more than likely in this instance that the oft-cited Dangerous Wild Animals Act of 1976 forced the owner of the big cat to set it free in order to avoid having to pay for the newly-required license. This explanation may have been true to a certain extent in the run-up to the act being passed, and for some time afterwards, but sightings in the decades prior to and following after it are less easy to explain.

It would be self-defeating and tedious to note every report of a black panther in Lincolnshire. In the late 20th and early 21st centuries, it has been seen in virtually every part of the county. The many names ascribed to the animal(s) by the local media in recent years is testament to the fact that it cannot be pinned down to one locale: the Lindsey Leopard, the Bassetlaw Beast, the Lincolnshire Lynx, the Fiskerton Phantom, the Gedney Beast, the Bourne Beast, the Wolds Panther, the Beast of Holton-le-Clay, the Grimsby Growler, and so on – not to mention the many other sightings within the counties that surround Lincolnshire. This evidence alone makes it clear that there is more than one 'panther' out there. But by its very nature the black cat has proved impossible to track down or reliably photograph. It is a ghost, or a Will o' the Wisp, glimpsed only by those lucky enough to see it – like Mr Till – before it vanishes again: seen, and yet invisible at the same time.

The surreal, comedic aspect of the whole Wolds Panther saga was illustrated in April 2003, when Christine Tye came upon the beast in Ludford, east of Market Rasen. The giant cat was sitting looking disinterestedly at her, and it showed no signs of budging, so she shooed it away in the manner one would when trying to get a tabby cat out of their garden. The Wolds Panther didn't budge, so it was Christine who ran off. She described the beast as four times the size of a normal cat. Its face was greyish and its long tail was black, and it had the sleek appearance of a puma.

Probably the nearest thing to 'proof' that the big cat has left for scientists concerns an incident in 2003. In Horncastle the mystery animal was playing with fire. On 11 July police marksmen were among a contingent of experts who descended on the garden of Sandy Richardson, of Green Lane, Hemingby, after he reported entering his back garden caravan to find it had been invaded. Sandy told the *Horncastle News* that he suddenly found himself sharing the confines of the caravan with a giant black feline the size of a large dog, with great yellow fangs and great big golden eyes, adding that it 'really is an impressive animal'. The beast moved towards Sandy, who gently backed out of the caravan

The approach to Laughton, surrounded by woodland.

and closed the door. Before he had any time to take anything in, a huge scrambling announced that the big cat had managed to bolt out the side of the caravan. The subsequent search for the Wolds Panther was as fruitless as all the others. Sandy's wife commented that they had never liked the children playing at the woodside end of the garden, so they had told them that lions and tigers were in the trees – never dreaming that a panther would wander out of that very same woodland one day.

DNA samples that had been taken on animal hairs found after the caravan invasion in July had indicated that the sneaky culprit was indeed a wild cat, of a type belonging to the leopard family. The samples have been forensically tested at laboratories in Essex and the US, and wildlife experts were gradually conforming to the idea that it was at least *possible* for animals such as pumas and black panthers to survive in the area, as they would be able to live off the rich food source the Wolds provided. The Richardsons had themselves subsequently maintained a vigil on their property and managed to grab photos and some video footage of the beast that, for one reason or another, preferred their garden: Julie Richardson was quoted by the *Horncastle News* as saying, 'You can tell it's not a normal cat because the pictures and the video footage we have clearly show its ears are forward and it has a hump on the back of his head, indicating it's a male black leopard.' The couple had managed to take the footage of the animal when it returned to their caravan the very day after Sandy Richardson's original encounter, and the video film, though blurred, was impressive enough for the *Horncastle News* to hand over a reward and proudly claim 'A BIG CAT *IS* ROAMING THE WOLDS!!!' This claim was somewhat over confident, perhaps, as the concrete, indisputable proof was still lacking. As one sceptical reader of the *Horncastle News* pointed out, possibly unfairly, video footage can be forged, and hair samples can be obtained...

But the big cat(s) does not merely confine itself to sneaking about under hedgerows in the wilds of Lincolnshire. For example, in 2000 businesswoman Diane Flear-Charlton and her partner Malcolm Moss were walking their dachshunds in Higson Road, near the old St George's Hospital in northern Lincoln when, to their amazement, their eyes fell upon an immense black feline that resembled a panther slinking down the steps. The animal gazed at the dog walkers and for a second Mrs Flear-Charlton thought it might attack and eat the dogs, but it merely lost interest and padded off.

The panther/puma story is a firm favourite with the local media and they occasionally report other tantalising clues as to the 'proof' of the creature's existence: in October 1998 it was suspected of being the culprit that attacked a rabbit hutch, tore open the mesh front and absconded with the two pet rabbits inside on Doddington Park, a suburban housing estate on the western edge of Lincoln. Other 'kills' of livestock and mutilated forest animals are occasionally blamed on the big cat. In October 1998, a week after a sighting in Minting, three mutilated sheep were found in fields in the vicinity of Baumber, torn to pieces. Confused experts could attribute the mess to nothing other than some kind of wild animal attack.

On 11 August 1998 a close encounter at 20 feet with the giant feline near Gainsborough prompted an RSPCA investigation. Three days later two large paw prints, five inches by four inches, were found in cut grass on farmland in the district of Bassetlaw, near Gainsborough, and in the vicinity of the sighting. Photographs and plaster casts were taken and RSPCA inspector Steve Foster identified them as belonging to either a puma or a lynx. In southern Lincolnshire in February 2002 a family, the Mundy's, had heard a disturbance outside their house near Gedney one evening but had ignored it. The following morning they were startled to find several sets of large paw prints on their property, and plaster casts of the prints have led the authorities to identify the beast as a puma, about the size of a large Labrador dog. The paw prints were about the size of a human hand, and the creature that had left them appeared to be some five feet in length. Its route around the Mundy's land was clear, and at one point it appeared to have gone down a dyke and then jumped across it. It had had enough sense to stay away from an electric fence on the property.

It is interesting to note of the big cat called the Wolds Panther that, after the spate of sightings in the mid-to-late 1990s, there appears to have been a lull in sightings until the early 21st century and the 'bumper year' of 2003 in the Horncastle area. This lull coincided with a telephone call to the *Market Rasen Mail* by a man who stated matter-of-factly, 'You know that panther? I've shot it!' And what of the Lindsey Leopard? On 20 April 2004 workers driving through Harpswell, east of Gainsborough, thought they spotted the body of a huge black panther-like animal (the witness was positive that it was not a canine animal) on the roadside, presumably some kind of roadkill. However, when they approached the same spot later in the day to inspect the specimen more closely, they found that persons unknown had removed the body.

SHADOW, THE BEAST OF NORTH SCARLE

On 24 March 2006 the *Lincolnshire Echo* ran as its banner headline 'THE BEAST' and pictured an intimidating photograph of a black panther next to the text. Although there was a degree of sensationalism, something was, again, being seen in the region west of the city of Lincoln. By the time the newspaper ran the story the mystery animal had been spotted so frequently in the area that the locals had nicknamed it Shadow. It haunted a nature reserve at North Scarle called Lowfields Country Retreat off Eagle Road. Within a week of the report 'Shadow' was seen again, on the other side of Lincoln at Bracebridge Heath. Thirty-year-old IT worker John Robinson had been cycling along Viking Way at about 8:30pm. He was with a neighbour, and both had very strong lights on their bikes.

The panther's haunt? View of the Lincolnshire Wolds from south-east of Nettleton.

A big, black animal suddenly crossed their path, and of course the pair thought they had come across a dog; however, as the creature slunk by and then bounded into a field (where it turned to look at them before moving off), John realised that perhaps he had just witnessed the famous black panther of North Scarle. It had certainly not been a dog...

And so it goes on, and one cannot help but make some fascinating observations at this juncture. The case of the Lincolnshire ABCs presents no coherent structure: masses of evidence and yet no *absolute* proof, and genuine uncertainty as to the number, location and even the species of the elusive beasts. Explanations for the sightings, such as they are, and alternative possible identifications of the animal (a Horncastle local claimed the Wolds Panther was a rare blue fox, bred for the fur trade during World War Two) are consistently trotted out with such lameness and are so lacking in follow-up detail regarding where, what, when and how, as to make the ABC explanation, in some cases, more plausible. Some link the big cats to the UFO phenomenon, claiming they are displaced animals that have been 'abducted' from their natural habitat only to be mistakenly returned to the wrong country. Some things can be tentatively regarded as 'definite', however, which is that unless every single witness is either hallucinating, mistaken or lying, then some kind of gigantic cat, or cats (for there are surely more than one), prowls the Lincolnshire countryside. The nearest thing to a genuine explanation is a *claim* that, in the 1970s, a female black panther was released into the wild by employees at Sotby Zoo Farm under a veil of secrecy; of course, that animal would be long dead by now but if it had mated with a male escapee then it could perhaps be a partial explanation for the scores of big cat sightings in Lincolnshire these days. That is, if the claim is true.

But Shadow, the beast of North Scarle, just like all the other panthers, will never be caught or conclusively photographed or filmed. A few footprints may be found, although these will be contentious. There will, however, be much reliable witness statements. After the flap has died away he will vanish into history, only to appear somewhere else in the county some years later, and it cannot help but be noticed that in this respect these animals are phantoms not too dissimilar to Hairy Jack himself. Although this generation lives by the internet, the DVD and mobile phones – and likes to think itself less superstitious than generations gone – this is modern folklore in the making, happening now to people who you probably know or live near. If Hairy Jack were a spiritual, ethereal hound, could it be that these animals are his modern incarnation? Until one of the big cats *are* caught, who can tell?

A MENAGERIE OF MYSTERIES

On 14 October 2003 it was reported that a giant *white* cat-like beast had been spotted near Mablethorpe. An anonymous witness spotted a great white feline, as large as a great dane, dash from right to left across the road in front of her car in the region of Saltfleet, just north of Mablethorpe on the Lincolnshire coast. A couple of days earlier video footage had been snatched of what was presumably the same mystery animal skulking about in woodland at the foot of a garden in Minting, so the 'Snow Leopard', as it has been christened, had apparently traversed the terrain of the Lincolnshire Wolds in two days. The albino panther of Minting is occasionally still seen, but panthers, pumas, leopards and lynxes are not the only mystery animals lurking in the Lincolnshire countryside.

On 24 July 2002 a wallaby was spotted hopping along Roman Bank in Long Sutton: this turned out to be an escapee from a local wildlife park. The wallaby's name was Jake, and he was the smallest of the three wallabies at the Long Sutton Butterfly and Wildlife Park. There was plenty of grass for Jake to munch on in the wilds outside his pen, and the main concern of the police and search parties was that the timid creature might end up being killed on the county's roads.

It was something of a mystery how Jake managed to get free of his pen. Investigators at the park could find no holes through which he could have hopped, and the 2ft 6in-tall animal was unlikely to have been able to somehow leap the 6ft surrounding fence.

While this sighting was partly explained, some others are not so easy to explain away. For example, in the late 20th century there was a report that an animal that resembled a small bear was roaming Fiskerton. The reports all came from the same night, and the animal earned the nickname the 'Fiskerton Phantom'. A group of young girls from South Yorkshire who spotted it claimed that it stood about 1 metre high, was jet black and 'bear-like' in appearance. The four girls first spotted the 'bear' when their attention was drawn towards rustling bushes as they enjoyed a steady holiday walk through Fiskerton. The nickname of the beast is somewhat misleading, as the animal was not an apparition; indeed, it was eating a pheasant as the girls looked on in wonder. Nine-year-old Nicola Proctor told the *Daily Star* newspaper of 27 August 1997 that the animal had 'very big teeth and great big claws', and when they saw it they collectively froze for a few seconds before all running off in fear.

With youthful fascination, the group of youngsters returned to the spot a while later, only to find that the 'bear' had ambled off, although they claimed that they found the paw prints that it had left behind. The girls then ran back to the caravan park where they were staying.

The caravan park was adjacent to the Tyrwhitt Arms public house in Short Ferry, and that strange evening pub manager Dave Brumhead found himself at the receiving end of the weirdest story he had ever heard: the girls had dashed into the Tyrwhitt Arms to find an adult, and they told Dave about the 'bear' they had just seen. He told the *Daily Star* that the girls had been genuinely shocked, and it was quite clear to him that it had not been a prank. Furthermore, that same evening a motorist reportedly had to apply his brakes in the middle of the road after spotting something like a large animal in the same area where the girls had seen the 'bear'.

There have been similar unverifiable sightings of monkeys in the county too. In August 1976 a monkey was spotted in fields near Gainsborough, and then what was presumably the same animal was seen a few days later twice more in the Blyton/Northorpe area of Lincolnshire. Witnesses described the monkey as being about two-feet tall and it appeared very timid. It had bright eyes, pointy ears and a square face, and after this the enigmatic animal was seen no more, nor was there ever any forthcoming explanation. In February 1991 a coatimundi – a 2ft-long (with the tail), long-nosed, tree-dwelling marsupial native to Belize – was seen in Spilsby. The following May what could (or could not) have been the same animal was captured alive in Wrawby, North Lincolnshire, although rumours persisted that the animal originally seen in Spilsby had been shot somewhere in Lincolnshire.

And on one occasion an animal that looked like a lemur was witnessed at Waddington Cliff, a scenic area of high ground to the south of the city of Lincoln. The sighting took place in 2000 and was made by two women out walking over the fields. Their journey took them to the top of Waddington Hill to a clump of trees and a security fence bearing a 'DANGER: KEEP OUT' sign. Their journey thus terminated, the two friends peered over the fence and saw a rather large animal with a face like a lemur. It had a small round head and grey ears. It had a white stripe down its body and long legs, and its 'very long' tail was striped grey and black.

Also in the early 21st century the police were contacted by a man who claimed that he had just seen a mysterious mammal on the grassy area of Cartergate in Grimsby, near the Deansgate Bridge. The out of place animal resembled nothing so much as a hyena.

On 13 August 2002 the *Grimsby Evening Telegraph* reported on the hunt for what was thought to be a North American garter snake. It had been spotted the previous day in the Boulevard Avenue area of Grimsby and was described as being about three-feet long with black and yellow spots. The slippery customer was assumed to have been an escaped pet.

South of Horncastle, a woman was driving a friend along the B1183 in the vicinity of Revesby one evening in June 2004 when both women were shocked to see a huge cat disappear into the bushes. Yet another ABC sighting...except that in this case both women were convinced that the monster they saw was a lion. It had massive paws, and the women described how they had clearly seen the tuft of fur on the end of its tail.

Is there a never-ending silly season in certain parts of Lincolnshire? Or is this story just possible? Scores of ABC reports mention that the beast witnessed resembles a 'lioness', and there had been recent sporadic reports of a big cat that looked like a lion which was roaming the wilds of Norfolk...

Maybe even Noah would have had his work cut out in Lincolnshire! But while proof of pumas, bears and even 12ft-long shortfin mako sharks off the east coast may be lacking, there is at least occasional evidence that we do indeed have alien, non-native animals roaming the wilds of Lincolnshire. In 1883 a ferocious wild cat was flushed out of Rand Wood at Bullington, west of Wragby, by a startled farmer who shot it. The animal was stuffed and mounted, weighing in at 18 pounds and being 46 inches long. The surprising thing about this was that not only had the native wild cat been extinct in Lincolnshire for 40 years, it had been declared extinct in England at large three years earlier.

The sharp-toothed and potentially-aggressive raccoon is native to North and South America. But on 8 October 2005 the *Lincolnshire Echo* reported on the bizarre experience of a retired farmer who had gone to his pigeon shed in Osgodby when he saw a large animal jump up into the roof and perch there. Thinking a fox had gotten in, he grabbed a pole and bashed it on the head as it tried to dash past him out the door.

The pigeon shed had been the repeated target of an animal that had so far eaten 13 pigeons and some of their eggs. But when the farmer realised what the animal was that he had killed, he was dumbfounded: for it was a raccoon. Raccoons are omnivores and will eat birds when they can catch them.

Where the raccoon came from is something of a mystery. But interestingly it was not the first to be found in the county. In March 2004 an injured raccoon was found lying by the side of the A46 near Nettleham, a considerable distance from Osgodby. The female animal was in a four-day coma, but was eventually nursed back to health and taken to a wildlife hospital in Peterborough, Cambridgeshire. Where this raccoon came from is also a mystery, and one is left wondering how many others are perhaps out there.

VULTURE CLUB

Reminiscent of the curious avian visitors to Lincolnshire's shores noted earlier is the letter submitted to *Bird Watching* magazine in December 2006, which noted the unexpected experience of a landowner in Lincolnshire who had chanced upon a buzzard feasting on a pigeon in one of his fields. This incident, noteworthy only as a reminder of how cruel nature can be, was soon overshadowed, quite literally. A large, dark bird began to circle in the sky above the buzzard, its carrion feast and the mildly curious farmer; at this the buzzard took off suddenly, only to be replaced by a gigantic vulture-like bird that swept down and took its place feeding on the remains of the pigeon. The strange bird's appearance so startled the landowner that he contacted an ornithologist friend of his who subsequently appeared on the scene. She in turn took a photograph of the great bird feasting and identified it tentatively as a turkey vulture.

Turkey vultures are classed as new world vultures and hail from warm climate areas of the Americas, and the bird gets its name from the adult's bald red head and its very dark brown plumage. While soaring, the adults will tip their wings into a characteristic V-shape (their wingspan is some six feet) and naturally such a creature, even if a scavenger, is exceptionally impressive.

Even more so, then, for its out-of-place appearance in the wilds of Lincolnshire. *Bird Watching* magazine published a clear photograph of the creature, commenting (only naturally) that the bird was supposedly an escapee from somewhere. That it almost certainly is, but it is noteworthy that the Lincolnshire incident coincided with a 'flap' of sightings of other out-of-place vulture-like birds across the UK, leading some to speculate on a possible cryptozoological or paranormal explanation for the sudden glut of sightings.

CHAPTER 10

ALL MANNER OF MONSTERS

INTRODUCTION

O ne of the misericords (small, wooden shelves on the underside of church seats, provided for leaning against when the seat is folded up during hymns while standing) in St Botolph's Church, Boston, depicts a mermaid and two fishermen in a boat listening to her piping. Despite Boston's proximity to the Wash, the misericords date from the mid-19th century and there sadly appears to be no legend behind this carving; indeed, another depicts a knight using his sword to kill a Griffin, the mighty winged lion/eagle creature of myth.

However, there are numerous other legends of strange and fantastic creatures from across Lincolnshire. Creatures from myth and folklore have long been speculated about by county folk. As one would guess, there is a story behind the name of Dragonby, the small North Lincolnshire hamlet to the north of Scunthorpe. About halfway down the only road through the place (off the A1077 to Winterton) there is a gap in the houses to the right; on the open ground beyond can be seen the 'dragon', a strange-shaped natural rock formation that snakes its way up the hill for 90 feet. Local tradition confirms that the geological anomaly was once a dragon that guarded treacle mines until a wizard turned it to stone. The Dragon Rock is commonly thought to have been the object of Pagan veneration and displays signs that it has been slightly 'helped' by humans to achieve its serpentine appearance. But no matter, for in honour of the petrified monster the local landowners – the Elwes family – recently changed the village's name from Conesby Cliff to Dragonby.

Elsewhere, a knight called Sir John de Buslingthorpe (or Boselyngthorpe) is said to have killed a dragon near Lissington, possibly sometime in the 1300s. For this Sir John was presented with some 400 acres of local land; the now-defunct church at Buslingthorpe still retains memorials to the family, who were lords of the manor until the 15th century.

South-east of Louth lies Castle Carlton, today a small hamlet where its old motte and bailey can still be espied. In the early 12th century a monstrous creature roamed the area, killing villagers with great blasts of poisonous breath. Folklore describes this entity in detail. It had an immensely-long, green and grey scaly body in the usual tradition of a dragon, with a powerful serpentine tail that it was able to use as a weapon. However, this monster had only one eye in its head, an eye the size of a pudding bowl that blazed like fire. It had clad its four short legs in iron, and its one reputed weak spot – a small wart on its right thigh – was adequately protected by three layers of brass armour. Its lair was at a place called Wormesgate, which some consider to be modern-day Walmsgate, south of Louth. A landowning knight called Sir Hugh Barde is held to have eventually slain the creature during a thunderstorm somewhere on a beach on the east coast. It is claimed that Sir Hugh collected the head and presented it to an astonished King Henry I of England at the royal court in London, which puts this event sometime during his reign of AD1100–35. The carcass of the creature was buried in the long barrow south of Walmsgate.

Some of the ancient stories present themes that horror fans of today would be familiar with. Legend says that strange things occurred during a ferocious outbreak of the plague in Boston in 1585. Some 460 people lost their lives, and terrified locals whispered in hushed voices how coffin lids had been seen to be thrown off by the apparently deceased victim within, who would then proceed to clamber out of their own coffin. In the churchyards the ghastly hands of those who had fallen victim would break through the soil, clawing as though trying to escape from their graves under the earth...

In 1854 labourers engaged on road works at Yaddlethorpe Hill, Bottesford, unearthed the sinister skeleton of a man with a wooden stake driven through his chest. It is assumed that the man had been a suicide, but the condition of the skeleton is a curious reminder of the superstitious belief of days gone by. In the case of a suicide it was common practice to hammer a wooden stake through the heart and then dump the body in a hole at a crossroads and cover it with quicklime to assist its disintegration. Whoever buried the corpse at Bottesford clearly believed that it could rise again: Gutch & Peacock's *County Folklore* found that, centuries later, there was still a primitive fear that the dead would somehow climb out of their coffin. The book, published in 1908, noted the practice of tying the feet of the corpse together '...else the dead may return, or some other spirit may take possession of the body for his own purposes'. There is clearly an origin in beliefs like this for the 20th century's horror icon: the zombie.

But this chapter is largely concerned with the creatures of myth and cryptozoology. It seems that if it can be imagined, then it has been seen – or there is at least a story concerning it. Some of the strange creatures reported defy explanation; some of them even defy belief.

THE HOWLING

Read's Island lies about 50 metres into the River Humber, with a stretch of the water known as the South Channel separating it from South Ferriby in North Lincolnshire. It covers an area of about 200 acres, and more than a decade ago a strange story concerning this place was passed on to me by a friend in Holderness, East Yorkshire. The legend doing the rounds among students at Hull University said that Read's Island had once been the lair of a wolfman. I vaguely recollect the story going something like this.

The tale dates from 'about 400 years ago' and concerns a travelling vagabond, who had set up a dismal shelter on the island and looked to the great Humber estuary for a means of eking out a living. He made a pittance as a boatman, ferrying travellers across the waters in a small vessel, and it was said that during his residence on the island scores of people from the surrounding area vanished in mysterious circumstances. Eventually, acting upon the evidence given by one of his passengers, the vagrant was arrested and dragged before magistrates to answer allegations that he was a murderer who survived by cannibalising his victims. An investigation reputedly found that Read's Island was a veritable bone yard, with carcasses and skeletons scattered around his grim hideout. During his trial in East Yorkshire, it was afterwards repeated in hushed voices that the vagrant had collapsed vomiting on to all fours, howling like an animal. His appearance began to take on the form of a monstrous wolf and there was an immense struggle to subdue him. Eventually he was restrained and dragged off into the countryside, where he was strung up and hanged.

There are signs that Read's Island was inhabited at one point. A 1734 census had it named as Old Warp, and there are the remains of an isolated farmstead there. But the story is likely to be an outrageous piece of folklore created by superstitious villagers to scare their children into being good, or otherwise a complete fabrication.

However, it is not the only rumour of the were-folk in Lincolnshire: Christopher Marlowe's *Legends Of The Fenland People* (1926) noted several such anecdotes. A bizarre piece of folklore claims that in the mid-1700s, the people of Gedney Dyke would keep themselves locked in their hovels and houses at night, terrified of a barking, howling creature that roamed the area where a witch called Old

The Dragon Rock at Dragonby: a petrified dragon?

Mother Nightshade lived. The people gave the woman a wide berth...all, that is, except a young man named John Culpepper. Culpepper was a simple youth, and he had been spurned in his quest to find true love with the village beauty, so his answer was to seek the advice of the witch.

One day Culpepper found himself in the witch's den. Two insane, hissing cats and a scruffy jackdaw in a cage were Old Mother Nightshade's companions (or familiars), but the boy, being a simpleton, was unafraid. He merely asked the woman how he could take revenge on the village beauty for spurning him and breaking his heart. Old Mother Nightshade gave him a box of sweetmeats and said he should present them to the object of his unrequited affections. Then, a few days later, he should report back to the witch where he would learn something very much to his advantage.

John Culpepper did as he was bid. A few nights later, under the full moon, he made his way back to the witch's dwelling to learn what would become of the woman who had spurned him. The old witch beckoned him in, then told the youth to sit tight with his eyes closed until she told him otherwise.

Eventually a distorted voice told him to open his eyes. To his horror the youth found himself gazing at an immense wolf-like creature reared up on its hind legs in front of him. The beast was covered in thick, brown hair and as the snarling, drooling monstrosity moved towards him it dawned on the simple youth that it had all been a trick...he had been lured back on the night of the full moon.

That night the locals blocked their doors and fastened their windows shut to keep out the horrific howling and screaming that was carried on the wind from Old Mother Nightshade's hovel. The following day at dawn the villagers formed a mob and marched to the cottage, but it was too late: the witch had fled, and all that remained of the unfortunate youth was a pile of blood-soaked skeletal remains and bloodied paw prints around the mess as of a giant beast. The village parson was fetched, but he refused to have anything to do with such supernatural ungodliness, so the assembled crowd burned the cottage to the ground.

Old Mother Nightshade was never again seen, but it is said that for some time afterwards the distant howling of the wolf was to be heard rolling across the Fens on the nights of the full moon. It is said that the foundations of the burnt-out cottage are in the vicinity of the Chequers Inn, and Marlowe noted that even as he wrote, the people in Gedney still claimed to sometimes hear the blood-curdling howl of a wild animal.

Another such legend concerns a terrifying encounter with a were-creature sometime in the early-to-mid-1800s. The tale relates how a young student of archaeology came across an ancient skeleton with the body of a human and a wolf's head, while digging in peatland at Langrick Fen, near – appropriately enough – Dogdyke. He took the sinister skull back to his cottage where he studied it, but he could make nothing out of his find and rationalised it as belonging to an exhibit perhaps abandoned by a travelling fair.

That very night a rapping at the windowpane roused the young man out of his sleep to investigate. Outside in the darkness of the back premises his eyes fell on a moving, black shape; peering closer the form defined itself as a human being with a wolf's head, which was looking at him through the glass and snarling viciously. The creature drew back its clawed arm to smash the glass, and at this the terrified young man regained the power of movement. He threw himself into the kitchen and stoutly barricaded the door while all manner of smashing and commotion sounded from behind.

For the rest of the night the archaeologist sat frozen with fear as the sounds of the animal moving around outside, trying to find a way to get to him, met his ears. When first light fell he cautiously ventured out of the kitchen to find the house a shambles. Hastily collecting the skeletal remains, he took them back to the peatland where he had discovered them and fearfully reburied them exactly as he had found them, deep in the ground. The creature never returned to the cottage after this.

Marlowe also noted a rumoured incident that had taken place in a hamlet near Crowland in the late 19th century. A lady artist, from London, had taken herself off into the Fens to make sketches. She was staying with a farming family, and on her way home in the dusk she encountered the farmstead's live-in helper – a young, attractive widow – in the lane. The widow acted strangely and gradually fell behind the lady artist, who turned to peer into the gloom for her mysterious companion. What she saw was the young widow drop on to all fours and transform into a terrifying wolf-like creature, which now bounded at her. The lady artist shone a 'pocket torch' at the monster's eyes – upon which it vanished instantly. When she arrived back at the farmstead the artist found that the young widow had never left the building...but had fallen to the floor in front of the farmer and his wife screaming that she had been blinded by lightning. Marlowe suggested that the widow was telepathically 'projecting' herself in the form of a wolf to attack the lady artist, but to what end he could not say.

There are, it should be noted, similar stories attached to the giant phantom black hound known as Hairy Jack: in Blyborough a Victorian woman wielding an umbrella lashed out at the beast, only for her 'weapon' to pass through it. But Hairy Jack was rarely considered bloodthirsty. So stick to the path...and beware the moon...!

SPRING-HEELED JACK

The name of the diabolical, laughing bogeyman is well known. He held England in a grip of fear for some 67 years, leaping out of the fog to attack before bounding with superhuman strength back into the mists of Victorian London. But this creature appeared in other parts of the country, and he even put in a brief – but spectacular – appearance in Lincolnshire.

He was Spring-Heeled Jack, and even today no one really has much idea who (or what) he was, where he came from...or where he went to. The best description of this fiendish entity came from a young girl in London, who, in 1838, stood before a magistrate in Lambeth and described the hideous form that had attacked her in February of that year. Jane Alsop had been brought rushing to the door of her back street house in Bow by frantic knocking from outside.

A figure stood in the gloom at the front gate. 'I'm a police officer,' the form said, 'For God's sake bring me a light, for we have caught Spring-Heeled Jack in the lane!!'

Young Jane rushed for a lantern and took it outside to the policeman. Her heart pounded, for legends of the strange humanoid figure bounding through the air in great leaps, terrifying women and travellers, were sweeping the area. As she handed the lantern to the man, the court in Lambeth was told, he had grabbed her head and torn at her dress and body. Jane had managed to escape, but as she fled screaming the thing rushed up behind her and grabbed her hair. But the young girl's screams had alerted her sisters in the house, and other folk were attracted by the noise of the commotion. The attacker – whoever he was – shot away into the darkness and escaped.

As she stood in court, Jane described her attacker thus. He had worn, she stated, a sort of helmet on his head, and a tight-fitting white costume like an oilskin covered his body. His face was that of a demon, and his eyes blazed like red fireballs. The hands that had torn her dress in the attack had been icy cold claws and the thing had spat blue and white flames at her. His frame had been tall, thin and strong.

Over the years this demonical vision was variously reported at places as diverse as Aldershot, the English midlands, Sheffield and Caistor in Norfolk in 1877. By the time this laughing, monstrous entity arrived in Lincolnshire, its appearance had changed somewhat. By this time, perhaps reflecting his rustic surroundings, the phantom was reportedly wearing some kind of sheep or goatskin. There is some confusion as to whether the creature appeared in Caistor, Lincolnshire, and it is likely that the reports of his appearance there had become confused with the alleged appearances of the demon in Norfolk. Rumours were spreading across southern Lincolnshire of a bounding entity that would leap out of the darkness to terrify the local folk – and his abilities had grown in stature too. He no longer merely leapt great distances, soared over walls or melted into the darkness; he was now reported as leaping over small buildings, and bounding from cobbles to rooftops and back again.

The *Illustrated Police News* of 3 November 1877 covered this story extensively, citing as its source a stringer in Lincoln who contributed the details of Jack's visit for the publication. It was claimed that

Newport Arch, Lincoln, allegedly scaled by Spring-Heeled Jack.

for some nights the neighbourhood had been greatly disturbed by '…a man dressed in a sheepskin, or something of the kind, with a long white tail to it. The man who is playing this mischief has springs to his boots, and can jump to a height of 15 to 20 feet.' Recently the creature had jumped upon a college and managed to get inside a window on the roof. Once inside he had terrified the young girls: one girl had apparently been severely traumatised by the incident (which is in keeping with the entity's apparent deviant behaviour towards women). Large groups of men formed nightly, but could not catch him. Two men, armed with guns, fired at him as he leapt up Newport Arch, but it appeared the sheepskin that he wore had somehow deflected the bullets. He disappeared over the rooftops and soon appeared in another part of the town, where another crowd gathered as he was seen running along 'the wall of the new barracks'. A publican fired at him but again the shot appeared to have no effect.

The question of what this terrifying monstrosity was remains a puzzle. It apparently spoke good English, as Jane Alsop's testimony indicates, but if it were human then by the time it terrified the good folk of Lincoln it would have been terrorising for some 40 years, and any human perpetrator would have had to be 60. The creature's behaviour is what we would now recognise as being that of a sexual predator, and perhaps hysterical shock accounted for much of the reports of his abilities. But his alleged gravity-defying leaps and demonic appearance appear to suggest something else. Added to this is the detail that soldiers at Aldershot, as well as the vigilantes in Lincoln, opened fire with no result. Spring-Heeled Jack's visit to Lincoln is likely destined to remain an enigma, for when explanations for him include a marooned space alien, an eccentric young Victorian Marquis, an insane acrobat, an escaped kangaroo and a hideous demon, you know you are truly in the world of the unanswerable.

THE WILD MAN OF THE WOODS

If there is one type of cryptozoological creature that is not easily associable with the British Isles, then it is giant, hairy man-beasts such as the Yeti of the Himalayas, the American Sasquatch or the Australian Yowie. However, some may be interested to know that such primitive throwbacks to a different era have every so often been reported here. Maybe the most famous British man-beast is the fabled Big Grey Man of Ben McDhui, although there are recent reports of a giant, hairy man-like figure that haunts the Peak District. I have heard rumours of a Sasquatch-like entity that is said to live in Sherwood Forest, Nottinghamshire, although perhaps such urban myths are bound to link themselves to any large body of woodland. Lincolnshire also has an ancient legend of such a creature.

Some 300 years ago a wild man roamed the thickly-forested woodland near the isolated hamlet of Stainfield, east of Lincoln. Like some prehistoric relic from the caveman era, he wandered among the trees armed with a great club and local folklore describes him as a naked semi-human, covered in hair. One Francis Tyrwhitt-Drake was presented with the task of hunting down the wildman after it had long terrorised the area, killing and making off with livestock, and even killing humans with its great club. He stumbled across the caveman in the depths of the woodland when his attention was drawn towards the angry twittering of a group of peewits – the bird's nest had been disturbed when the wildman had laid himself asleep on a bank by a pit. Wasting no time, Tyrwhitt-Drake drew his sword and ran the creature through.

Pub sign at Short Ferry displays the supposed 'wild man-beast'.

The story is recounted in the Revd James Alpas Penny's *Folklore Round Horncastle* (1915), but an article in *Lincolnshire Life* (Feb 2005) effectively dissected Penny's story. A funerary helmet (long held to be part of Tyrwhitt-Drake's armour) once hung in St Andrew's Church, Stainfield, and was adorned with a wild man motif. This motif is now thought to have been a representation of the mediaeval woodwose, symbolic of fertility, strength, etc. Likewise, peewits which adorned the family coat of arms in memory of the strange event are more likely there in memory of another Tyrwhitt legend – that the first of the Tyrwhitt's was located unconscious after a heroic battle, by the fuss a group of lapwings were making around him. Tattered rags that also hung in the church – said to be the creature's clothing – were the remnants of banners created by the Tyrwhitt ladies. Furthermore, the Tyrwhitt-Drakes were not resident in Stainfield and played no part in local politics.

But maybe the wildman story *did* have some basis on an actual event – only the incident took place earlier than the 300-odd years ago as put forward by Revd Penny in 1915. Far to the north of Stainfield in Bigby there is a tantalising piece of evidence that lends just the tiniest bit of credence to the old tale. In the church of this small town east of Brigg there can be found the impressive monument to Sir Robert Tyrwhitt and his wife Elizabeth Oxenbridge. Images of their 22 children have been carved into the base of the monument, and curiously what can be described as a large hairy man can be seen laid across Sir Robert's feet. Sir Robert died on 10 May 1572, and the Bigby tomb dates to 1581, indicating that the Tyrwhitt association with the slaying of the wild man was well established by the late Elizabethan era.

What is interesting is the way that variations of the old tale appear to reinvent themselves for successive generations, with many locals (as adults) recalling first being told the legend of a hairy man-beast that was supposed to inhabit the thickly-wooded land in the gloomy countryside between Stainfield and Langworth; although, as stated earlier, maybe such rumours will always be common currency near such places as Stainfield Wood and Hardy Gang Wood. The Tyrwhitt Arms at Short Ferry displays the Tyrwhitt crest as its pub sign, and the man-beast, or woodwose if you like, can be seen thereon. This alone perhaps ensures that stories of man-beasts in the forests of the area will not die out.

If the savage man of Stainfield ever existed, perhaps he was indeed little more than a vagrant, outlaw or shipwrecked foreign national, who had reverted to a wild and lawless existence. Nevertheless, it is all too tempting to speculate that he may have been a relic of prehistoric man, a throwback to the Neanderthal age...and it is this fanciful idea that has kept the tale of the Stainfield wildman cropping up every so often in various guises throughout the generations. And the mythology of the uncivilised primitive man persists even to this day, with claims that he (or a descendant) is 'out there'...

MARINE MONSTERS OFF THE EAST COAST

The River Welland rises near Market Harborough, Leicestershire, and flows in an easterly direction for some 35 miles, passing through Stamford and then out into the Wash by way of Market Deeping, Deeping St James, Crowland, Cowbit, Spalding and finally Fosdyke. Beyond the banks of the River Welland lies fertile arable land, much of it marine silt, which is ideal for the bulb production that Spalding is so famous for. But this stretch of water through South Holland is allegedly inhabited by a gigantic marine animal, which some say is none other than a plesiosaur. There have allegedly been sightings of this monster for generations, if not centuries, and as with Nessie far away to the north in Scotland, the River Welland creature has earned the nickname 'Welly'. The legend of Welly is highlighted in a suspiciously tongue-in-cheek article by the *Stamford Mercury* on 31 March 2001. A statement proffered by an expert on such prehistoric relics at the University of Leicester Archaeology Department claimed that the best time to see Welly would be between 10:00am and noon on 1 April – the date clearly giving the game away there. The article in the *Stamford Mercury* focussed on the disappearance of an angler a few days before, and it is quick to make a connection between the missing angler and the voracious carnivore said to dwell within the river's depths. The article begins with the words 'Has a local angler become a victim of Stamford's oldest mystery?' According to the article, Welly has been linked to the disappearances of many anglers and animals along the banks of the River Welland. One assumes that the whole story of Welly is an April Fool's joke, although perhaps tales locally of 'something' in the water *do* go back generations, and the *Stamford Mercury* used the legend as the basis for a jape.

More substantive is the mysterious, giant creature periodically witnessed off the east coast of England. The creature's first appearance off the Lincolnshire coast was brief. A Mr R.W. Midgeley, from Boston, was holidaying in Trusthorpe in 1937 or 1938, and he was looking along the sea wall when he saw something 400 yards or so from the water's edge. Four or five 'half links' protruding out of the sea indicated to Mr Midgeley that he was looking at a huge serpentine monster that was only partly visible, the rest – including the head – being submerged. After five minutes it disappeared under the water from view, and Mr Midgeley's experience was published in the *Skegness Standard* of 6 November 1966. Mr Midgeley was quite sure that what he saw was a solid, living creature and, furthermore, he was positive it was not a school of dolphins or porpoises swimming in single file. It was apparently moving northwards towards Yorkshire, for it was also spotted around this time by folk in Easington, Yorkshire, who stared aghast at a strange snake-like sea animal with a flat, serpentine head. It had a greenish colour to its skin. As it shot across the water in humped glides, this marine mystery appeared to be gasping for air.

What could be the best description of this creature was reported in the *Daily Telegraph* on the 1 March 1934 and concerned a local coastguard named Herbert, who spotted it as he walked the seafront at Filey, between Scarborough and Bridlington in Yorkshire, one evening. Unnervingly, the monster had come ashore on to the beach, and Mr Herbert's encounter was at a frightening distance of about six yards away from it.

He described his encounter thus. In the darkness of the night on the beach he heard a bizarre growling sound, which to his ears reminded him of a dozen dogs, and at this he switched on his torch. To his astonishment the light illuminated a huge serpentine neck, eight-feet tall and a yard thick. It had large, saucer-like eyes and a mouth a foot wide, and in the semi-darkness behind the neck Herbert estimated a large body some 30-feet long lying on the sand. The frightened man picked up some stones and threw them at the beast, and his appearance seemed to startle it – for it moved away slowly, rolling its bulk from side to side and growling defensively. It did not appear to have a tail. The black bulk of its body appeared to have two humps, and the creature had four short 'legs' that ended in gigantic flippers. Once it took flight, it moved quickly, rolling its body until it reached the water's edge and slipped into the sea. From a vantage point on a cliff top, Herbert saw the two large eyes of the beast shining 300 yards out to sea.

There were on-and-off sightings of a gigantic, unidentified dark-coloured marine creature in the choppy waters off Skegness in 1960. But in 1966 the sea serpent made a quick appearance in the waters off Chapel-St-Leonards, south of Mablethorpe. On 16 October of that year a couple from Sheffield spotted a creature with six or seven humps 100 yards from the shoreline as they walked along the beach. It came from the direction of Chapel Point. The thing produced a serpentine head as it swam at about 8mph parallel with the shoreline, before it was lost from sight as it went in the direction of Ingoldmells. The gentleman concerned affirmed himself a non-believer in such things as sea monsters, but after attempting to rationalise what he had seen he eventually gave up and had to admit to himself that he had seen some giant form of unknown sea creature. His wife was equally adamant in her assertion that it had not been a whale, seals, a flock of birds on the surface of the water, a torpedo or even a miniature submarine. It had been a living, unidentifiable sea creature, and their account of this appeared in the *Skegness Standard* of 19 October 1966.

So what was – or is – this monster of the deep? Conventional wisdom dictates that it was an animal known to us – perhaps Mr Herbert's flashlight fell upon a rearing Elephant Seal or a large Stellar Sea Lion, although both of these would in themselves be noteworthy for their out-of-place appearance along England's east coast. But if the various witness descriptions are anything to go by then the animal appears to resemble a plesiosaur, a small-headed, long-necked sea dragon with a short, round body and four flippers, from the Cretaceous period of 130 million years ago.

In 2002 an amateur palaeontologist found the four-metre long skeleton of such an animal sticking out of a cliff just south of Filey, but is it possible that remnants of the species survived into the 20th century? Could such a thing happen? Perhaps the countless investigators who have camped on the shore or submerged the peaty depths of Loch Ness are looking in the wrong place, for it would appear that the east coast sea serpent is due an appearance very soon.

The blustery coast of Anderby Creek, just north of Chapel-St-Leonards.

CRYPTOZOOLOGY

Outside of folklore, one of the earliest accounts of an unknown creature in Lincolnshire comes from the 18th century. In 1743 an 'amphibious freak' was discovered asleep in the 'Fossdyke Wash' – presumably meaning along the banks of the Wash as it snakes inland past Fosdyke in the Lincolnshire Fens. The creature was captured by fishermen: it was some eight-feet long and had webbed feet. This is not a million miles in description from a rumoured creature which Ethel Rudkin wrote in 1936 was still feared by keelmen at the Jenny Hurn bend in the River Trent, between Wildsworth and Owston Ferry far away on the other side of Lincolnshire. The creature would emerge from the murky water and crawl up the bank into the fields to feed. Descriptions of this thing were unclear, although it apparently had large eyes, long shaggy hair and – bizarrely – tusks like a walrus. Keelmen would relate eerie tales of something in the water that would bump the side of their boats while they sat anchored, awaiting the turn of the tide. Few apparently cared for this stretch of the Trent at night.

In the annals of the paranormal, the tale of the night the Devil walked in Devon is a classic mystery; *The Times* of London reported that during the evening of 8–9 February 1885, there was a heavy snowfall and the inhabitants of various Devonshire villages awoke to find the new snow marked with the footprints of some 'strange and mysterious animal, endowed with the power of ubiquity, as the footprints were to be seen in all kinds of mysterious places...' The tracks appeared to be 'more like a biped than a quadruped, and the steps were generally eight inches in advance of each other. The impressions of the feet closely resembled that of a donkey's shoe'. This description gave rise to the fearful suggestion that it was Satan who had patrolled the snow-covered landscape of Devon.

A report on the 'footprints' in *Notes And Queries* in 1889/1890 by R.H. Busk, entitled *Phenomenal footprints in snow, S. Devon*, drew on contemporary accounts for its investigation, and the explanations – both natural and unnatural – put forward since could fill a small book on their own. However, Busk's inquires turned up late evidence that such a phenomenon was also observed in snow at Weymouth (in Dorset) and in Lincolnshire. The creature they called the Devil had stalked the land that winter, not merely Devonshire.

Rudkin's *Lincolnshire Folklore* (1936) also noted how a Mr B of Willoughton had seen the strangest of creatures one evening while cycling along the Kirton Low Road. A little creature, about the size of a rabbit, had jumped into the road out of the hedge: it was bipedal and the witness noted that the little being had horns on its head. The creature appeared 'on the west side' and started running in front of him. Whenever he manoeuvred his bicycle the thing skirted the road so he couldn't pass it. It moved at quite a speed, eventually hopping on to the grass verge and out of sight as the cyclist neared a group of people coming from the other direction. This incident probably occurred around the early 20th century, although there is precious little detail – such as whether the little horned creature wore clothes, what its face looked like, etc. But despite the pointlessness of this encounter, there is a certain ring of truth about it – he told Ms Rudkin that '...its feet clattered on the road'. One is left with the feeling that Mr B either told Ms Rudkin an outright lie, or else he did see something very strange on the road that evening.

In mid-June 1977 a group of boys from a boarding school were going into Bardney one afternoon when they caught a glimpse from their bus of a weird entity that they could only describe as a 'stick man'. The thing was sighted from roughly 150 metres away, and it was difficult to see as it moved along on the other side of a hedge.

Details were difficult to make out. The thing moved in a spasmodic fashion, perhaps moving as though a puppet on a string might, and it appeared to be black or dark in colour. Its head was circular and the boys could make out no features on the face.

There is some suggestion that this sighting was linked to a worldwide 'flap' of UFO reports involving all sorts of weird humanoids, but the story of the Bardney stick man involves no mention of an accompanying flying saucer.

During an investigation into the disused church at Skidbrooke, which was, in a former life, St Botolph's, the Bassetlaw Ghost Research Group (BGRG) unearthed evidence of something quite unexpected. The gloomy church was investigated because of alleged hauntings and satanic activity, but the group claimed they had filmed something equally unusual. They claimed to have filmed the so-called 'Rods'.

Evidence of Rods, or Roswell Rods as they are sometimes known, was first discovered by a Mexican named Jose Escamilla in the 90s. They are thin, unidentified organic life forms that move through the air quicker than the human eye can perceive – but can be captured on camcorders and the like. They appear as string-like lines playing among the clouds and it would seem they can be anything up to 100-feet long.

The Jenny Hurn bend is the site of a lonely pumping station these days.

Some claim that Rods are a form of fish-like organism in the sky, while others reckon that they are possibly invertebrates. Whatever they are, they are among the most exciting cryptozoological 'discoveries' of recent years – and it would seem that the strange creatures are around all of us. What are thought to be Rods have been filmed in the United States, Canada, New Zealand, Iraq...basically worldwide.

In all, some 200-odd Rods were filmed shooting about the night sky at Skidbrooke. Parapsychologist David Wharmby told the *Louth Leader* in January 2004, 'They are about four inches to a foot in length and are not visible to the naked eye. They could be flying insects, aliens or something of a paranormal nature.' Strange flashes were observed in an otherwise calm sky, and David Wharmby claimed his footage is the first-ever example of the Rods to be cited in the United Kingdom.

The BGRG may be a little premature in claiming they have captured Rods on film, but their assertion is none the less fascinating. If Rods can appear anywhere in the world, then why shouldn't they have been at Skidbrooke Church at that time?

THINGS THAT COME FOR US

I was told this story several years ago and it still makes me think about things I would rather not, given that I – like many others – have suffered from a sleeping disorder called sleep paralysis.

Sleep paralysis is sometimes characterised by an overwhelming knowledge that something horrible is making its way towards you while you slumber, and that unless you can force yourself awake then the 'thing' will kill you in your sleep. The fear is terrific at the time, and sufferers will torment themselves, twisting to and fro in a terrible effort to awaken themselves before it is too late. This goes beyond a mere nightmare, as the sufferer is *convinced* there is something coming up the stairs or is actually in the room with them. Upon waking, however, the preceding terror is often more-or-less forgotten.

The disorder is a relatively common one, but in some cultures (including western) it is believed that the torment is caused by a demon, ghost or a witch, sitting on the sufferer's chest. Sometimes it is called Old Hag Syndrome. In Turkey it is thought a jinn causes the condition. That sleep paralysis is something other than a medical condition is a worldwide belief and it is with this in mind that D told me a truly-unsettling story dating from the mid-1970s when he lived alone on the outskirts of Tattershall.

D was at that time in his mid-30s and suffered regularly from sleep paralysis, characterised by the certainty that something small and hideously ugly was in the house, and that he had to wake up and fend it off. Mostly, upon awakening, he forgot the torment he had suffered in his sleep, but on one occasion he awoke with the reason for his terror very vivid in his mind.

D referred to the 'thing' that tormented him as the 'Pumpkin Man', and he assures me that as he made his way on to the landing he is absolutely positive he was awake and not still dreaming. As his eyes grew accustomed to the gloom, his heart leapt into his mouth when his vision fell upon a bulbous, white face that poked through the rails of the banister. The head was facing in his direction but did not seem to be looking at him, for its eyelids were puffed up and its eyes closed. The thing's lips were huge and purple, and its nose crooked and pointed. The head was shaped like a small pumpkin.

In his utter fright D turned the landing light on and at once the face vanished. Petrified, he made his way down the stairs and through the house, switching lights on as he went, but could not find the creature. In the kitchen he heard a noise, as of an animal skittering across the flooring, but he was forced to return to bed very afraid – leaving every light on in the house.

I do not doubt the story for a minute, but whether such incidents are hallucinatory, dreams, or – heaven forbid – real is an unnerving question for sufferers of sleep paralysis. D told me that the following morning all the lights in the house were still switched on, and he recalls the strange 'Pumpkin Man's' face very clearly. Perhaps he caught a glimpse of one of the bogles that worldwide folklore claims create sleep paralysis…so they can come and take their victims in their sleep.

THE DEAD HAND

South-west of Lincoln lies the village of Whisby, and 1989 found me in employment at Whisby Garden Centre for my first Saturday job, aged 15, while still attending school. The place was a lot smaller then, both in staff and scope, but – just as today – was surrounded by drains, wetlands and vast, flooded sand and gravel pits, some of which encroached on to the garden centre and its farmstead. These pits are known as the Whisby Pits, a hangover from the last glaciation, and while some have been given over to fishing and water skiing, for the most part the area is now managed by the Lincolnshire Wildlife Trust and is classed as a Local Nature Reserve. While idly walking along the edge of one of these great ponds as a young man in 1989, I was warned by an aged fellow employee not to get too close to the edge; the man (a typical Lincolnshire octogenarian, tough, weather beaten and smoking woodbines, whose name I sadly cannot recall) told me that if I went too close to the water then 'the Dead Hand would get me'.

I recall asking whether a murder had been committed there, but could not get any more information out of the old man. As a youth, I was left with the image of some zombie-like corpse crawling out of the water, but as an adult I have found the possible explanation for this cryptic comment even more fascinating. M.C. Balfour wrote an article for *Folk-lore* in 1891 called *Legends Of The Lincolnshire Cars Part II*, in which she narrated the legend of a foolish lad called Tom Pattison who, long ago, had ventured into the wild, swampy morass of darkest northern Lincolnshire and where he was allegedly attacked by a dreadful creature from the wetlands called the Dead Hand, or Dead Fingers. It was, '…the Dead Hand itself, with the rotting flesh dropping off the mouldy bones and its dreadful fingers gripping tight hold of Tom's hand as if they were growed together,' which pulled the unfortunate lad into the swamps.

The Dead Hand may be a local variant of a creature from Celtic folklore known as Rawhead and Bloody Bones, or Tommy Rawhead: an Irish hobgoblin who punished naughty children by dragging them away into swamps. The legend of this malignant creature spread to northern England, and in the 'modern' era he became a bogle who hid in the grime under sink pipes and dragged children to a grisly fate down the drains and through the sewage system.

It would seem the old man was recalling the ancient legend of the Dead Hand, or of Tommy Rawhead himself, but as to whether he *believed* in the creature's existence I severely doubt. I suspect, if anything, he was remembering a turn-of-phrase perhaps passed through generations of his family, maybe going back to an era centuries ago when people genuinely believed in the Dead Hand, or Tommy Rawhead – some descriptions of whom allude to the entity as a burnt, scabbed or hideously scarred mutation of a man, or a gremlin with twisted flesh.

CHAPTER 11

MYSTERIES OF THE SKY

INTRODUCTION

O n 28 July 1995 people across the county of Lincolnshire looked to the skies in awe and not a little fear – for it must have seemed like the invasion of earth by some terrifying species from outer space had begun. The skies were lit up, according to the *Lincolnshire Echo*, by 'a mysterious spectacle of bright lights and flashes'. One man who lived in Monks Road, Lincoln, rang RAF Waddington to report that he had seen a bright light shoot from the sky and land behind Lincoln Cathedral. In Boston, the emergency services received reports of a fiery object that had fallen from the sky and crashed in the marshland north-west of Long Sutton and north of Holbeach.

In Nettleham an inspector at the county police headquarters saw the strange lights in the sky, and the phenomenon was also seen by his fellow officers, who radioed in incredulous reports of extraterrestrial activity.

In this instance, a spokesperson from RAF Waddington later told the *Echo* that there had been no alien invasion that weird night: the lights were merely a meteor shower known as Aquarids. The flashes were caused by the rocks burning up when they entered the earth's atmosphere. The spectacle always took place on or about 28 July every year, and it was well observed in 1995 because of the clear skies and hot evening temperature.

For the most part, however, aerial curiosities in Lincolnshire are concerned with strange lights and unidentifiable objects in the sky. In 1947, as war-weary Britain braced itself for one of the worst snowy winters ever recorded, there was another emergency taking place behind the scenes – the raids by so-called 'ghost planes' along the eastern coast of England. The RAF were aware of them, fighter jets were scrambled on a number of occasions…yet nothing was ever seen, other than on radar, or caught. During this period the east of England received visits from what the RAF termed unidentified high-flying aircraft, although such incursions had already taken place in late 1945 to early 1946. But the mystery first came to the attention of the British public on 29 April 1947 when the *London Daily Mail* included on its front page the headline 'Ghost Plane Over Coast, RAF Spot It – Can't Catch It'. It claimed that the Royal Air Force had monitored a 'blip' on their radar that had made several sorties into England at a high altitude, crossing the coast at roughly the same spot. It then passed near Norwich, through East Anglia and penetrated deep inland before vanishing. The object moved at some 400mph and although the RAF scanners watched in the hope they could catch it on its return journey, they never did so. The invasions took place at midnight, and, according to the *London Daily Mail*, its speed far outstripped that of the UK's top night fighters of the time, the Mosquitoes. The UFO was labelled 'X 362' and the flight path became so familiar to officers in Fighter Command's operations room that it was nicknamed 'Charlie'. It was assumed to be hostile. Although the assumption at the time was that the mysterious craft were pilots on Soviet reconnaissance missions, or smugglers, nothing was proven – and who, or what, the 'ghost planes' were remains unsolved, as does the reason why they were never spotted making 'return journeys'.

Since then, there have been an almost never-ending avalanche of UFO reports covered by the local media, growing in intensity and frequency every decade. The phenomenon peaked, perhaps, in the late 1990s/early 2000s, with a substantial 'flap' in north-east Lincolnshire: a wave effect of anomalous reports of weird sky phenomena that presented no coherence other than their locality. Nick Pope adds a sensible note of caution about UFO encounters in his *Open Skies, Closed Minds* (2000), in which he reminds readers that Lincolnshire is a county studded with airbases, notably RAF Waddington – which is home to the early-warning Sentry aircraft. These have a large, saucer-shaped radome mounted on the rear of the fuselage and Pope recounts how the base's community relations officer was travelling by Waddington's perimeter one evening as a Sentry was coming into land. A red Metro up ahead, apparently distracted, flew off the road and came to a stop in the ditch. When the officer approached the crashed car to offer help, she was met by the insane sight of the driver babbling incoherently that flying saucers and aliens were coming to get him. Slightly more perplexing, however, although still apparently terrestrial, was the report of a truly-gigantic triangular craft resembling a Delta or Vulcan bomber, that allegedly swept silently and slowly over Alford late one night in 1978. The craft was some four-times larger than a normal Vulcan and flew frighteningly low, about 50 feet above ground, before swooping majestically in the direction of Spilsby. No noise, smoke or vibrations followed in its wake, and two dazzling lights at the front blacked out much detail of the strange craft. In Lincolnshire RAF circles, perhaps not surprisingly, the story of the 'Gigantic Vulcan' is familiar, and it is almost classed as modern folklore these days.

Some aerial oddities are of a different calibre again. Take the following enigmatic report that appeared in the *Daily Graphic* on 22 March 1919, which apparently formed part of a letter to an unknown Lincolnshire newspaper, date also unknown. The report turned up in a Bible owned by one Bill Creasey of Horbling, who served in the Lincolnshire Regiment in World War One. It was submitted to *Lincolnshire Life* magazine by Bill's son-in-law. The report read:

'An inquest was held at Rauceby, near Sleaford, yesterday on Captain Robin Jaspar Lunn, Lincolnshire Regiment, and 2nd Lieut William Pegg, 10th Warwicks, who were killed as they were following the meet of the Belvoir Hounds along the main road at Rauceby in the trap in which they had driven from the Caythorpe Court Convalescent Home. It is alleged that an aeroplane swooped down on the trap fatally injuring the two officers, and then rose again and proceeded on its journey; The inquest was adjourned.'

How could such a thing be possible? Unless by some million-to-one chance the 'aeroplane' clumsily landed on the trap and crushed the two men before alighting again, in the manner of those primitive machines in the early days of flight. Such an accident seems very curious though, to say the least.

But some of the encounters noted here are certainly not of terrestrial origins. Hovering glass discs, silver spheres, abductions by aliens, Men in Black and oddly-behaving light formations that cause power cuts do indeed suggest something truly out of this world.

ATMOSPHERIC ODDITIES: THE END OF THE WORLD?

One Henry Wilson recorded in 1719 *A Strange and Wonderful Account of the Appearance of a Fiery Meteor in the air: which was seen by many Hundreds of Spectators, at the town of Boston in Lincolnshire etc. Stamford, Lincolnshire.* Wilson was perhaps a man with scientific leanings, for he appears to note the event was an astronomical wonder. No doubt the people in southern Lincolnshire, perhaps more superstitiously-minded, thought the world was coming to an end, as is evidenced by a doom-laden prophecy from Gedney dated 1745. This warned of fires and lights dancing in the sky above St Mary's Church, which, it seems, heralded the raising of ghosts.

Five years later in 1750 a spectacular aurora borealis occurred in Spalding during nationwide earth tremors on 23 August. Sometimes called the Northern Lights, auroras are natural light displays that often appear as a bright-reddish glow, creating the impression that the sun is rising from an unusual direction. The phenomena can be seen at the North Pole and has been witnessed in the UK, but mainly in Scotland.

In the year 1799 strange phenomena in the sky frightened the people of England. On 19 September many looked skyward at 8:30pm and witnessed in terror a 'beautiful ball blazing with white light', which passed from the north west to the south east. It moved speedily and noiselessly, with a 'gentle tremulous motion' and scattered red sparks in its wake. On 12 November a violent electrical storm presaged the appearance of what appeared to be a large pillar of red fire. It passed north to south over Hereford and frightened the people who lived in the Forest of Dean. This was at 5:45am, and on this night the moon shone with fierce brilliance. On 19 November the people of Huncoates in Lincolnshire witnessed a ball of fire that shot across the early morning sky at 6:00am for 30 seconds, leaving a showery trial of sparks and flashes behind it.

This strange tale of what was presumably some kind of natural phenomena was recorded in an issue of *Gentleman's Magazine* at the time. With typical foreboding some claimed that the aerial display announced the end of the world, and there was much fear across England that autumn.

The Huncoates Fireball, although in all likelihood a natural fireworks display, is often cited as an early example of possible UFO activity; however, it is unclear where 'Huncoates' in Lincolnshire actually is.

THE PHANTOM SCARESHIPS

The phantom 'scareship' mystery first gained public attention across the Atlantic Ocean in 1896. The first shaky test flights by airships in Europe were some way off, but in the Autumn of that year people in San Francisco, California, were reporting that huge cigar-shaped objects with bright lights were to be spotted floating in the sky. In 1897, with genuine airship activity still some months away, another wave of mysterious 'phantom airship' sightings were reported across the western and mid-western states. Rival newspapers speculated wildly as to what was going on and unknown, unnamed 'eccentric inventors' claimed the airships were their handiwork. But the sightings died away.

The unexplainable sightings proved to be a bizarre indication of what was to come in other parts of the world. For, in 1909, mysterious phantom Zeppelin invasions were reported in New Zealand, Australia and in particular the UK.

The first major sighting of a scareship in Britain came on 23 March 1909, when PC Kettle's ears were alerted to the steady buzz of a high-powered engine while he patrolled Cromwell Road in Peterborough. Looking skyward he was utterly dumbfounded – and not to say a little unnerved – by the sight of a gigantic oblong-shaped thing with a light attached to it, which sailed speedily through the sky. Although this sighting was at first dismissed as nonsense, it was followed by reports of giant airships from all over the UK in the months that followed. They were seen in Lincolnshire: over the Wash and in Lincoln itself. On 9 May the phantom airship was seen over Burghley House on the southern edge of Stamford. A Mr Cole told the *London Evening News* that he was in the park at 11 o'clock when he saw a light on the edge of the woodland which came from up in the night sky. The light rose and fell seven or eight times, and gradually Mr Cole realised that the searchlight was attached to a giant, dark cigar shape. The object sailed quickly from one edge of the woodland to the other and then a few minutes later turned back again. Mr Cole then watched it for 10 minutes as it gradually flew in the direction of Peterborough, Cambridgeshire.

Speculation was rife as to who piloted the scareships. In Lincolnshire there was direct suspicion that they were piloted by spies on reconnaissance missions. In 1909 the *Northern Daily Mail* reported how men working at Killingholme Marshes, near the strategic port of Immingham in north-east Lincolnshire, had been approached by unidentified men in a car who asked them if any airships had been noted in the area, and whether there were mines laid in the waters of the River Humber. Around the same time, a PC reported that at about 2:00am on 22 May he had witnessed a phantom dirigible hovering over Immingham Docks. He had been patrolling near the banks of the Humber when he had seen a light extending over the docks from the sky. Looking up, he saw 'a car, which was swaying gently in mid-air'. The searchlight remained for an hour until the constable went off duty. Was all this not evidence that the Germans were carrying out night-time spying manoeuvres? It is highly doubtful as to whether the Germans had the technology at this time. And while Immingham Docks would conceivably be of interest to foreign spies, what possible interest could they have had in Burghley House in Stamford? There the scareship gave itself away by shining a searchlight into the forest, a strange thing to do if on a 'secret mission': unless, perhaps, it was looking for something – or someone.

Three years later there was another wave of phantom airship sightings that began with a report of one over Sheerness in Kent in October 1912. In 1913 they were reported from Dover, Merthyr, Swansea, Liverpool, Manchester, Scarborough…and on 22 February an impressive sighting took place in the north-east Lincolnshire region. At 9:15pm the steamer *City of Leeds* was leaving the mouth of the River Humber. In the darkness of the night Captain Lundie, Second Officer Williams and the crew picked out something high in the sky over East Yorkshire. The object, said the captain, 'resembled a shark in appearance'. Furthermore, the thing had wings on either side and all witnessed the tail of the machine. No lights or searchlights were visible on the airship, which was clearly illuminated by the moon.

The airship was observed for about five minutes through binoculars, during which time it maintained its distant position in the sky. It crossed the River Humber and sailed in the direction of Grimsby before the captain and his men lost it from sight.

So who sent the scareships? The first and most obvious answer would be that they were, indeed, German Zeppelins. But by 1909 there were only three working dirigibles in Germany, owing to financial difficulties and a series of crashes. Only two were in the hands of the German army, neither of which were thought technologically capable of travelling as far as the British Isles or of undertaking the complicated manoeuvres the British scareships had done. Perhaps, then, the scareships were prototype British army airships? Again, this is unlikely, as the army's two airships – the *Nulli Secundus I* and the *Nulli Secundus II* – had been dismantled by 1909. By 1913 the British public at large were increasingly familiar with concepts such as flight and Zeppelins, and in the tension of pre-World War One Europe the question of the mysterious airships ended up being debated in the House of Commons. When questioned about an unidentifiable dirigible spotted in Glamorganshire, MP Mr Joynson-Hicks replied, 'I don't doubt the report at all, for though our own aircraft can only do 30 or 40 miles, the Zeppelin vessels can cross the Channel. I believe, in fact, that foreign dirigibles are crossing the English Channel at will. It is a very serious matter.' But the true answer as to where these phantom scareships came from, what their purpose was and who peopled them remains an enigma, tantalisingly out of reach. By 1916, when Europe was in the grip of World War One, there was certainly the capability *at that time* for giant airships to attack Lincolnshire: on 31 January it was noted that they passed over the county and dropped an incendiary bomb over Digby, which set fire to a barn. But if the technology and capability had simply not been there in 1909 nor as late as 1913, what were the scareships?

THE EARLIEST UFOs

One of the first of what would be considered 'modern' UFO sightings (i.e. post-1947 after Kenneth Arnold's highly-publicised sighting of nine flying saucers over Washington) in Lincolnshire occurred on 12 August 1954, when a man in Gosberton, south-east Lincolnshire, claimed he had spotted a glowing white disc flying rapidly at an altitude of about 40,000 feet. It was early evening, and the UFO left no vapour trail in its wake. It was totally noiseless.

It was early November 1954 when reports began circulating that the skies above Lincolnshire were not quiet. The UFO – labelled 'The Thing' – was first spotted by a farmer and his wife late one evening, whose attention had been alerted by a strange, skyborne sound 'like a humming top'. The farmer, 42-year-old Albert Smith, looked up and saw The Thing, as did his wife. This occurred at South Carlton, north of Lincoln, and as the strange object faded from view two Americans drove up to the couple. Mr Smith asked them if they had seen anything unusual in the sky just then, and the two Americans agreed that they had seen something in the sky that had quickly been lost from view. Detailed descriptions of The Thing were lacking, but Mr Smith told the *Lincolnshire Echo* some days later, 'It was definitely a flying saucer'.

Mr Smith later expanded on his description of the object. It had been, he stated, a big saucer-shaped craft with an orange light that flashed into life on its top. It appeared to have two smaller craft following it.

An investigative *Echo* reporter interviewed other witnesses to the UFO. In nearby Nettleham at around the same time as the South Carlton sightings, two men who had been sitting indoors had suddenly found themselves listening to a bizarre noise from above that sounded like, 'this weird humming-top noise'. The sound was so curious that the two men went outside to see what was causing it. As they stood there, their ears still detected the humming noise about them…but whatever was causing it could not be seen, either on the ground or in the air.

The reporter also located a Saxilby housewife who told him that earlier that very same evening she had been getting ready to go to a Women's Institute meeting when a bizarre chug-chugging noise roused her curiosity. The sound came from above, high in the sky, and it appeared to be travelling in a westerly direction. But the lady could not spy anything to account for the sounds. She was certain that the noises were not made by an aeroplane.

Reporting on the mystery, the *Lincolnshire Echo* speculated that The Thing could be some form of prototype RAF aircraft, adding that there was evidence to suggest that the Government had decided to spend more on modernising the RAF with speedy new aircraft and higher production of sophisticated guided missiles. But the RAF either could not or would not explain the sightings, claiming that all the aircraft at the nearest RAF base, Scampton, had returned by 9:30pm – well before Mr Smith had his encounter.

Quite possibly the Government were experimenting with prototype aircraft north of Lincoln that day. But one wonders what technology could render the aircraft apparently invisible to the witnesses in Nettleham and Saxilby?

THE CLEETHORPES 'GLASS DISC'

On 22 September 1956 the townsfolk of Cleethorpes, north-east Lincolnshire, looked skyward and witnessed what they could only describe as a 'glass disc' that hovered enigmatically.

It was Saturday afternoon, and in an article on the incident in *Flying Saucer Review* it was stated that 'thousands' observed the strange object that day. Some 54,000 feet in the air above the promenade they watched a glittering, spherical glass globe hovering against a backdrop of blue sky; the UFO seemed to have 'something white' inside it according to one witness. It remained stationary for about an hour, despite the estimated 40mph winds that gusted that day.

To the south, RAF Manby also picked up the thing on its radar and estimated it to have a diameter of about 80 feet, and a Meteorological Office spokesman at Manby stated categorically that it was not a balloon, after studying the UFO through a telescope. Two fighter jets were dispatched to investigate, but by the time they arrived in the area the strange disc was long gone. Neither could the object be seen from the ground by this time.

A contemporary report in the *Sunday Times* two days after the mystery sightings indicated that as well as being observed by radar from Manby, it could also be witnessed with the eye from the same location. What it was remains unexplained, although I understand that perhaps it made one last appearance *c*.1957 when two young lads playing on the West Common, Lincoln, saw what looked like a 'cloudy glass globe' in the sky.

THE SIXTIES AND SEVENTIES

Perhaps the most astonishing account of a UFO in 1960s Lincolnshire was the one submitted anonymously to the office of *The Unexplained* magazine in 1981. The witness began their strange tale with the words 'What I am about to tell you is the absolute truth.' His experience had taken place around 1968 as he had been making his way to the local shop in Susworth, a small village on the Lincolnshire side of the River Trent south of Scunthorpe.

It was summer, and at 6:30ish in the evening it was still light. As he walked, the witness became aware – perhaps subconsciously at first – of a totally unnatural stillness in the air: no birds or insect noises, etc. He theorised that this was perhaps what prompted him to look skywards.

When he did so, he saw something amazing. Half a mile or so in front of him was a 'big black object, something like the spinning tops we used to play with when we were children'. However, the mysterious craft appeared not to be spinning; indeed, no noise, lights or anything could be observed. It merely stayed still, hovering in the sky.

After a few minutes of staring at the object in fascinated wonder the witness was jolted by the sound of jet aircraft approaching from his right. Two jets passed right by him and then banked back towards the UFO. As they did so, and in the space of a few seconds, the object appeared to shrink away into nothing, and by the time the jets circled back it was nowhere to be seen.

But it was in the 1970s that the UFO phenomenon really began to take on a life of its own in Lincolnshire. One summer night in 1975 a slow-moving brilliant white light that passed over Ashby and Bottesford in North Lincolnshire appeared to be affecting the National Grid, for, as it moved across the landscape, all electrical power in its wake failed, and road by road the area was plunged into darkness.

In January 2005 the release of the UK National Archives revealed a spectacular UFO sighting had taken place over RAF Waddington in 1977. At about 10:20pm on the night of 21 May, three airmen at Waddington saw what they described as a 'triangular' white light that moved erratically over the airbase. In East Yorkshire RAF Patrington picked up the UFO on its radar. The object was also being monitored by radar at Waddington itself, but after four minutes the radar screens were partially obliterated by an electronic interference, which seemed to correct itself once the UFO had disappeared. An investigation found the radar equipment at Waddington to be fully functional, and it has been speculated that the UFO may have been taking an interest in the squadron of nuclear-armed Vulcan bombers that were then stationed at the base.

Just three months after Steven Spielberg's classic movie *Close Encounters of the Third Kind* descended on cinemas across the world, it would seem a close encounter was also taking place in Lincolnshire, as noted by *Strange Magazine*.

On 1 February 1978 a witness claimed that they saw a large silvery disc-like object fly overhead and alight in woodland at Laughton, near Gainsborough. Upon closer inspection two strange figures were spotted close to the grounded craft, moving among the trees. The humanoids were described as about six-feet tall, man-like in appearance and wearing silver suits. Shortly afterwards the UFO was spotted shooting away from the area at phenomenal speed.

Perhaps to some extent helped along by the success of the movie, reports of these silver-suited spacemen swept Britain, and indeed the world at large appeared to be gripped by a 'flap' of humanoid sightings. For instance, three silver-suited humanoids, seven-feet tall, were spotted walking across a field beneath a silvery sphere in Anglesey, Wales, in September. But although these entities bore some resemblance to the Gainsborough humanoids they do not really validate them: for it should be noted that in that year all kinds of strange lights and weird entities were reported from the British Isles.

SEARCH FOR MYSTERY AIRCRAFT

On 2 May 1972 the *Scunthorpe Evening Telegraph* carried a story entitled 'Search For Mystery Aircraft In North Lincolnshire'. There is no suggestion that the mysterious craft concerned was a UFO, but there is a certain enigma about the whole affair nonetheless.

The radar operator at RAF Coningsby, south of Woodhall Spa, had picked up a blip on his monitor which looked like an aircraft approaching the east coast. After a few minutes the blip vanished from the screen, and it was assumed that the craft had flown beneath radar cover and landed somewhere on the coast.

It was thought that a plane load of illegal aliens had arrived in the United Kingdom, and numerous police cars and personnel were dispatched to the area in which it was thought the aircraft must have landed. However, thorough searches turned up nothing: no evidence, no tracks, no marks, no witness statements, indeed nothing to indicate that anything had *actually* taken place. But it had – such major search operations are not conducted merely on a whim...

THE BLACK TRIANGLES

While ufology in Lincolnshire, as elsewhere, is largely concerned with miscellaneous silver discs, jumping stars, brilliant pulsating spheres or balls of orange light, there is a UFO which seems to have been spotted regularly since the mid-1980s: the black triangle.

Local newspapers and speculative Lincolnshire folk had been reporting the mysterious craft since at least 1984, when a gigantic black triangle with multicoloured lights at each point was seen to make its way into Lincolnshire. It was visible from the A46 Newark-Lincoln road, and as it passed over Heighington in its wake there followed a second such triangular craft. Both shapes appeared to be entirely soundless. As the craft flew into the distance, many people claimed to see what looked like F4 Phantoms apparently in pursuit, or maybe monitoring them. It seems that the two triangular objects then headed south-east over the Wash and hence were lost from sight beyond Hunstanton, Norfolk.

This bizarre incidence was repeated in February 1993. The story began one very cold and frosty night in February when a Mablethorpe family claimed to have seen a large, dark, triangular craft moving southwards towards the giant BT mast in Trusthorpe, south of Mablethorpe. The family saw no aircraft lights or navigation lights, and they were so struck by the strange, silent black object that they exited their car to look at it more closely. However, as it passed slowly overhead they saw one long static red light in the object's centre, surrounded by many smaller white lights, perhaps 15 in all. The object moved totally soundlessly over the mast and then hovered there for about 20 seconds before moving off in the direction of Sutton-on-Sea. But it was not over; after a while two helicopters with powerful searchlights appeared and shone their beams around the mast as though investigating, before shooting off southwards towards Sutton-on-Sea as the black triangle had done.

Such events occurred surprisingly regularly through the mid-1990s, with many being reported in a wave of excitement to eastern Lincolnshire newspapers like the *Louth Leader*. Indeed, the *Leader* was almost literally deluged with claims of sightings of the mystery flying triangles. At 2:55pm on about 12 February 1997 a man walking on the beach at Mablethorpe found his attention drawn to something unnatural in the east-coast sky. What he found himself staring at in disbelief was a small triangular black UFO sweeping low over the North Sea; weirder still, it was apparently being 'escorted' by an RAF Tornado jet interceptor. The strange craft being escorted was silent and had no visible means of propulsion; furthermore, it *apparently* operated totally independently of the RAF jet. Later that year in July, another of the strange Black Triangles was sighted. This one was encountered a few miles from New Leake, north of Boston, and displayed an erratic flight path. It shot backwards and forwards, and several times it was lost from sight — only for it to reappear somewhere else in the sky. Before each short, sharp manoeuvre it emitted a greenish glow or heatwave beforehand.

The mystery surrounding the apparent covert knowledge of these strange craft and their 'escorts' continued. At around 10:25pm one night in September 1998 a witness spotted what appeared to be two Tornados in the company of a strange craft. The witness guessed that the UFO was triangular based on the lights at each corner, each of which glowed green. As he looked through his sunroof the witness noticed that the triangular craft was about three quarters of the size of the two jets accompanying it. This sighting happened in the vicinity of Spilsby, four miles past Ulceby Cross. And Ministry of Defence archives reported that on 9 September 2001 a call was logged from someone in North Hykeham who had witnessed a triangular object hovering in the sky. The caller claimed that several white lights illuminated the UFO and it had coloured lights on its base. 'Intermittent lightning' flashed around it.

It appears that, for the most part, the patterns were the same. And much like the Lindsey Leopard or the Wolds Panther, the Black Triangles have now become part of modern Lincolnshire folklore. In an article looking back over the panic, the *Louth Leader* speculated that perhaps ultra-secret, technically-advanced triangular aircraft called TR-3B were responsible for the rash of strange sightings. It was apparently one of the American government's so-called Black Projects, and it has been theorised, naturally, that many UFO sightings in Lincolnshire are test flights of as-yet unannounced secret aircraft. Until they are revealed conclusively, however, the speculation and the mystery must remain. UFO investigator Jenny Randles noted that the Lincolnshire triangles could either be '...a prototype Stealth aircraft similar to those alleged to be under development by British Aerospace — and widely believed to be operating from their plant at Warton in Lancashire — or an Unmanned Aerial Vehicle (UAV) piloted by remote control, which was taking part in a covert training operation'. But could such explanations account for every single UFO sighting in Lincolnshire, North Lincolnshire and north-east Lincolnshire? Clearly something was, or is still, going on.

THE SKEGNESS ENCOUNTER

Early in the morning of 5 October 1996 something airborne visited the east coast of Lincolnshire and set into motion one of the county's most baffling and plausible UFO encounters.

It all began at 3:14am that morning when RAF Neatishead, near Wroxham in Norfolk, picked up a mysterious blip on its radar; something was hovering over the Wash, the great bay of shallow seawater off the south-east coast of Lincolnshire. The thing was also picked up by the radar at Great

View of the Wash, as seen from the mouth of the River Nene.

Yarmouth coastguard station on the Norfolk coast and at RAF Kinloss in Scotland. A short while later, the tanker *M/V Conocoast*, out in the North Sea, also reported visual and radar contact with the object.

Simultaneously the police in Skegness had been contacted repeatedly that night by people who wished to report that there appeared to be a huge, rotating bright object over the coast. The police themselves were able to view the object, which they described as a large UFO about a mile up in the sky with multi-coloured lights that flashed blue, white, red and green. It was directly south-east of Skegness and made no sound at all.

Cross correspondence ensued between the various parties, and the radio transcripts reveal some fascinating pointers. Although the RAF stations were picking up a stationary blip, they were in contact with the Skegness police and the *M/V Conocoast*, both of whom were able to actually view the UFO with the naked eye. At 4:08am – nearly an hour since the first radar sighting – those aboard the *M/V Conocoast* could still see the object, which they described as stationary, at a very high altitude north of themselves and flashing various bright colours. Whatever it was, it seemed to be completely noiseless. At 4:45am something amazing happened.

The strange object appeared to split into two, for by now those aboard the *M/V Conocoast* stated that there were two lights that were distinctly visible to the naked eye. Both flashed red, green, blue and white.

Back on land the Skegness police confirmed that they too could still see the UFO with the naked eye, although to them it seemed to be just one very large bright light. This is perhaps accounted for by the greater distance they were observing the craft from, and RAF Kinloss commented that whatever the object was, it must be quite a size to be visible from Skegness. Further southwards, the strange bright light was also visible to the people of Boston.

Kinloss also noted that there should have been neither military aircraft nor civilian flights in the area at that time, and if by some weird, unlikely combination of circumstances the UFOs were helicopters then they were fast running out of flight time, as the objects had now been hovering for some two hours.

At 5:52am (two hours and 38 minutes after the first radar alert) the *M/V Conocoast* reported that it could still spy the two flashing lights in the sky, but now it appeared that they had retreated to a higher altitude and were becoming increasingly difficult to view. The brilliance of the lights also seemed to be dimming.

At 7:08am RAF Neatishead radioed that they had recieved an unconfirmed report that a civilian flight had earlier sighted multi-coloured, stationary flashing lights in the area from a great distance. That report had been passed on by RAF Northwood in Middlesex. There is also some indication that the UFO was still there by 11:09am, although no longer visible to the naked eye.

When news of the sightings came out it created a sensation in Lincolnshire, with the *Lincolnshire Echo* carrying the UFO story as its front-page lead. Flight Lt Keith Sweatman at RAF Neatishead commented, 'The number of independent reports we have had suggests that there was something to follow up. We will be investigating the matter thoroughly and we are already collecting the information.'

Every good UFO tale produces its share of ridiculous official 'explanations', which only serve to fuel speculation as to what the object *really* was, and the Skegness case is no different. On 11 October a local TV news report on the incident aired on Anglia TV claimed that the stationary 'blip' that radar operators were seeing at their stations in various parts of Britain was nothing more than a 'shadow' of the Boston parish church spire, while weather experts claimed that the flashing lights visible to the human eye were nothing more unearthly than an electrical storm. It was suggested that this was the 'official' explanation, produced by the Ministry of Defence after analysing the 'UFO alert'.

And there the matter rests for the moment…although there is some suggestion that the RAF requested that Skegness police take footage of the UFO, further indicating just how seriously everybody was taking it. Any video footage shot of the object would perhaps not reveal much, maybe just a very bright stationary light in the distance; nevertheless, if such footage *does* exist, that light may well represent the closest thing to a 'real' UFO that has been captured on film anywhere in the United Kingdom.

ABDUCTIONS AND MEN IN BLACK

Very strange things were happening to Peter Gregory, of Mablethorpe, in April 1993. On 16 April he had gotten out of bed at 2:30am to go to the bathroom and had witnessed through the window a ball of light which floated towards the seafront, where it vanished. The object had been so bright that its image had remained on his retina for five minutes afterwards.

The following night Peter had a strange experience, which although totally visionary, as though a dream, was so intense that he commented to prolific UFO researcher and writer Jenny Randles that the memory of it would remain with him for the rest of his life. He 'saw' himself in a room which was full of strange equipment. A humming noise filled the air and the whole room swirled with a blue haze. In this environment, Peter saw several figures: they were quite tall and human-like, and their hair was shoulder-length – but they were possessed of piercing blue eyes. He wanted to talk to them but felt like a phantom in their world, and when he tried to touch one of them his hand passed through the figure as though it were a projection. Although this appears to be a vision, in the light of the other phenomena he experienced, could the 'dream' have been some kind of residual memory of an abduction he underwent? How would he know?

The strange incidents continued. Peter saw a ball of white light moving through the evening sky above Mablethorpe on 31 May and was lucky enough to capture some camcorder footage of it. Jenny Randles herself saw this film and found that, although the light was difficult to pick out against the pale blue of the sky, there was no doubt in her mind he had filmed a real object. On 21 June 1993 Peter Gregory managed to film several seconds of a UFO that flew over Mablethorpe. The footage, he claimed, showed an enormous, flattened triangular spaceship with red and yellow lights at the edges. It was very low down in the sky, yet so large that as he stared out of the bedroom window it almost filled his view with its bulk. As it passed by overhead it left a 'trail of light' in its wake.

On 24 June two very smartly-dressed men arrived at Peter's home. Claiming to be from a certain Grimsby-based UFO research group, they stated that if Peter would hand over his video footage then they would have it subjected to professional analysis and computer enhancement. Grimsby was Peter's home town and he took the two men into his confidence completely, entrusting them with the invaluable evidence. The two men were very enthusiastic about the whole affair and asked many questions.

But as time went by and he heard nothing, Peter checked out the UFO group and found that it was non-existent. The address they had provided was similarly bogus, and his tape was never returned.

Such claims take the standard 'weird light in the sky' sighting to another level, and they are not unique. By 2000, north-east Lincolnshire was in the grip of a 'flap' of sightings of weird objects in the sky, which ranged from a formation of three pulsating lights seen over Immingham in October 1997 to a 'lovely silver object', cigar-shaped and with a pinkish glow seen hovering in the sky in April 2000 above Humberston, tipped at an angle. Every kind of aerial phenomena was reported during this period, from what were undoubtedly unusual natural displays to claims that 'something in the sky' fired a two-inch, spherical ball of red fire into the chest of a man standing at his window in

Cleethorpes. In the midst of this madness, Elaine King, a 40-year-old woman who lived in Tetney Lock, (who claimed several previous contacts with extra-terrestrials) was abducted by aliens from her bed on or about the 24 April 2000. She found herself unaccountably transported – presumably in her pyjamas – to a great alien spacecraft constructed entirely of 'steel-like material'. She could not explain how she had gotten there. While in bed she had felt herself getting weaker and weaker as though she was going into a faint: the next thing she knew, she blinked her eyes open and found herself in the corridor of the spaceship. In an 'operating room' of white mesh metallic walls with curved white supports, humanoids gathered about a bearded man laid out on a table. Of the humanoids themselves, none of the beings talked; they 'talked sort of through your mind'. They appeared not to care that she had come into the room where they were seemingly operating. Ms King described them as bald and with no noses. They were about five-feet tall. One particular humanoid which had shown concern for Ms King's distress had 'this sort of robe-like clothing on' and was taller and bigger than the rest. Ms King had felt sure that she was doomed to die on the spaceship, and also that the aliens had no real concept of time – other than that if she was not returned home within a certain 'window' of time she would never be able to return. The taller humanoid, who had hair, had made a comment to the effect that 'too many humans' were dying because of what they, the aliens, were doing to them. Ms King's final memory on board the UFO was of gradually growing weaker and weaker before slumping against the side of the walls.

One wonders what the point of such vivid encounters are. Jenny Randles mentioned Peter Gregory's tale in *The Truth Behind Men In Black* (1997), but it is noteworthy that when Mr Gregory's story was originally published by *The People* newspaper of 20 February 1994 it read as an actual abduction, whereby he was shown the end of civilisation by beings from the 37th century. At the time the east coast of Lincolnshire was in the middle of a 'flap' of Black Triangle sightings, but Mr Gregory's was the only allegation that took the encounters to the 'next level', just as Ms King's encounter was the ultimate encounter during another 'flap' in north-east Lincolnshire.

In 2006 a book claimed that a mass abduction scenario had occurred in Grantham on 9 November 1965. And whether such claims are the 'truth' of people who have *genuinely* had something strange happen to them or are just those of UFO-obsessed publicity seekers, is always going to be open to debate.

INTO THE 21ST CENTURY

These days, there is quite literally a never-ending stream of UFO incidents from the River Humber to the Wash that are in the public forum, thanks mainly to local newspapers, word of mouth and other media. It would be quite an impossible job for UFO researchers to make any sense out of any of it, were it not for the fact that some stories stand out as having that unmistakable ring of truth about them. Of course, that does not mean the thing sighted is an alien craft – merely that it is a 'real' unidentified flying object.

For example, MoD archives released under the Freedom of Information Act in 2005 showed a call logged from a worried resident of Gonerby at about 7:30pm on the evening of 6 November 2001. The caller's house had begun to shake and there had been a sudden power cut. Rushing to the window, the witness saw a glowing object shoot over his house at terrific speed. It resembled no known aircraft and, indeed, did not have any wings. Searching for an apt description, the witness stated that it resembled a missile. The simultaneous power cut had affected the general area and other people were out in the street looking skyward at the curious object.

In January 2000 came claims that an unidentifiable craft had been observed hovering in the vicinity of Holbeach one dark evening. The UFO had displayed a powerful, torch-like white light in its centre and appeared to be 'scanning' the region for some 10 minutes, from a vantage point of about two and a half miles up. Other, smaller lights flickered around the main beam. Whatever had fascinated the UFO in this thinly-populated area of south-east Lincolnshire, it apparently soon lost interest: it dipped slowly and then rocketed up into the sky at a speed reckoned to be at least 4,000mph.

And so the phenomena continues unabatedly. In the very early hours of a February 2005 morning, a night shift delivery driver pulled his truck over in a dark country lane at Pinchbeck and watched a circular object, possibly metallic, which pulsed with light. It had been stationary, as if a star. But when it moved it shot over the countryside in a matter of seconds, in complete silence but making the ground vibrate noticeably.

The witness had attempted to navigate the country lanes in an effort to keep the object in sight, and became absolutely sure it was some type of controlled object – solid, metallic and very large, with five distinct lights on its underside.

In cases such as this it is difficult not to believe the sincerity of witnesses. People, on the whole, are not fools. They have enough intelligence to recognise very rare natural phenomena for just that (such as the green fireball seen sweeping low through the night sky on 3 December 2006 over the Wolds), without jumping to the automatic conclusion it was a UFO. So while there are doubtless those out there for whom every light in the sky is a spaceship, many people only talk reluctantly of the erratically-moving lights they have seen, fearing ridicule: credible witnesses, for the most part, who have to be assumed capable of reliably relating what they think they have seen – or actually *did* see.

MYSTERIOUS MISSILES

Perhaps evidencing the previous point, there have occasionally been reports of unidentified sky-borne objects that resemble not so much a UFO or craft, but more a kind of man-made object gone awry. In 1954 the *Lincolnshire Echo* published an account of an ex-fighter pilot who had looked out of the bedroom window of his house in Nettleham Road, Lincoln, and seen a golden sphere – like a small sun – flash through the heavens from north-east to south-west. It shot through the sky at roughly 1,500 mph at an altitude of 5,000ft and was only visible for three seconds. It had made no sound. It has been suggested that perhaps the object was a rocket fired from a test base, maybe at Faldingworth to the north-east of Lincoln. But to test fire it over land would be lunacy, unless it was a miscalculation or an accident.

There were echoes here of the incident in 2001 in Gonerby noted earlier, the Gonerby incident, however, being marked apart by the mysterious power failures it brought with it as it passed overhead. An incident at around the same time, though, does appear to bear the hallmarks of something more terrestrial. Once again, the MoD were alerted to a mysterious object that shot through the sky in the mid-afternoon of 2 November 2002. The object was witnessed from Scawby, a village south-west of Brigg in North Lincolnshire, and appeared to be a very dark blue solid object, torpedo-shaped and followed by a thick plume of whitish smoke.

As the *Scunthorpe Evening Telegraph* ruefully noted on 26 February 2007, 'The last sightings of flying-saucer-type objects in our region were almost five years ago.' In truth, the Scawby object almost certainly appears to be man-made – a rocket or missile perhaps mistakenly shot over land, like an immense firework, which landed who-knows-where?

CHAPTER 12

INEXPLICABLE INCIDENTS, BIZARRE BEHAVIOUR AND PECULIAR PLACES

INTRODUCTION

On 14 March 2005 it was reported that Jason and Claire Foster, who lived near Market Rasen, were suffering a mystery plague. On a regular basis since the previous December, and usually on a Sunday, someone – for reasons best know to themselves – was taking the trouble to dump pairs of shoes at their remote farmhouse. Sometimes as many as four shoes were left for them at a time. But this was no dumping of old or out-of-fashion footwear; some shoes were cheap and retailed at a low price, while others were more expensive designer brands. By April over 30 shoes had been dumped…some were single, some were in pairs and they were in a variety of styles, sizes and condition. Even pairs of roller blades had joined the collection on some occasions.

Mrs Foster said that the incident had been quite scary at first, owing to the fact that it simply made no sense. The couple managed to snatch video footage of the culprits, yet this only added to the bizarre nature of the incident. For they were no scallywags dumping stolen goods they had not been able to flog at car boot sales – the footage showed that an unidentified elderly couple in a green vehicle were behind the deposits.

East Lindsey District Council described the case as one of fly tipping, but although there was a legal term for the offence it did not lessen the totally arbitrary nature of what was happening.

Charles Hoy Fort (1874–1932) would have found the above story typically irreverent. The New Yorker, from Albany, was a compiler and chronicler on all things supernatural, nonsensical and out of place. He has given his name to such occurrences and allegations – they are sometimes referred to as Fortean events – and the man himself was certainly familiar with Lincolnshire.

Charles Fort was always fascinated by million-to-one coincidences, particularly coincidences where patterns appeared to emerge. In his collection *Wild Talents* (1932) he recorded a spate of deaths and serious injuries that occurred in various parts of Britain during foxhunts. Drawing on an article entitled *Chapter of accidents* that appeared in the *New York Times* on 26 January 1873, he reported how during the Pytchley hunt, one General Mayow collapsed dead from the saddle of his horse, while about the same time in Gloucestershire the daughter of the Bishop of Gloucester was seriously injured in a hunting accident. That very day somewhere in the north of England a Miss Cavendish lost her life in a hunting tragedy. Not long afterwards two hunters were thrown from their horses and seriously injured near Sanders' Gorse. Added to this list of foxhunting-related catastrophes is the case of a clergyman killed while out hunting in Lincolnshire at about the same time. Although Fort acknowledged the incident belonged to the realm of coincidence, there was nonetheless an 'incident force that is related to the common character'. He goes on to mention that there had always been 'intense feeling, in England, against fox hunters' and there were always those who desired to sabotage it: food for thought for those who consider hunt sabotage and the volatile situation regarding the controversial tradition a current phenomenon. Fort's discussion of the incident almost reads like he believes an invisible, travelling saboteur could have been at work!

But for Charles Fort, the study of the phenomenal transcended general human weirdness and crossed the border into the paranormal. Ghosts, folklore and UFOs aside, there are countless stories from Lincolnshire of things that do not appear to make sense in any conventional way, from earth mysteries and strange places, to psychic abilities and general curiosities.

Fort realised that such things surrounded us every day. In May 1880 a chicken was hatched at Epworth which had two bodies, but only one head. In January 1954 there was the report of a unique egg being found by Mr H. Baldock, a farmer making the weekly collection from his fowls. The *Market Rasen Mail* reported that among all the other eggs was found a massive egg, which weighed five and a quarter oz and measured seven and a quarter inches in circumference. This oddity, not remarkable in itself, was found to have another complete egg floating within the egg white. Inside this second egg there was a complete yolk. To cap it all, the outer egg was white shelled, while the inner egg was brown shelled. On 10 June 1976 an unusual male foal was born at Hibaldstow, North Lincolnshire. Owner Bill Sargent stated, 'I've been breeding horses for years and I've never seen one like it. It's only once in a lifetime owt like this happens, I reckon.' For the foal's white coat bore elongated black blotches that merged in some places to form stripes. The foal, which was healthy, was christened 'Zebradia'. Similarly, a very rare pure-white albino seal pup was found exhausted and washed up on the beach near Sutton-on-Sea in December 2006. The little fellow was being cared for by the Natureland Seal Sanctuary and was named Whitebeam. No doubt in centuries gone by such rarities would have been considered portents by the folk of Lincolnshire.

Very early one morning in November 2002 65-year-old Derek Harris heard a loud, high-pitched whistling noise which ended with a thump in the vicinity of his back garden in St Clement's Road, Ruskington. The noise woke him up, and from the sounds he heard he immediately considered the possibility that his property had been struck by a small meteorite. When he got up he excitedly combed his back garden for any signs of disturbance, but his search was futile. Nearly a year later, however, while digging in the garden, he turned up a small piece of rock: it was about one and a half inches wide and weighed more than 3oz, and it resembled nothing so much as a tiny moon with lots of craters. Furthermore, it was formed with three different-coloured layers.

On Friday 27 October 2006 a Lincoln man told how his battery-powered clock hanging in the kitchen began to slow down, which he naturally took to assume meant the batteries were running out. It fell an hour behind – and then promptly started working normally again, meaning that it had somehow *turned itself* back exactly an hour for the benefit of the clocks going back on Saturday 28 October.

After witchcraft, ghosts, UFOs and monsters, this chapter is concerned with all the rest: all that does not quite fit the preconceived order.

THE NATURAL LANDSCAPE

The county of Lincolnshire is a mystical landscape, criss-crossed with ley lines and alive with mysterious earthlights.

In Lincolnshire the Will o' the Wisps (strange, ghostly lights sometimes seen at night flickering in forests or over swamps) went by many names: Will o' the Wykes, the Lantern Man and Peggy with the Lantern. Despite plausible scientific explanations for the phenomenon, much folklore is attached to the Will o' the Wisp: 'If you follow a Will o' the Wisp it'll lead you into a bog.' This detail sounds suspiciously like the claims levelled against other inhabitants that were held to haunt the boglands south of Scunthorpe, namely the Shag Foal and the Lackey Causey Calf.

Some first-hand stories do indeed give the impression that there was something supernaturally playful, or even sinister, about the lights. The supposition that they resulted from ignited marsh gas does not explain all the 'behavioural patterns' of the Will o' the Wisp. Ethel Rudkin noted that one could be seen in Willoughton near the crossroads of Ermine Street (A15) and Old Leys Lane, which took one westwards to Willoughton Cliff and Willoughton itself. In winter time it would appear nightly in the stretch of road between Old Leys Manor and the crossroads, and it flickered about the same height from the ground as a bicycle lamp would do. It was also the same colour and seemed to appear in the road between eight and 10 o'clock at night. It frightened people, and Rudkin wrote that it did not 'dance' but moved in a steady way, some three feet off the road, adding 'Nowadays there is so much more traffic down Old Leys Lane that it would not be so noticeable.' Around 1913 a young fellow who had been courting a girl in Kirton-in-Lindsey was chased by a 'Willie Wisp' that appeared as he made his way home southwards along (what is now) the B1398. It kept pace with him as he ran back to Willoughton. To the west, on Blyton Carr, south-west of Blyton, they were redder in colour and danced closer to the ground, as of a man carrying a lantern. Just south of Willoughton can be found Harpswell, and one villager told Rudkin that when he used to live at Harpswell, at the foot of the hill, he regularly saw a Will o' the Wisp which followed a set pattern. It would come across a field known as the Fish Pond and across the grass to the foot of the hill. Sometimes it would get so far and then change direction, moving towards the white cottage to the south of the field, where '...the Serpentine runs, a stream with a good flow of water'.

Broadly speaking, this phenomenon falls under the umbrella term 'earth lights', and it may be related to ball lightning and earthquake lights – but does not seem to require an electrical storm or an earthquake to actually appear. Typically, earth lights manifest themselves as 'globes' of light, although they can take on any shape and have been seen to perform mesmerising aerobic manoeuvres, including hovering and merging together. (NB. This reminds me of a story I heard years ago about a lightning bolt that hit a cottage in Lincolnshire. It flashed down the chimney and into the kitchen, where it hit an uncooked joint and roasted it perfectly. This may be an urban myth though.) The exact nature of the earth lights' energy is not known, but it is fascinating to note that the lights can and do haunt localised regions, where in some place they are seen for generations. The places where they appear may have certain geological characteristics such as geological faulting, seismic history or simply mineral deposits or bodies of water.

An even more bizarre – and apparently natural – phenomenon are the so-called 'mystery flares': phantom lights out at sea that the coastguard are alerted to – only to find nothing to account for them. Such lights were witnessed and reported off the coasts of Lincolnshire, Norfolk and Northumberland in 1974, as well as off the Welsh coastline. It is interesting that in the case of the 1974 sightings the phantom flares appeared off Lincolnshire and Norfolk, and it has to be wondered how close they were to the sandy banks of the Wash; the Welsh spooklights were frequently reported by sand dunes and, as at the Wash, a connection was put forward between combustible methane, waterlogged sandhills and decaying organic matter.

LINES ACROSS THE LANDSCAPE

On a more mystical level are the conundrum known as ley lines, or leys, which take the form of arrow-straight alignments between ancient sites often stretching for miles across the landscape and passing through such sites as long barrows, churches, Pagan burial grounds, prehistoric mounds, etc. They were first 'discovered' (although rediscovered is perhaps a better word) in 1921 by Alfred Watkins, a 66-year-old businessman. On a bright June afternoon he sat in his car gazing over Hertfordshire from his Blackwardine home. Comparing what he saw with the map on his lap he suddenly noticed how all the prehistoric earthworks, standing stones and churches appeared to be aligned in a dead straight path across the county. Watkins speculated that perhaps the leys were ancient trade routes, but this was against the fact that some leys travelled up difficult steep hillsides which would have been transparently easier to go around. More modern thinking has speculated that leys are 'lines of power' linking sacred prehistoric sites, following lines of cosmic energy within the earth which could be detected by dowsing rods. In the 1960s leys, like the earth lights, became entangled with the UFO mythology.

Ley lines are a worldwide phenomenon and given the thousands of years of history in Lincolnshire it is hardly a surprise that they have been found here as well. The Guru Nanak Sikh Temple on Normanby Road, Scunthorpe, has been found to have at least two ley lines passing through the site; this is perhaps a modern example of subconscious construction on a sacred site, for the temple occupies what was originally a bungalow and warehouse built in the 1950s. Alignment (A) is eight miles in length and may possibly be aligned with the mid-winter moonrise, and it takes in such sites as St Michael's Church, the ancient relic known as the Crosby Stone, the Guru Nanak Sikh Temple, an old Mesolithic settlement on Risby Warren, the Norman church of St Bartholomew and a crossroads high up on the hill at Saxby All Saints. Alignment (B) touches an ancient Iron Age/Roman-British settlement at Dragonby, passes through the so-called 'Dragon Rock', through a Mesolithic settlement at Sheffield's Hill and the 14th-century St Mary's Church at Roxby, before finally terminating at a well to the north of Winterton. Both alignments appear to converge at the site of the Guru Nanak Sikh Temple.

There are other sites that are suggested to fall into the path of ley lines in Lincolnshire, although sometimes these lines have been referred to as 'spirit lines' due to the more folkloric attributes rather than its ancient route: a line from Stow to Lincoln for instance, along which it was held that fairies carried blocks to help build the cathedral. The witch-infested hill at Dorrington and the Drake Stone at Anwick are also reputed to fall in the path of an alignment. An energy line through Kirton-in-Lindsey, which stems from the church, is reputed to pass through the allegedly-cursed vicarage.

Old Leys Lane, Willoughton: where Will o' the Wisps would chase the locals.

Tradition also tells us that Hairy Jack, Lincolnshire's phantom black hound, favours patrolling ley lines among other select places. And roads at Saltfleet on the east coast (north of Mablethorpe), which have been paved with coffin-shaped stones, may have been corpse ways. Corpse ways often emerged when funeral cortéges from outlying farms took the shortest, straight-line route to the parish church rather than the impossibly out-of-the-way road system. There was a belief (widely held until recently) that if a corpse was carried over private land it established a right-of-way forever, and corpse ways have often been theorised to follow ley lines in their route. Clearly, then, these curious arrow-straight alignments are linked to a significant proportion of the phenomena featured in this collection.

Closely associated with the ley lines is the practice of dowsing. Pippa Hanbury, from Legsby near Market Rasen, first chanced upon a theory that there were such a thing as 'black streams' of negative energy running beneath the ground when she moved the bed at her house and found her pet dog curiously reluctant to sit on it in its new place. Speaking on BBC Radio Lincolnshire, Pippa stated that she believed that a black stream running under her farmhouse was the reason and employed the tactic of dowsing to 'heal' the area using a set of brass dowsing rods around the perimeter of the property thus: if the rods remained unmoved then it meant the property was clear, but if they reacted then she would have to heal the site with an archaic ritual involving crystals and flower essences.

Pippa explained that pets are very sensitive to black streams. Dogs avoided them like the plague, but cats would seek them out and make them a favourite spot to lie on. Horses, too, were wary of them and would start behaving unpredictably if they were moved and one was nearby. These sites of geopathic stress under the earth could also be responsible for a change in family patterns such as an increase in arguments, total lethargy and unexplained personality changes should the household move home or even rearrange their current one.

In 2006 property developer Tony Peart noted that the locations of churches south of Lincoln formed a mystical pentacle – a five pointed star with St John the Baptist Church near Temple Bruer at one of its five points. Mr Peart believed that all the locations of the churches were on ancient Pagan burial grounds, and some of the arrow-straight alignments from one point to another (such as the alignment that stretched from the church at Bassinghmam to Temple Bruer, and then extended to the church at Ruskington) were in fact set on ley lines. The mystical symbolism of the pentacle was not lost on Mr Peart, nor were the ancient rumours that the 'true' Grail is buried somewhere in the vicinity of Temple Bruer.

PLANT LIFE

It was believed that certain trees, like the elder trees, in Lincolnshire were themselves possessed of 'life', in the form of a spirit they called The Old Lady Of The Elder Tree, Elder Mother or Elder Queen. She lived at the roots of the tree and was the mother of the Elves. If one cut the branches of the elder tree, it would bleed real blood, and those who did so without the permission of the Elder Mother risked blindness and the loss of their health, livestock and children. If an elder tree was wounded, then the Elder Mother had to be appeased with charms and offerings. Similarly, if a child offended the tree, the parents would present offerings to it and beg forgiveness off the Elder Mother. In Lincolnshire permission had to be gained to use its wood, with words such as these, 'Owd Gal, give me some of thy wood, and Oi will give thee some of moine when Oi graws inter a tree.'

In 1908 folklorist Miss Mabel Peacock recorded that an old man was presented with a sizeable piece of elder wood by a party curious of this ancient belief in plant life. The old man was chopping fire wood at the time and agreed that he would cut the elder wood and add it to the pile, as it was 'already dead' – but if it had been 'alive' and still on the tree he would not have dared to cut it off without asking the permission of the Old Lady. Miss Peacock wrote that a rocker for a baby's cradle had been mended with ill-gotten elder wood in Lincolnshire and the unfortunate infant had been pinched mercilessly while it lay in the cradle.

But there are other tales of curious plant life. One tells of how in May 1606, an ash tree in Brampton, between Gainsborough and Lincoln, began to excite local villagers who claimed it was a 'talking tree'. In a letter dated 7 July 1606 it was written that the '…ash tree shaketh in body and boughs thereof, sighing and groaning like a man troubled in his sleep, as if it felt some sensible torment'.

The ash tree moaned, muttered and grumbled, and those gathered around it strained their ears in an attempt to hear what it was saying. Several people climbed to the top of the tree, where the noises it made were apparently more audible. One fellow, when at the top of the ash, reportedly spoke to the tree; what he heard back left him a traumatised wreck, grovelling speechless at the foot of the tree for three hours before recovering and saying, 'Brampton, Brampton, thou are much bound to pray!' All were intrigued, and efforts to get the ash to speak up failed so the locals thought if they could drill a hole in the trunk it would allow what the tree was trying to say to escape. A hole was drilled, watched over by the Earl of Lincoln, but although the tree continued to 'talk' more audibly in a 'hollow voice', no one could understand it and attempts at translating the mumblings were in vain.

In Nettleham churchyard there can be found a simple headstone bearing the inscription '*Tho. Gardiner. Post boy of Lincoln. Barbarously murdered by Isaac and Tho. Hallam. Jan. 3rd 1732. Aged 19.*' The unfortunate post boy had had his throat cut by two highwaymen, who had also killed another traveller in a light open carriage near Faldingworth so violently that they had almost severed his head. The crimes shocked Lincolnshire and roused much emotion: as the murderers were carted into Lincoln to be executed a mob of post boys jeered their entry by blasting loudly on horns. But this sad, violent episode did not end there. For an entire generation, it is said, the grass would not grow at young Gardiner's gravesite and the ground surrounding the plot remained barren, solid earth. This type of phenomenon is commonly recounted in folklore as taking place at the graves of poor murder victims, but in reality the tramp of hundreds of feet to the site probably explains most of these types of incidents. There is certainly plenty of grass growing in Nettleham churchyard these days, where the unfortunate youth's tombstone can still be seen.

A curious tree with a folkloric background is the out-of-place palm tree which is to be found to the right of the porch at the St Peter and St Paul Church in Ingoldmells, north of Skegness. I have been told that it is said the palm spontaneously grew upon the death of a squire's daughter, who had died very young – heartbroken that her lover, the houseboy, had left for an island in the Pacific after their romance was discovered by her father. But in all likelihood this story is a local myth, perhaps created to account for the mysterious 'Lonesome Palm Tree' that nobody had an explanation for.

A kind of 'life' seems to have possessed a group of elm trees in the grounds of the tiny thatched church of St Peter's at Markby near Alford – the desire to fight back against the axeman. In 1988 a workman hired to cut down the dead elms was thwarted at every turn. It was claimed that a falling branch moved horizontally and snapped the ladder the man was on, and gusts of sawdust unaccountably blew into his eyes, nostrils and mouth. When he attempted to lift logs that had been cut his strength vanished, and upon managing to get the dead wood in the back of the van, the vehicle broke down three times as he tried to leave. The workman was forced to abandon the contract half finished, and if all this sounds like the excuses of a lazy workman then perhaps another explanation should be considered. A second workman brought in to complete the job also found this straightforward contract no easy task, running into many problems himself. During the incident, horses in the fields began to act as if they had gone mad whenever the old elms were being cut, and a woman painting in the churchyard was frightened when her pet dog suddenly froze on the spot, its hair on end and its eyes staring at something invisible.

Like the elder trees in days gone by, it seems that to some, in Brigg at least, trees are still an age-old object of veneration. On a cold and crisp October morning in 2003, walkers across the recreation ground found that a giant tree standing on its own had been bedecked and dressed with 'offerings' by persons unknown. A bemused witness took photographs of the strange offering and submitted them on the internet, commenting, 'People – on the whole – are strange creatures. It seems traditions appear out of nowhere or are kept alive long after the original reason has been forgotten.' However, the tree in question was not a sycamore or an ash – traditionally trees regarded as potent symbols in folklore – which only added to the mystery.

WEIRD HARVESTS

The *Cardiff Evening Express and Evening Mail* of 1 July 1919 reported on the strange case of a fallow field that had mysteriously produced a fine and full crop of wheat. The field was 10 miles north of Lincoln between the villages of Stow and Sturton-by-Stow, and it belonged to Mr Edward Calvert – although there had been barley grown there before it was 10 years since wheat had been sown. Even more remarkable was the fact that the field had been left fallow that year, so to find it full of wheat was truly astonishing.

The unaccountable crop was described as, 'a fine crop of wheat of apparently more robust growth and better quality than some in the cultivated fields around.'

Many farmers and agriculturalists made pilgrimages to view the field and its mystery crop; none could provide an explanation as to how it had happened.

These days the mystery of harvest time is the more-familiar crop circle. On 15 August 1996 a spectacular crop circle formation was discovered in a field in south-east Lincolnshire at Scremby, comprising of two circles with diameters measured at 92 feet and 34 feet. Strange patterns in crops are regularly reported. On 23 April 2005 what appeared to be crop circles were seen and photographed in a field of oil seed rape in Brigg. Then, on 18 June 2005, a random scattering of circular depressions was found in a barley field at Burwell, lending the field a crater-filled, moon-like appearance. On 4 July 2005 a picture of weird patterns in a wheat field next to Rocal Panels on the Ancholme Industrial Estate was posted on the web. The pattern of the circles (20 feet by 6 metres across) appeared to be regular, and it diminished in size from east to west. No footprints or other tracks led to the crop circles.

Although the phenomenon is a real, tangible one, the question of what causes them is the subject of intense debate. The issue has become inextricably linked to the UFO story, with unlikely claims that the depressions are caused by spacecraft landing, although most serious researchers consider some kind of bizarre weather explanation is behind it. Others have gone for the explanations rooted in the animal world, such as deer and vixens trampling the crops (making perfectly-circular designs?) in order to give birth to and raise their young.

There are other competing theories, with the suggestion of a hoax often being levelled at the harvest-time patterns. In the last week of June 2003 a mysterious circle appeared in the Gonerby Moor field at Great Gonerby and caused much excitement for travellers on the A1 passing the site. However, a neighbouring farmer was less than impressed, claiming that at first he had thought the circle was caused by a tractor turning and then he had seen what he thought were footprints in the 'tramlines' in the field, which indicated trickery at the circle. The sceptical farmer commented wryly, 'I'm sure it's a fake. If you don't see me for a few weeks, then I've been abducted by aliens.' It seems

Thomas Gardiner's sad headstone.

that some, at least, agree with Dana Scully's comment in an episode of *The X-Files* entitled *All Things*. When Mulder announces he is going to England to investigate crop circles and asks his partner if she wants to come along, Scully replies, 'I'm not interested in tracking down some sneaky farmers who happened to ace geometry in high school!'

INDELIBLE BLOODSTAINS

Closely identified with the aforementioned phenomenon of 'grass that will not grow' at gravesites is that staple of folklore, indelible bloodstains.

T.F. Thiselton-Dyer's *Strange Pages from Family Papers* (1900) recalls the story of a master workman who created one of the magnificent rose windows in Lincoln Cathedral. His apprentice worked alongside him, creating his own rose window using bits of glass that his master had thrown away. When the work was completed, to the shock of the workman, his apprentice's work was judged to be the better. In a fit of anger he threw himself from the gallery and was killed on the stone floor beneath his second-rate window. The blood from the incident spread across the floor and was said to be indelible: no amount of scrubbing would remove it.

According to an ancient legend, sometime in the decades prior to the English Civil War a Lincolnshire innkeeper's wife murdered a traveller for his money. Her guilt was proven by dark tell-tale stains on her smock – which, apparently, she had scrubbed and scrubbed without success. The bloodstains had proved literally impossible to remove, and they were widely seen as the work of providence.

Blood from the murdered Mary Kirkham could not be washed off the steps of the Sun Inn, Saxilby, and there are similar gruesome stories from Kirton-in-Lindsey. *The Book Of Days* (1869) noted how around 1819 a woman at a dance burst a blood vessel and expired there and then, and blood could still be seen in the room where she had been laid out, nearly 50 years later. In *c.*1849 an old man and his sister were murdered in the village with such brutality that their cottage was 'deluged with blood, the stains of which are believed yet to remain'.

The hamlet of Farforth is to be found in the Lincolnshire Wolds, between Louth and Horncastle. These days Farforth House is a hotel, but in 1927 a Mrs Johnson reported that she and her eight-year-old daughter had witnessed on several occasions the sight of a Grey Lady; the phantom was dressed in grey and had a 'big white collar' like that worn by a Quaker. Strangely, a bedroom above the east window had a mysterious stain 'as of blood', which could not be removed despite vigorous scrubbing.

In 1971 Hugh Martineau wrote an article for *Lincolnshire Life* about the Farforth House ghost. The then owner, Mrs Hardy, was unaware of any ghosts, and the bedroom with the supposed stain had long since been carpeted over. But Mrs Hardy had complained that that particular room had a smell of decay which no amount of airing could remove.

STRANGE RAIN

Thomas Cooper (1805–1892) was an enormously popular 19th-century lecturer on Christianity, an extremely well-educated man who spoke six languages and became a lay preacher in 1829. By 1836 he was writing for the *Stamford Mercury*, but an ambition to write books took him to London in 1839. A sympathy for those living in working-class poverty led to his joining the radical Chartist movement and his speeches – where he preached for equal opportunities, electoral reform and the right to basic living conditions – attracted enormous crowds. When a riot erupted at Hanley, Staffordshire, Cooper was jailed for two years.

Cooper's sympathy for the working classes was born out of his own miserable upbringing in Gainsborough, Lincolnshire. Although he was born at Leicester, the son of a Yorkshire Quaker, his mother took him to Gainsborough (her home town) upon his father's death and the young Cooper spent his childhood among the dimly-lit alleys by the River Trent while his mother eked out a living.

Thomas Cooper was a very bright child, however, and he attended the Blue Coat School in Beaumont Street, joining his friend Joseph Foulkes Wink's Mutual Improvement Society (MIS) as a teenager. This latter move was the first big step in the direction his life was to take, and what all this illustrates is that an event experienced by Thomas Cooper during his time in Gainsborough is not merely the story of a slum child but the statement of a highly-intelligent youth who went on to achieve great things.

Cooper declared, 'I am as sure of what I relate as I am of my own existence.' He was talking about an occasion when, quite simply, it rained frogs.

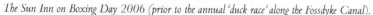

The Sun Inn on Boxing Day 2006 (prior to the annual 'duck race' along the Fossdyke Canal).

There is no date for this incident, merely that it took place in his boyhood. The amphibians showered from the heavens, attested Cooper, and they were clearly alive as they came jumping and tumbling from the sky. They '...fell on the pavement at our feet, and came tumbling down the spouts from the tiles of the houses into the water tubs'.

Although the power of wind is not to be underestimated during an outbreak of bad weather, it clearly takes a special kind of wind that sweeps up merely one kind of creature. Although in some cases a thunderous outbreak of rain may actually mean that hordes of frogs emerge from holes in the ground as the rainwater enlivens them – thus giving the impression they fell with the rain – in this case, they didn't. As with the Epworth Poltergeist, it is the integrity of the witness that speaks for itself against all the scientific arguments in favour of a 'natural' explanation.

LIVING FOSSIL

The phenomenon of living toads found to be alive after being liberated from the boulders and rocks they were solidly encased in is one of the world's enduring mysteries...and 19th-century Lincolnshire produced its own example of this staple of Fortean strangeness.

On 31 October 1862 the *Stamford Mercury* reported that during an excavation underneath a tavern in Spittlegate, Stamford, workmen found a live toad to be securely entombed in stone bedrock. The incident is all the more remarkable in that this amazing find was made seven feet underground as the men worked in a cellar.

In 1862 the Great Exhibition in London had proudly displayed a controversial exhibit in its eastern annexe: a lump of coal with a clearly defined toad-shaped depression within. The preserved body of the little fellow found in the hole was also displayed. The baffling indication was that toads and frogs had a legendary ability to live encased in rocks, somehow staying alive and somehow leaving the impression of their body – almost as if the rock or lump of coal had been formed around them at its genesis.

The Stamford curiosity came on the back of the controversy surrounding the Great Exhibition find, and those who wish to debunk the whole thing as preposterous have pointed to this 'suspicious timing'. But the Stamford toad appears to be a genuine mystery, with the timing merely a coincidence.

MYSTERIOUS HUMS, FUMES AND FAILURES

The *Daily Mirror* of 26 October 1991 briefly reported on the singular experience of the Lindley family of Horncastle, who stood and watched as their house and everything around them began to turn silver before their eyes.

Household furniture, doors and windows began to change colour and start to shine, and then food such as jellies and tomatoes began to change colour. Unnervingly, the feet of their 11-year-old daughter took on a silvery hue. With the whole house shining the Lindleys raced outdoors, but this was no bizarre sunshine effect on a bright day. Closer inspection revealed that their house had been thoroughly coated with a kind of silvery dust.

Other houses in the street had been left untouched by the mysterious substance, and the report in the newspaper rounds it all off by saying that 'council officials' came and took samples away for testing.

In May 2004 the *Grimsby Evening Telegraph* reported on the mysterious humming that had plagued a pensioner called Margaret Belton at her home in Pretymen Crescent, New Waltham, north-east

Lincolnshire. The strange noise had given Margaret sleepless nights for months, and it was described by the newspaper as sounding like a big, invisible tumble drier. The noise appeared to be airborne rather than under the ground, and there were also 'vibrations' which could be detected when the noise was sounding. An investigation established that the noise was not in Mrs Belton's head. Others had also heard the hum: a friend of Mrs Belton's, who was deaf, could detect the vibrations that accompanied it, and the 'whirring' sound detected within the hum greatly disturbed a dog two doors away down the street.

There are numerous contemporary stories of similar phenomena. Typically, on 2 March 2005, Dollond and Aitchison in the Hildreds Centre, Skegness, was evacuated as staff and shoppers were overcome by fumes. Two dozen people were hospitalised amid fears that fumes had contaminated the area, and emergency crews in special protective suits searched the area for the source of the noxious smell. To date, no explanation has been found for the entire affair. The emergency services have halted their investigations and there is a feeling of unease among those involved that perhaps they are not being told the whole truth.

On 13 September 2005 a 74-year-old ex-serviceman was motoring some 300 yards short of the A16 roundabout near Kenwick Hall south of Louth when in a second, something happened in front of the car. There was what he could only describe as a red fireball explosion, about the size of a football, which filled his field of vision. The suddenness and intensity of the phenomenon hurt his eyes but there was no noise or smoke and upon investigation the car was found not to have been scorched. Furthermore, he recalled that two years previously he had been driving an extremely reliable Saab car which had never failed him. Yet at that same spot its engine died completely and as it slowed to a halt he noticed that another motorist was at the roadside. The other man was stood with the bonnet of his car up looking puzzled, and the ex-serviceman assumed that he had experienced the same strange engine failure. Strangely reminiscent of this mystery is the instance of a driveway at a property in Gosberton, where, it was reported in 2006, cars simply refused to start. They had to be pushed off the drive and along the street – whereupon they would miraculously start up again.

At 2:19pm on Wednesday 11 January 2006 Spalding and the surrounding area was shaken by a massive boom which caused buildings to shake. Pedestrians in Spalding's town centre stopped in their tracks at the bang and several cars pulled over in the sheep market. The noise was heard in Gedney, Bourne, Boston and as far away as Eye in Cambridgeshire, although most agreed the immense bang had come from somewhere in the sky directly above Spalding. Neil Pulford heard the bang and felt the ground shake as he was walking his dogs in Deeping High Bank. The trees nearby all moved as the vibration swept through them and continued across the field, scattering a flock of sheep. The force of the bang was so powerful that it somehow turned off fridges in a newsagents in Sheep Market, Spalding. The usual 'sonic boom' theories were mentioned, but a spokesman for RAF Wittering, Tony Walsh, denied that Harrier jets were behind the noise. There was, he stated, no military activity in the area that could have been responsible, and the residents of Spalding were left perplexed – and more than a little worried – by the mystery.

Spontaneous Human Combustion

It is reported that a servant girl spontaneously combusted during the poltergeist affair at Walk Farm, near Binbrook, but Charles Fort noted in his book *LO!* (1931) that around the same time there had been another mysterious fire in the area. The servant girl concerned in the Binbrook incident had been taken to Louth Hospital, and Fort recorded that on 5 February 1905 *Lloyd's Weekly News* reported that there had been a strange fire death at the same hospital concerning a Mr Ashton Clodd. The 75-year-old had died of severe burn injuries after falling against the fire grate while putting coals in it. For some reason – perhaps because of his rheumatism – he had been unable to get back up and had been fatally burned. But a witness at the inquest was quoted as saying in bemusement, 'If there was a fire in the fireplace, it was very little.'

The implication here is that the severity of Mr Clodd's injuries was not consistent with any fire he may have got going. Indeed, there was a suggestion that he may not even have gotten around to lighting the fire in the first place.

There were echoes of these strange events on 2 December 2005. A 38-year-old Lithuanian called Ovidijus Kemzura was observed to leap from his red Vauxhall Astra engulfed in flames at Bull Ends Lane in Swineshead. Horrified passers-by who were first on the scene smothered the screaming man and put out the flames; Mr Kemzura was taken to Boston's Pilgrim Hospital but died of his injuries the following day.

On 7 December Boston coroner Jim Bradwell said that he had taken statements from the people first on the scene who had put out the flames, and who had witnessed the event first hand. Mr Kemzura, a worker for a market gardener, had been due to return to Lithuania for a Christmas break with his family and the fact that he had exited the car indicated an attempt at self-rescue. In short, it did not at first glance appear to be a suicide. Similarly mystifying was the fact that Mr Kemzura had been engulfed in flames when he fled the vehicle, the blaze apparently starting *on him* rather that the car being on fire and then *spreading* to him.

An inquest in March 2006 established that at the time a gas bottle had been wedged between two seats, but it also established that it had not been faulty. Mr Kemzura was a smoker, and there were faint traces of petrol on his clothes, so all the ingredients for a fire were there: but as Boston and South Holland coroner Maureen Taylor commented, 'Thorough investigations have been carried out but at the end of the day we have no idea why this occurred.'

I WILLED MYSELF OUT OF MY BODY...

At the end of August 1888 Miss Ethel Thompson paid a visit to a friend in Lincolnshire, Miss Edith Maughan, who lived at East Kirkby Vicarage near Spilsby. The two women were interested in spirituality and that evening discussed the possibility of one leaving their own body and appearing to someone else in their 'astral form'.

One night during her visit, Miss Thompson – being a naturally-bad sleeper – found herself still awake at two or three in the morning. She was perfectly wide awake, and then, in her own words, saw '....Miss Edith Maughan standing by my bedside in her ordinary dark dressing gown. The moonlight came in at the window sufficiently for me to distinguish her face clearly, and her figure partially.' Miss Thompson was rattled by the intrusion and scalded her friend, thinking she was playing a trick.

However, her friend did not reply to her words and Miss Thompson lit a match to light a candle. In the time it took to strike the match the silent figure vanished from the bedroom, and at this Miss Thompson screamed out loud. Eventually, though, she managed to recover her nerves, her last thought on the subject being the rapidity with which Edith Maughan had managed to get out of the room.

The following morning Miss Thompson brought the matter up at breakfast. Edith Maughan flatly denied having ever entered her friend's bedroom. However, she too had been having difficulty sleeping so had merely *thought* about going to see Miss Thompson – before deciding against it, as her friend might be asleep.

Edith Maughan, in trying to relax, then deliberately adopted a sleeping position, which she had been told was adopted by eastern peoples when they wished to concentrate fully on something. Thus, hands clasped and feet crossed in a special manner, she had laid there on the bed and simply willed herself to leave her body and materialise in the other room. When she awoke, she was still in the same position as she had been when she attempted her experiment.

The two women were questioned about this episode at length by an investigator called Mrs Sidgwick, who found them sincere in their belief as to what had occurred: astral projection.

'SLAIN BY LIGHTNING'

English teacher Margaret Baker underwent hypnotic regression in 1978, and while under she told a remarkable story concerning the life and death of one Tyzo Boswell, a horse dealer from Lincolnshire born in 1775.

Margaret began speaking in guttural, coarse tones of the past life she had lived when she had been Mr Boswell. It appeared Mr Boswell had been a gypsy, for many of the phrases that came from Margaret's mouth ('motto' for drunk, 'mello' for dead and 'chopping greis' for selling horses) were Romany. Margaret even referred to her interviewer as 'gorgio', which apparently meant non-gypsy. Needless to say, Margaret was totally unfamiliar with this kind of language. There is a suggestion that she was not even particularly familiar with Lincolnshire.

In his rough Romany accent, 'Boswell' explained much about his life for the benefit of the interviewer. He described in detail his dealings as a horse trader, and his death in 1831 when he was struck by lightning and killed at the Horncastle Fair.

Afterwards, Margaret attempted to find out more about the unfortunate Mr Boswell. She eventually found his grave in St Mary's Church, Tetford, Lincolnshire, where the stone records that he was 'slain by *lightning*' on 5 August 1831.

FUTURE ECHO?

A bizarre experience claimed by a young man who lived on the Glebe estate in Lincoln has all the hallmarks of what may be some kind of time slip. It was January 2005 and the young man was awaiting his father's arrival at his house, as his father intended to help him renovate the garden. At about 9:30am the young man watched from his living room window as his father's silver D-reg Vauxhall Astra swept up the driveway. At last they could get started!

The young man grabbed an ashtray off the coffee table and took it into the kitchen where he emptied it into a bin, an action that took mere seconds and involved him ducking out the living room and then walking back in. Looking out the window he now noticed that there was merely his own car on the driveway, and his father's silver Astra was nowhere to be seen. The close was wide and the road that led to it was long, yet no car – silver Astra or otherwise – could be seen reversing out the driveway or speeding off up the street. It appeared to have vanished.

At first the young man began to doubt his sanity. He had witnessed the silver Astra pull up on to his driveway through open Venetian blinds, but this had in no way obscured his vision. With hindsight he recalled that the interior of the Astra had appeared exceptionally dark on that cold, clear January day, and he had not *actually* witnessed his father at the steering wheel; in fact, he had seen no one. But it had been his father's car, he was certain of that.

An hour passed and the young man began to get worried. Finally his father's Vauxhall Astra pulled into the driveway and his father got out, apologising profusely for his late arrival. As the pair set to work in the back garden the young man asked his father if he had arrived at the property an hour or so earlier and then had to suddenly leave for some reason. His father merely replied that no, he had been delayed at home for over an hour, but once he realised he was going to be late he had had a split-second vision – perhaps born out of frustration – of his silver Astra pulling up on to his son's driveway.

There the matter concludes, perhaps an example of a so-called 'future echo', or perhaps some kind of bizarre astral projection by a frustrated father made telepathically 'real' by his son on the other side of the city.

A Small Conclusion

In years of researching folklore and the paranormal, I have found Lincolnshire hides a wealth of curious anecdotes and odd historical facts and exudes a sense of fascination and hidden treasures not immediately apparent to the casual traveller passing through the county (although wherever they are they cannot fail to be touched by the immediate landscape: the flatness of the Fens, the beauty of the Wolds, the occasionally uneasy, gloomy sense of rural isolation). Such curiosities have sometimes taken the form of oral tradition: underneath such places as Lincoln, Tattershall Castle and Stamford in particular, for example, there are held to be labyrinthine tunnel networks. Sometimes, tradition holds, people have found the secret trapdoors that lead to such networks and intrepidly set off, never to be seen again. Then again, sometimes the anecdotes have a historical basis, as in the story of a burglar named Prest who was hanged in Louth in 1348, only to be found unaccountably alive after the supposed 'execution'. He was later pardoned, it perhaps being feared that divine intervention had occurred. Sometimes the curios take the form of charming fairytales. A tiny little dwelling etched on to the ridge of a house in Tattershall's market place is said to have been the home of Tom Thumb. In the nave of the church of Holy Trinity by the font can be found his tiny resting place, his little gravestone declaring he died in 1620 aged a remarkable 101 years old. He is believed to have been a mere 47cm tall. Quite how or why Tattershall became the 'home' of the mythical Tom Thumb has been lost to the ages, but the people of the village have nonetheless 'adopted' him. Some anecdotes merely lift us briefly from the world of the banal: a correspondent noted in *Folk-lore* in 1905 how a match lit a peat bank in Cadney in 1902 which, after the initial blaze, continued to burn Hellishly for another 14 months just underneath the surface of the ground. Other tales, of course, entertain an eerier, paranormal theme.

After so much studying, all that can really be said about Lincolnshire's fascinating, mysterious and supernatural heritage is this. Some small evidence can be found that certain beliefs of bygone generations persist unchanged, but anecdotal evidence indicates that new variations of such folklore are replacing them. A generation these days is growing up in Lincolnshire with modern legends of huge black panthers, mysterious flying black triangles and mischievous poltergeists, which is somehow reassuring in such a digital age; it can only be wondered what form these enigmas will take in subsequent generations. I have pondered long and hard about the need for belief in such things: maybe all the stories contained herein had a basis in fact, which over centuries grew in a status that took it far beyond the original event. Maybe the boredom of life in certain isolated communities, coupled with the rumour mill, provided some of the stories. Maybe the folk of Lincolnshire just love a good story to ponder over. And maybe some of the events contained in this book are truthful accounts which do indeed present anecdotal evidence of real, supernaturally bizarre and downright weird incidents in the county. Hopefully complete scepticism of such oddities will not overtake us too soon.

Printed in Great Britain
by Amazon.co.uk, Ltd.,
Marston Gate.